Creating Conversations

Improvisation in
Everyday Discourse

Perspectives on Creativity
Mark A. Runco (ed.)

Reclaiming the Wasteland: TV & Gifted Children
Bob Abelman

The Motives for Creative Work
Jock Abra

Remarkable Women: Perspectives on Female Talent Development
Karen Arnold, Kathleen Noble, and Rena Subotnik (eds.)

Creativity and Giftedness in Culturally Diverse Students
Giselle B. Esquivel and John Houtz (eds.)

Investigating Creativity in Youth: A Book of Readings on
Research and Methods
Anne S. Fishkin, Bonnie Cramond, and Paula Olszewski-Kubilius (eds.)

Enhancing Creativity of Gifted Children: A Guide for Parents
and Teachers
Joe Khatena

Style and Psyche
Pavel Machotka

Social Creativity Volumes 1 & 2
Alfonso Montuori and Ronald Purser (eds.)

Creativity Research Handbook Volume One
Mark A. Runco (ed.)

Creating Conversations: Improvisation in Everyday Discourse
R. Keith Sawyer

The Young Gifted Child: Potential and Promise—An Anthology
Joan F. Smutny (ed.)

forthcoming

Critical Thinking and Reasoning: Current Research, Theory and Practice
Daniel Fasko, Jr. (ed.)

Critical Creative Processes
Mark A. Runco (ed.)

Theories of Creativity Revised Edition
Mark A. Runco and Robert S. Albert (eds.)

Underserved Gifted Populations
Joan F. Smutny (ed.)

Creating Conversations

Improvisation in
Everyday Discourse

R. Keith Sawyer
Washington University in St. Louis

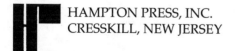
HAMPTON PRESS, INC.
CRESSKILL, NEW JERSEY

Printed in the United States of America

Library of Congress Cataloging-in-Publication

Sawyer, R. Keith (Robert Keith)
    Creating conversations : improvisation in everyday discourse /
R. Keith Sawyer
        p. cm. -- (Perspectives on creativity)
    Includes bibliographic references and index.
    ISBN 1-57273-329-2 -- ISBN 1-57273-330-6
        1. Conversation. 2. Discourse analysis. 3. Creativity (Linguistics)
    I. Title. II. Series

    P95.45.S29 2001
    302.3'46--dc21

                                                                00-054217

Second Printing 2003

cover: Wassily Kandinsky, "Komposition X"
© 2001 Artists Rights Society (ARS), New York / ADAGP, Paris
Kunstsammlung Nordrhein-Westfalen, Düsseldorf, owner
Walter Klein, Düsseldorf, photographer

Hampton Press, Inc.
23 Broadway
Cresskill, NJ 07626

To my parents, Bob and Joyce Sawyer

Contents

Acknowledgments

This book draws on the research of scholars too numerous to mention here; I have done my best to acknowledge them prominently in the text. Over the years, I have spoken directly with many of these scholars; I am grateful to all for collegial interaction and productive conversation. As this book makes clear, I believe that each of these conversations contributed to my own creative process.

I began and completed this book while in the Department of Education at Washington University in St. Louis. I would like to thank the department and particularly its chair, Jim Wertsch, for providing a collegial environment that encourages productivity, creativity, and interdisciplinary scholarship.

I would like to thank those colleagues that read and commented on portions of the book: Andy Clark, Lauretta Conklin Frederking, Dan Goldstein, Rob Henke, Philip Laughlin, Ingrid Monson, Robert Moore, Allen Orr, Whit Schonbein, and Michael Silverstein. I am particularly grateful to Mark Runco, series editor of Perspectives on Creativity, and to Barbara Bernstein, my editor.

Prologue

This book is about the casual, unplanned conversations that we have many times every day—with coworkers between cubicles or over lunch; with strangers while standing in the elevator or on a bus; with family over dinner, or friends at a party. When we meet someone in the hallway and stop for some casual small talk, neither of us knows what we're going to talk about ahead of time. Instead, we improvise these everyday conversations—that's why I call them *creating* conversations.

We don't take these conversations very seriously. The fact that we often call them *small talk* shows how unimportant we think they are. Although these casual conversations may seem trivial and unimportant, social scientists are finding that they have great meaning in our lives. Small talk with a colleague over dinner can help you to cement a relationship that could have unpredictable benefits down the road. Brainstorming with a friend can lead to the solution to a problem that has stumped you. And unplanned, meandering conversation is the essence of friendships, of marriage, and of family life.

This book explores the creativity of these everyday conversations. My scientific research has focused on both conversation and creativity, so it's not surprising that I would attempt to write a book that integrates these two topics. But in fact, this book was originally inspired by my experiences as a musician. I've been a jazz and rock musician for over 20 years, starting with classical piano lessons as a child, then teaching myself jazz while playing in my high school band. In college, I started listening to improvisational folk and blues—the virtuoso bluegrass of The Seldom Scene, the extended blues-inspired improvisations of the Grateful Dead. In the years after college, I played in a series of jazz and blues bands.

Many jazz musicians describe their musical interaction as a kind of conversation. So when I began my research into creativity and conversation at the University of Chicago, it was natural for me to study the similarities between music and language, and I chose to focus my research on the improvisational creativity of everyday conversation. In my first project, I spent about five years studying children's preschool pretend play, as they improvised mini-dramas at the sand table or with blocks; this research led to my first book, *Pretend Play as Improvisation.* Drawing on this experience, I started my second research project in 1992: a study of the spontaneous dialogues of Chicago improvisational theater groups. These two research projects exposed me to some of the most creative examples of conversation, and provided me with a unique perspective on everyday conversation. *Creating Conversations* explores the similarities between play, improv theater, and everyday conversation.

Since Chomsky first presented his influential theory of generative grammar in the 1950s, linguists have realized that language use is fundamentally creative; many of the sentences that we speak have never been spoken by anyone in the history of the language. The goal of Chomskian linguistics is to explain how we can create an infinite variety of sentences out of a finite vocabulary. When we think about conversational creativity, we often think of a person who creatively uses language—someone who can come up with just the right thing to say, or tell a joke well, or entertain a crowd with a funny story.

But unlike these solo verbal performances, conversation is fundamentally *collaborative.* Conversation is not like stand-up comedy; it's always improvised in a group. No one takes on the role of the "director," telling everyone what to say and when to talk; these decisions are collectively made, often without explicit discussion. Because conversations are collaboratively improvised, it's difficult to understand what's going on by focusing on any one participant; instead, we have to examine the entire group, and the interactional dynamics of the ensemble. Because no one can shine without the right partners and setting, being a creative conversationalist doesn't mean you'll have a creative conversation. That's why traditional psychology and linguistics haven't been very successful at understanding conversation; the study of conversation can't be solely psychological, because we can't reduce the study of conversation to the study of the behaviors or skills of any one participant. Likewise, theories of language that look to biology can't help us to understand these collaborative social dimensions of language use. The study of conversation requires a fundamentally *social* science, and that's why this book draws not only on psychological research, but also on the research of sociologists and anthropologists, and even communication research and literary theory.

There's another reason why I've drawn on sociology and anthropology: When we study collaboration and conversation, we find significant differences from culture to culture. Unfortunately, some of most widespread theories of conversation—developed primarily by American and British researchers—are implicitly based on Anglo-American concepts of how conversation works, and don't transfer very well to conversation in other cultures. In *Creating Conversations*, I'll explore these cross-cultural differences by presenting examples of conversational creativity in other cultures, taken from the field reports of linguistic anthropologists.

This book is in a long tradition of writers who've compared everyday life to stage performance. This approach to everyday social life is associated with influential modern thinkers including Erving Goffman, Richard Schechner, Victor Turner, and Kenneth Burke. However, all of these writers—by basing their metaphors on conventional, scripted performance—neglected improvisational creativity. Scripted metaphors for everyday life can be traced back at least to 1600, when Shakespeare wrote the famous lines "All the world's a stage / And all the men and women merely players."[1] In writing "merely" players, Shakespeare meant that none of us have much of a chance to be that creative, or to influence the course of events. Theater metaphors were quite common during Shakespeare's time, reflecting the widespread belief in predestination, and in an omniscient God who directed life's play.

In our own time, the sociologist Erving Goffman developed an influential *dramaturgical* theory of social life, starting with his 1959 book *The Presentation of Self in Everyday Life*. In a career spanning three decades, Goffman worked out a theory of how our everyday actions are dramatic. Goffman is the intellectual grandfather of this book, and without his insights, this book would not have been possible. Unlike the predestination implied by Shakespeare's metaphor, Goffman realized that the performances of everyday life involved creativity. By treating interaction as a kind of game—focusing on an individual's strategies and moves during interaction—Goffman explored the creative options available to individuals. Although his game metaphor acknowledged the creative potential of interaction, Goffman preferred to emphasize that our everyday performances are highly constrained by the scripts that we learned from our culture, and that we are a lot less spontaneous than we like to think.[2]

In contrast to these scripted theater metaphors, my use of the theater metaphor emphasize *improvisational* performance. This focus on improvisation leads me to focus more closely on dialogue than most of these theorists, because the defining feature of improv theater is that the actors create their dialogue on stage, rather than reading from a script. An improvisational performance theory must focus primarily on the creativity of conversation. In developing such a theory, my research has drawn primarily on two traditions: first, creativity research, which has focused on the sciences and the arts; second, the linguistic anthropology of verbal performance—the study of language use in rituals, jokes, storytelling, and gossip. Although addressing similar themes, these areas of research rarely overlap; linguistic anthropologists do not draw on psychological theories of creativity when they analyze verbal art, and creativity researchers have rarely studied performance. However, by the mid 1990s, there had been over 30 years of research into verbal creativity in oral traditions, and much of this research provides insights that extend to creativity more generally. I first tried to bring these fields together by editing the 1997 book *Creativity in Performance,* and I started writing *Creating Conversations* while this earlier volume was taking shape.

Creating Conversations is written for a broad audience. I hope that researchers in several different disciplines will benefit from its integrative treatment of a large body of research on conversational creativity. However, no prior knowledge of research in the field is necessary to understand this book; it would also be appropriate for an educated reader or an undergraduate student interested in finding out more about conversation research.

I introduce each topic by focusing on examples and anecdotes—bits of conversation from everyday life, cartoons, television sitcoms, or from my past research on play and theater. The creativity of these conversations is almost always hidden under the surface of what is said; it's not found in the literal meaning of language. It takes some close analysis to fully tease out what's going on; in many cases, the participants themselves can't tell you exactly what they were doing, because their creativity was subconscious and implicit. A researcher has to replay the tape more than just once or twice, spending days to fully understand even the briefest of conversations. After each of my conversation examples, I'll engage in this sort of in-depth interpretation of the dialogue, demonstrating how conversation researchers tease out those aspects of the interaction that usually remain unstated and beneath the surface.

Following each analysis, I'll show how the example connects to central concerns of social science theory, including psychology, linguistic anthropology, sociolinguistics, folkloristics, and performance theory.

The last 30 years have been an exciting time for researchers who study conversation, because a wide range of social theorists have realized that conversation is one of the keys to understanding social life. Consequently, although it's not a major theme of the book, we'll indirectly touch on many current issues in social theory.

Improvisation is the central theme running through all of the chapters, and in Chapter 1, "Scripts and Improvisations," I describe improvisational theater and I explore the many parallels between improvised stage dialogues and creating conversations. In everyday conversation, we are like actors without a script—we make up our dialogue as we go along. That's why conversation requires creativity, and the ability to work together with others—no one creates a conversation single-handedly. I describe the unique approach to conversation that improvising actors have developed—a set of guidelines that help them create dialogues on stage. We'll gain a deeper understanding of what goes on in improvisation, and we'll begin to understand how much creativity is required when we speak without a script and without a director.

Chapter 2, "Dialogues," continues on this theme, exploring specific techniques that conversation researchers have studied, and showing how creating conversations proceed differently in different cultures. We aren't consciously aware of most of the tools that we use to help us improvise conversations, but these principles and rules are part of our shared cultural knowledge. Although conversation works differently in different cultures and different countries, we'll see that all human societies share some basic techniques.

Chapter 3, "Audiences," focuses on the listener. We often think that conversation is simple communication: We have a thought, and then form a sentence to deliver it to our audience. But conversation researchers have discovered that the audience has a significant effect on what we say, while we're saying it. We aren't consciously aware of how much of an influence our audience has on our words, because we instantly change our conversation to match whoever is present. In this chapter we'll see many examples of people changing their talk to fit the audience—with a special focus on the most creative types of conversations, those that involve *indirect audiences, overhearers,* and *multiple audiences.* Perhaps more than any other chapter, these examples emphasize that all conversation is collaboratively created.

Chapter 4, "Rehearsals," is about how conversations change over time, with a focus on three kinds of change. The chapter begins with several examples of individual learning—how children learn to create conversations, and how we continue to change and develop as adults. If conversation is so difficult, then how come we can all do it? We don't remember how much work it was to learn how to create a conversation; we learn it early in childhood, with our families and during play with friends. But individual learning is not the only way that conversations evolve over time. Social groups can learn, through a kind of ensemble rehearsal. And conversation itself changes over time—it takes on a life of its own, and evolves just like other aspects of our culture.

Chapter 5, "Characters," is about creating conversations and the self. Everyday conversation is the most important way that we present ourselves to the world; it's how people develop first impressions; it's the way our friends get to know us. Our talk also says a lot about how we want to be perceived—the persona that we create for different people, different situations, and different social goals. In this chapter, we'll explore how we use conversation to tell people about who we are—with a focus on how our conversations change to present different aspects of our personality in different contexts. This focus will show us that, in an interesting sense, our self-creation is also collaborative.

Chapter 6, "Settings," is about how conversations change in different situations, and how we can even create the context with conversation. Our conversations take place in many different settings—at the office, at home, with friends. We don't talk the same way all the time; in fact, we frequently change our conversational style to match the situation. What are the subtle shifts in conversational style that let everyone know what kind of situation this is? Even more intriguing are those ambiguous settings where no one is sure exactly what's going on. In such conversations, people creatively negotiate what the setting will be; in a very real sense, they collaboratively create the conversational context. In Chapter 6, we'll explore how our words tell people what kind of situation we think we're in, and how often our words themselves creatively define the situation.

In Chapter 7, "Performances," we'll weave together everything we've learned about conversation, connecting it all to the main theme of the book—that conversation is improvised, and is collaboratively created by all of the participants. We'll bring these insights to bear on the most common everyday conversations—dinner conversation at home, collaborations and meetings at work, small talk with friends, and the educational conversations that take place in classrooms. We'll see that improvisational creativity is important in all of these conversations.

Conversational researchers have made great strides forward in the last few decades. This is a young field on the verge of a rapid expansion in knowledge; there's an exciting sense of unexplored possibility, particularly with respect to the most creative uses of conversation. I've tried to share my enthusiasm about the creativity of conversation, and if I communicate some of the excitement of this research, I will have been successful.

Chapter 1

Scripts and Improvisations

Scripts even in the hands of unpracticed players can come to life because life itself is a dramatically enacted thing. All the world is not, of course, a stage, but the crucial ways in which it isn't are not easy to specify.
—Erving Goffman, *The Presentation of Self in Everyday Life*[1]

Our study begins with an exploration of two key facts about conversation—two characteristics that make it especially creative. These key facts become clear when we compare our creating conversations with the scripted dialogues of the theater.

Long before we see a play on stage, it starts in the mind of a playwright, who generates the script; and the script provides the actors with their lines. However, this leads to a problem with Goffman's classic metaphor of everyday life—because our everyday conversations do not have a script. This is the first key fact about conversations—they are creative *because* there is no script. Because we don't have a script, we have to *improvise* our lines.

The script is only the beginning of the long, hard work that results in a play. Before any of us can see a play, a large cast of characters has to turn it into a performance—including a director, a stage crew, and the actors. And each of these players has his or her own creative influence on the production that we see. If it's a first-time production of a new script, directors typically work collaboratively with the playwright to develop the initial script; the playwright may even sit in on the rehearsals, and make changes on the spot based on how the dialogue sounds.[2] Even if it's a classic play by Shakespeare, a director's interpretation can result in very different productions. The director's vision guides the actors, telling them how to phrase their lines, how to interact with each other—everything that's not in the script.

But in everyday conversations, we act without a director. This is the second key fact about conversations—they are creative *because* there is no director. Because we don't have a director guiding us, we have to collaboratively improvise the direction of our everyday conversations—for example, choosing a topic, choosing how serious or humorous we will be, choosing whether to be formal or informal.

These two facts—there is no script, and there is no director—show that our everyday conversations are fundamentally different from stage performance. So what was Goffman getting at in the above epigraph? What do scripts have to do with our creating conversations? Answering that question is the main topic of this first chapter. I'll begin by describing an influential psychological theory of social life—a theory that proposes that we develop mental models of the social world that look a lot like a script, with a different script for each type of social situation we might find ourselves in. This kind of theory seems to work for some sorts of social situations, but doesn't work very well in situations where there is no script—when we have to improvise our dialogue, in collaboration with others. To gain insight into the improvisationality of conversation, I'll describe *improvisational theater*—an alternative form of theater developed in Chicago—where the actors do not use a script, but instead generate all of their dialogue on stage in front of the audience.

We'll learn from this exploration that improvisation doesn't mean "anything goes." The most talented improvisers—jazz musicians and improv theater actors—know that no improviser invents everything from scratch in every performance. Creative improvisation depends on a lifetime of practice and rehearsal, and improvisers have a large body of material that they draw on during performance. It's the same in conversation; we don't invent everything that we say from scratch in every conversation, but that doesn't mean it's not creative. Even though our conversations are improvised, we still use small bits of structure that seem almost scripted. Exploring this tension between script and improvisation will help us to see what Goffman was getting at—to see how scripts are used in creating conversations.

I'll close the chapter by exploring the implications of these two key facts about creating conversations. How can we engage in coherent, seamless, and even artful conversation without the guidance of a script or a director? Answering this question will lead us to a discussion of some important contemporary discoveries in social science, discoveries that have influenced research in economics, artificial intelligence, and social psychology.

Both of these key facts about creating conversations—they are not scripted and not directed—lead us to the key theme of this book: Creating conversations are *improvisations*. This theme runs through all of the remaining chapters, and this chapter is an important introduction to everything that follows.

SCRIPTS

A few months ago, I visited Kansas City for the first time. When I visit new cities, I like to go without planning ahead. I don't read any tourist guides or ask for restaurant recommendations. I prefer to improvise my vacations, exploring without being tied to a schedule. On my last day in Kansas City, I decided to stop for lunch before the drive back to St. Louis; true to my improvisational style, I stopped in the first restaurant that looked interesting.

I paused for a moment after walking in, figuring out what kind of restaurant it was. As I stood inside the door, I wondered, was I supposed to seat myself, or wait for a hostess? Was everyone paying at the cash register or were they giving money to the waiter? Was there a blackboard on the wall with the menu or with the day's specials? I took all of this in before the hostess even had time to ask "One for lunch?"

Even after being seated, I still hadn't worked out which variation of the restaurant "play" I was in. Was it my waitress that had seated me? Or would a different person be coming over to take my order? Is this person who is filling my glass going to take my order or is he the busboy? Was I supposed to wait for someone to tell me the daily specials?

Of course, in spite of these uncertainties, I knew the rough outlines of what could happen. The restaurant is one of those everyday situations where we are aware that there's a standard sequence of events to be followed—almost the same script every time. You could almost write out the sequence of events in a computer program. In fact, two Yale scientists—Roger Schank and Robert Abelson—first tried to write a "restaurant" program in the 1970s. In a now famous 1977 paper, they proposed a computational version of Shakespeare's original metaphor, which they called the *script* model of everyday action.[3]

Of course we don't go through our everyday lives reading from a script. But Schank and Abelson observed that there are common sequences of events, conventional routines that we can rely on in certain situations. Although these are not word-for-word scripts, they are loose outlines that guide everyday performance. Although Schank and Abelson chose to call them scripts, other researchers have called these loose outlines *routines* or *event schemata.*[4]

Schank and Abelson demonstrated the script theory by using the restaurant example. All Americans, of a given social class and cultural group, have eaten in restaurants and know the routine. So when I was in a strange restaurant in Kansas City, I still knew what all of the possible script variations were. Schank and Abelson proposed that the restaurant experience was stored in your brain, and that it looked something like a computer program. Their computer version of the restaurant script looked like this:

Script: Restaurant
Roles: Customer, waitress, chef, cashier
Scene 1:   Entering. Enter restaurant, look for an empty table, decide where to sit, go sit down.
Scene 2:   Ordering. Receive menu, read menu, decide what to order, give order to waitress.
Scene 3:   Eating. Receive the food, eat it.
Scene 4:   Exiting. Ask for check, receive check, tip waitress, walk to cashier, pay cashier, leave.

But my confusion in the Kansas City restaurant shows that not all restaurants have the same script. First of all, this simple script applies only to certain kinds of restaurants. Some restaurants don't use a host, and expect you to seat yourself, thus altering scene 1. Some restaurants are buffet style, like Boston Market, where you get your own food before sitting down, changing all four scenes. In some restaurants, in scene 4 you're expected to pay the waiter, rather than paying at the cash register.

If we programmed a word-for-word script into a robot, it wouldn't be able to handle the slightest variation from the script—just like an actor stumbles when a fellow actor flubs a line. To handle variation, our everyday scripts must allow for a range of common possibilities, almost like a flow chart that represents each possible scene as a path leading from the prior scene. The script program is a way of describing a variety of possible restaurant experiences. If the possible sequences of events in a situation are limited, then we can imagine constructing a flow chart—a computer script—as a way to summarize all of the possibilities. To use a musical metaphor, the most common restaurant script is the *theme,* and the flow chart describes the *variations.*

The script theory is appealing because there are many everyday situations that have a conventional pattern. The psychologist Ellen Langer has drawn on the script model, proposing that each of us has a repertoire of thousands of scripts that are cued by certain situations. We form a mental script when we overlearn a task, and we "automatize" the sequence of behaviors. Langer observes that once we start performing one of these scripts, we can do it *mindlessly,* without conscious thought; and her research explores how often this can lead to mistakes, and how we can become more *mindful* in everyday life.[5]

Although we all use these scripts, many of the situations that we find ourselves in are much more unstructured, with no conventions about what events will occur and what order they will occur in. Most of our everyday conversations occur in unstructured situations: gossip, mealtime conversations, or party small talk. Improvisation is perhaps the most remarkable and important aspect of these creating conversations. And in fact, once we develop a deeper understanding of how improvisation works, we'll be better prepared to understand the role of scripts in conversation. I'll start by drawing on my own experiences with Chicago improvisational theater to show how creative improvised dialogues can be. Then I'll turn to an examination of those conversations that aren't so improvised—when we are more scripted. I'll show you that we're creative even as we weave scripted material into our conversational improvisations. By the end of this chapter, we'll have a more complete understanding of how scripts and improvisations are used to create conversation.

IMPROVISATION

La vie est plus belle quand on l'écrit soi-même (Life is best played without a script).
—Advertising slogan for the perfume "Champs-Elysees," Fall, 1996[6]

To help us understand performance in everyday life, we need to turn to a new kind of experimental theater—improvisational theater. Chicago is world-famous as a center of improv. When you enter the theater and take your seat, you see a stage that is empty except for a few plain, wooden chairs. On schedule, the house lights go down, and the actors— about eight men and women—run up to the bare stage, and ask the audience for a suggestion: "Give us a location!" Someone in the audience yells out, "A sidewalk!"

"We take you to—a sidewalk." The stage lights go down. The actors all wait at the sides of the stage. Then the lights go up—and the empty stage is like a blank canvas. Here's the beginning of a two-minute scene that the actors created at the Improv Institute, in 1993, in Chicago:[7]

(1) Andrew steps to stage center, pulls up a chair and sits down, miming the action of driving by holding an imaginary steering wheel)

(2) (Ben steps to stage center, stands next to Andrew, fishes in pocket for something)

(3) Andrew On or off?

(4) Ben   I'm getting on, sir (continues fishing in his pocket)

(5) Andrew In or out?

(6) Ben   I'm getting in!
             I'm getting in!

(7) Andrew Did I see you tryin' to get in the back door a couple of stops back?

(8) Ben   Uh . . .

The first actor to jump to stage front and start the scene can do almost anything. Apart from the location, nothing has been decided, no plot, no characters, no events. The first actors can take on any role, perform any action, and create any relationship between their characters that they like. For novice improvisers, this uncertainty can be terrifying. Actors call it "performing without a net," because there is nothing to catch you if you fail—no script, and no prompter to read you lines. But only a few seconds into the scene, the actors quickly establish a basic dramatic framework. Once this happens, the actors have to work within that framework.

By the end of this exchange, Andrew and Ben have developed a reasonably complex drama. They know that Andrew is a bus driver, and that Ben is a potential passenger. Andrew is getting a little impatient, and Ben may be a little shifty, perhaps trying to sneak on. But how do the audience and the actors know this? How was it decided? It's important to emphasize how unpredictable all of this is, how this tiny bit of dialogue could have gone in a hundred other directions. For example, at line (2), Ben had a range of creative options available. Ben could have pulled up a second chair and sat down next to the "driver," and he would have become a passenger in a car. At line (3), Andrew had an equal range of options. He could have addressed Ben as his friend, and Ben's hand in his pocket could be searching for theater tickets: "Don't tell me you forgot the tickets *again*!" These are just the most obvious of the dramatic options that can occur on stage. For a more crazy example, at line (2), Ben could have addressed Andrew as Captain Kirk of *Star Trek*, creating a TV-show parody. Look back over these eight lines and you'll discover more and more possible directions that Andrew or Ben could have suggested. Because each line provides its own unlimited possibilities, a combinatorial explosion quickly results in hundreds of other performances that could have been.

Because of the creative possibilities at every line of the dialogue, neither actor alone can decide what will happen and then impose the decision on the other actor. Andrew and Ben are working together in a collaborative duet. Even without a director and without a script, a dramatic scene emerges after only eight lines.

Chicago improvisational theater has its roots in a series of theater games developed for children by a drama teacher, Viola Spolin, in the 1930s and 1940s. Her son, Paul Sills, used these games to found the first improvisational comedy group, The Compass Players, at the University of Chicago in 1955. The Compass later evolved into the well-known improv group, The Second City, the model for the popular TV show *Saturday Night Live*. And improv's influence goes far beyond late-night comedy: Many critics believe that Chicago-style improv was one of the most influential developments in American theater; a long list of famous and talented actors started their careers in improv groups, including Ed Asner, John Belushi, and Alan Alda.[8]

Since its origins in the 1950s, improvisational theater has grown dramatically in Chicago and in other urban centers. With this growth has come a remarkable variety of styles and approaches to improvisation. These styles can be grouped loosely into three main approaches. The bus stop skit at the Improv Institute is an example of the first approach—*scene* improv. The actors take an audience suggestion, and then perform a dramatic scene, typically under five minutes long. The second approach, and the most popular, is *game improv*. Games are the most likely to get quick laughs from the audience, and that's why this approach is often called *improv comedy*. These groups break up the evening's performance into a series of short *games* of five minutes or less, which each start from one or two audience suggestions. There are dozens of different games widely used by improvisational ensembles; each game has a unique set of constraints on how the performance will proceed. A common game is Freeze Tag. After asking for an audience suggestion, perhaps a location or a starting line of dialogue, two performers begin to improvise a scene. The actors accompany their dialog with exaggerated gestures and broad physical movements. The audience is instructed to shout "freeze" whenever they think the actors are in interesting physical positions. Immediately, the actors must "freeze" themselves in position. A third actor then walks up to these two and taps one of them on the shoulder. The tapped actor leaves the stage, and the new actor must take his place, in the same position, and then begin a completely different scene with her first line of dialogue, playing on the ambiguities inherent in the physical relationship of the frozen actors.

The third style of performance, *long-form improv,* is the most experimental. These groups also start with an audience suggestion, but then they improvise a 30-minute play, complete with scene changes, multiple plot lines, and complex relationships. The original long-form improv, called "The Harold," was created by Del Close, one of the original Second City cast members from the 1950s. Both tourists and locals make the pilgrimage to Belmont avenue on the North Side to see performances of his group, the ImprovOlympic. You don't know what to expect from this group—you've only heard that it's not like any kind of play you've seen before.

Before the house lights dim, Charna Halpern, a co-founder, walks to the front and announces "The show you are about to see is completely improvised. Could we have a suggestion for a problem?" Audience members yell out suggestions immediately: "Dog with ringworm." "Lost my engagement ring." "Suicidal roommate." Charna raises her hand to silence the crowd, and says "I heard 'dog with ringworm' first." She leaves the stage, and the lights dim for a few seconds. Then, the stage lights rise, and we see the cast of nine actors and actresses in a semicircle, facing the audience. They begin a sort of group free-association, each saying one line related to the suggestion, "Dog with ringworm." Their lines follow quicker and quicker, building to a crescendo, until suddenly, the stage goes black again. A few seconds later, the stage lights are up again, and two of the actors begin to improvise a dialogue. The rest of the show continues—a full half-hour, one-act play on the theme—with the nine actors entering and exiting, improvising smooth scene transitions, creating multiple plot lines that interweave and characters with complex relationships.

These performances often are so good that many audience members assume a script is being followed. Yet this is never the case with authentic improv groups. The actors work very hard to avoid repeating even brief segments of a performance from a prior night. The first time I saw it, I thought *how can they do this without a script?*

Although working without a script is an unusual situation for most actors, it's not so different from what we do every day in creating conversations. In a book about improv technique, the actor Kim Johnson wrote, "Anyone can improvise. We all do it every day—none of us goes through our day to day life with a script to tell us what to do."[9] I'm fascinated by improv, because I think it has the potential to teach us so much about everyday conversation. Like improv, our everyday lives are unscripted, and we are often placed in situations in which we have to improvise.

William Calvin, a prominent neurophysiologist, argues that this improvisational ability is at the core of human intelligence. In his 1996 book *How Brains Think*, Calvin argues that "Intelligence is about the *process* of improvising," because it allows us to perform when we don't know what to do ahead of time. Intelligent improvising serves us well, but some days are so unpredictable that they overwhelm even the most improvisational among us. That's why we have to unwind with predictable, scripted entertainments: "After a hard day awash in unpredictability, you tend to seek relief in ritual, music, or sitcoms." (At the end of this chapter, we'll see just how predictable sitcoms are.) Calvin argues that there is biological and evolutionary evidence for the brain's improvisational nature, and connects intelligent improvisation with both creativity and play.[10]

The childhood disorder *autism* provides additional evidence that improvisational skill may be part of our biological make-up. A distinctive feature of autistic children is that their behavior is extremely ritualized and scripted; the psychiatrists' bible—the *Diagnostic and Statistical Manual of Mental Disorders*—describes the symptoms as "stereotyped and repetitive use of language," and "inflexible adherence to specific, nonfunctional routines or rituals."[11] Both of these behavioral symptoms suggest that autistics cannot handle improvisation, and thus use scripts to do the best they can. Their "conversations" sound very odd, because they are never collaborative improvisations—they cannot listen and respond appropriately. Some adults have a mild form of autism that results in a failure to communicate well with others, and they have trouble making friends. Some psychologists have begun to treat this condition by teaching them improvisational skills—how to give and take, when to talk and when to stop talking. The earlier in life that they are taught these lessons in treatment, the fewer the emotional scars.[12]

To learn more about improvisation, I joined an improv group as their pianist, and I performed with this group for almost two years. I attended rehearsals and training classes, interviewed the actors and directors, and videotaped all of their performances. At the end of this two-year period, I visited most of the major professional improvisational groups in Chicago, videotaping performances and interviewing actors and directors.

While performing improv theater, I discovered that the actors use a small set of guidelines to help them create better improvisations. In improv training classes, aspiring actors learn these principles. Every improviser that I've met, from San Francisco to New York, follows the same guidelines. I was a little surprised by this. Because there are so many different professional groups and so many different teachers and schools of improvisation, I thought there would be differences of opinion. But this remarkable consensus made me realize that I was on to something: If these guidelines are so universal, then they must have something to teach us about everyday conversation.

Improvisers have developed these principles through repeated experience with what entertains the audience, and what leaves them cold. Improvisational actors have to test their theories about conversation in front of a live audience, and that's why these theories can tell us a lot about creating conversations.

The First Rule of Improv: Yes, and . . .

The single most important rule of improv is "Yes, and." In every line of dialogue, an actor should do two things: Accept the material introduced in the prior line, and add something new to the emerging drama. It's extremely important to accept the material introduced by the preceding actor. Another way that actors say this rule is "Don't deny." To deny a fellow actor is to reject whatever he has just introduced into the dialogue. Everything that is introduced by an actor must be fully embraced and accepted by the other actors on stage. Denial stops a scene dead. In a scene at the ImprovOlympic theater in Chicago,[13] a man and a woman were taking a romantic stroll through the park. The woman had the idea that she would find a lottery ticket—a scenario rife with romantic possibility—but it didn't turn out like she planned. She initiated the scene change by pointing at the ground and saying, with surprise:

Woman: What's that?
Man: It's just a pile of shit.
Woman: (Frustrated) No, it's a lottery ticket!

This is an outright denial. Once the man has defined "it" to be a pile of shit, the woman has to forget her preconceived idea about the lottery ticket plot, and accept that it is now a pile of shit. The problem started with her first turn, when she broke the "Yes, and" rule by asking a question, because the question does not contribute anything new to the dramatic frame. She should have simply said "Look! A lottery ticket!" Good actors keep the scene moving by introducing something new to the dramatic frame with every turn. No turn is wasted. If an actor fails to add something, he is forcing the other actors to do more than their share of the creative building of the frame.

The "don't deny" rule encourages a democratic, collaborative performance. Performances are more effective if the frame is created collectively, emerging from everyone's creative input. Actors would rather create the drama collaboratively, rather than have one person making all the decisions and the others simply saying "Yes"; that's not the way that ensemble improv works.

Improvisational performances are unpredictable, and some nights are better than others. When I asked actors to evaluate the quality of different performances, they were pretty consistent in their judgments. The most common reason that they didn't like a skit was "There was too much denial." The "don't deny" rule is just as important in everyday conversation. When a conversation leaves us frustrated, thinking "What just happened?," when we feel as if we weren't connecting somehow, it's often because there was a lot of denial in the conversation. The "—And . . ." half of the rule is equally important. If the person we're talking to doesn't offer anything new during the conversation, we're likely to think it was boring.

The Second Rule of Improv: Don't Write the Script in Your Head

The second key rule of improv is "Don't write the script in your head." I heard this rule in the first improv class that I ever attended. My ears perked up, because here was an improv expert talking about writing a script! What was going on?

The lottery ticket/shit confusion is a perfect example of what happens when this rule isn't followed. When the woman pointed to an imaginary lottery ticket and said "What's that?" she simultaneously began to imagine a fairly elaborate scene, a romantic scenario of a couple finding a lottery ticket in the park. She was probably thinking that it would be a winning ticket. My teacher called this advance planning "writing the script in your head." For this woman, writing the script in her head put her on autopilot, focusing on herself, and caused her to fail to hear her partner's dramatic proposal, resulting in a denial. Her inward focus on her own creativity resulted in a lack of the necessary outward focus, toward the group creativity.

Imagine a scene that begins with a man and a woman on stage. The woman starts the dialogue by saying:[14]

Woman: I've missed you, dear.

If the woman were writing the script in her head, she might have initiated this exchange thinking that the man was her husband, in the navy, and just back from a six-month tour. Her mind would already be working on the romantic implications of the scene. But her line is compatible with several different plot lines. Here's what the man said next:

Man: Yeah, sorry I haven't called more often, Mom.

Now we can see that the woman's opening line could have been spoken by a wife, or by a mother. Because of the "no denial" rule, she has to proceed as the "mother" now. But if she had already started writing a different script in her head, she'd have to take a second to recover, and the scene won't flow as naturally.

The "don't write" rule encourages the collaborative creation of a performance. It forces the actors to "stay in the moment," another way of phrasing this rule, rather than thinking ahead to the rest of the scene. It's a hard thing to do, because it's so natural to think through the subsequent flow of an interaction. Try to imagine being the actress, on stage in front of an audience, saying "I've missed you, dear," and not having any specific idea of what your relationship is. Hard to do, isn't it? But that's exactly what a good improv actor will do. It involves a great deal of trust: The actress has to trust her partner to select the relationship. It involves relinquishing control to the group process, to trust that creativity will emerge from the conversation. Actors often talk in terms of "trust" and "losing one's ego."

These examples emphasize the paradoxical kind of non-planning, non-directing mindset that improv actors have to be in. It's simply not possible for any one person to single-handedly create the improv drama. Likewise, creativity in conversation is more than one person's creativity: It's always a collaborative performance.

The Third Rule of Improv: Listen to the Group Mind

Think of a conversation where you felt like the other person wasn't hearing what you were saying. Your comments weren't responded to; instead, that person seemed to be responding to something you didn't actually say. Often this is because that person was writing the script in his or her head, thinking ahead to the next comment rather than listening and responding to you. Or, think of a conversation that was very important to you, where you were thinking hard to make sure you didn't forget what you wanted to say. You're waiting for just the right moment in the conversation to bring up an important point. The problem is that you're not listening—you need to shift the focus from your own plan, to the *group mind*.

An example from jazz will show what I mean by "listen to the group mind." Like improv theater, jazz performances are group collaborations. When I was learning how to improvise jazz on the piano, I bought an album of songs by the famous saxophonist John Coltrane. But this was not your usual Coltrane album—it had no saxophone track, only piano, bass, and drums. When I turned the stereo balance all the way to the left, the piano dropped out, and I heard only bass and drums. Then I sat at my piano and played along with the stereo, imagining that I was Coltrane's pianist, McCoy Tyner. These albums—called *Music Minus One*—are learning tools, recorded by studio musicians. They copy famous jazz performances, but with the solos left out of the recording. A young saxophonist or trumpet player may not be ready to perform with other jazz musicians, but by improvising a solo over the record, he gets a taste of the experience of performing.

But any jazz musician will tell you that this is nothing like playing jazz with a live band. What makes it different? When all of the musicians are improvising together, everyone is responding to everyone else. You don't know what the drummer or pianist will do next; you have to be prepared for the unexpected. All of the musicians create something new together, and the performance emerges out of their musical conversation. When I played with the *Music Minus One* album, there was no collaboration, no group responsiveness—it was not really a conversation.

People who've never improvised often think of something like Music Minus One when they think of jazz. In a jazz club, they watch the soloist, and ignore the rest of the band; they don't realize how much conversation goes on between the musicians. The ability to listen is the hardest skill for a musician to learn, and I can always tell which jazz musicians are novices, because they play without listening—as if the rest of the band were a *Music Minus One* recording. The unique, defining feature of jazz improvisation is the importance of group interaction.

This is what actors mean when they say "listen to the group mind." Beginning improvisers have to be taught to listen. They often start out by saying whatever they want, because they think it's clever or a good one-liner. But it doesn't matter how much the audience laughs at your line if you've destroyed the group mind that everyone has been carefully crafting together.

When I played with the *Music Minus One* album, I didn't have to listen; no matter what I played, the recording would still be the same. The recording allowed me to focus on my own clever solo lines, and this is helpful for a beginner. But to be a good ensemble improviser, you have to shift your focus from trying to be funny or clever, to trying to listen to everyone else. Your lines should always work to further the evolving group mind.

Of course, we can't be completely open and flexible in all of our conversations. Sometimes our goal in the conversation is to say something very specific, and we feel as if we can't let the conversation go in just any direction. But in many of our everyday encounters, we could follow this improv rule more effectively—by relinquishing control of the conversation, listening to the group mind, and allowing the talk to emerge from everyone's creative contributions.

Think back to a time when the conversation was particularly interesting, when everyone was talking and the conversation flowed smoothly without pause. What made this conversation so memorable? It's because we followed the rules for good improvisation—no denial, don't write the script in your head, listen to the group mind. These rules should seem familiar, because in our most creative conversations, we follow the same guidelines.

The Improvisation Zone

After aspiring actors get through the first few months of classes, they've learned the above rules pretty well. They are already skilled at collaborating with their fellow actors to create a believable, improvised scene. When actors reach this intermediate level, they have a new kind of problem, one that you probably wouldn't expect—their performances get to be, in a sense, too good—too believable, too predictable. That's because they're all part of the same society, with the same language, the same TV shows, and the same movies. Improvising actors assume a lot of shared knowledge of each other—conventional situations like the restaurant script; all of the symbols of pop culture, including TV shows, movies, and advertising jingles. If the audience is asked for a location, and someone yells out "Restaurant," the actors will probably start out by enacting the standard version of the restaurant script.

But this alone would be a boring play; improvisers know that they have to muddy the waters early in a scene, to create tension and novelty. If the audience suggests "restaurant," for example, one of the actors will do something to radically break out of the stereotypical restaurant script. Think of all of the *Saturday Night Live* skits that start out with a couple seated in a restaurant. They always tweak the script—the humor comes from violating our expectations of what usually happens in a restaurant. One of the classic examples is John Belushi's "Samurai Waiter" character, a running gag with the 1970s cast. A couple would enter a restaurant and sit down. According to the restaurant script, the waiter should then approach the table. Instead, John Belushi, dressed as a Samurai warrior, would enter, brandishing a large sword, speaking in incomprehensible, guttural syllables. By the end of the skit, Belushi would cut the table in half with his sword, frighten the couple, and in general, completely demolish the conventional restaurant script.

In the kinds of improv performances that I studied in Chicago, if a scene started out with a couple in a restaurant, the actors would work hard to break out of the expected script, because they know that the expected sequence of events would be boring. Halfway through one scene that started in a restaurant, I saw one of the diners hop up excitedly, point to the back of the stage, and say "Look out! The porthole has broken and the ship is flooding!" Suddenly the actors are no longer in a restaurant—they have been eating on a ship, and their meal has been interrupted by a dangerous, unexpected event.

As with so much of comedy, the actors assume a shared knowledge with the audience. Only audiences that know the restaurant script, and all of its possible variants, will get the joke. The porthole is a pretty dramatic shift for a restaurant scene—but actors know just how far they can go. Once they've established that they are eating dinner, the actors can't do something that would be incompatible, such as, for example, bending down and starting to work on a car engine.

Actors know just the right degree of discontinuity and unexpectedness. They stay in the *improvisation zone* between complete predictability and going too far, between our shared knowledge about conventional situations, and doing something so inconsistent that it just doesn't make sense. Improvisational actors become highly attuned to this zone, and they are always trying to stay in the zone.

We also have to stay in an improvisation zone during our everyday conversations. If someone always says the predictable thing, we won't have a very interesting conversation with them; we'll probably think of them as a boring person. But if a person is always saying odd things, mouthing nonstop non sequiturs that don't connect, it may be very creative but we won't enjoy it very much. Creativity is important in conversation, but it has to be the right degree of creativity. It has to fall within the improvisation zone.

The challenge of staying in the improvisation zone is responsible for the experience of *flow* that we get from a particularly good conversation. The psychologist Mike Csikszentmihalyi defined "flow" as the state of mind we get into when we're doing something that really clicks, when we forget about the time and become absorbed by an activity. His research has shown that flow occurs in a zone as well, a zone where the challenges of the task are perfectly matched to the ability of the person. If the task is too challenging, we simply get frustrated; if the task is too easy, we become bored. Improvisational theater companies don't make a lot of money; the actors keep doing it because they experience a high on stage that they don't get from conventional, scripted theater.[15]

Different situations provide us with different opportunities for creative conversation. At some points in a conversation, we have a great deal of freedom to say whatever we want—to be extremely creative in introducing a new topic or making an unexpected comment. The improvisation zone is large—we have many different choices about what to say next. At other times, our range of options may be more limited; the improvisation zone is smaller. In each case, our creative task is slightly different; we have to be able to judge the range of creative options available, and say something that fits well into the unique demands of that conversational situation. In the most creative conversations, we experience the flow that comes from balancing all of these things—listening to the emerging, collaborative creation that is the conversation itself, and creating novel contributions that fit in, and yet further the conversation's creative movement. Through it all, we have to stay creative, speaking like the improvising actors that we are.

We've all had the experience of being in a wonderful, flowing conversation, one that we would have no trouble calling creative. But at other times, we have boring, predictable conversations. And we can't always be as improvisational as we would like. In many everyday situations—like going to a restaurant—there's a basic script that everyone expects to be followed. Even scripted situations vary in how much individual creativity they permit. In a casual restaurant we might joke with the waiter, but in a formal restaurant we probably wouldn't.

Of course, we all know that conversations can be more or less creative. When you're buying stamps at the post office you won't try to be all that creative. If you are, the clerk will think you're weird, and the people waiting in line behind you will get impatient. You're expected to stick to predictable lines that anyone would say. In contrast, at a party, we're expected to be unscripted and improvisational. If you can't match your degree of conversational creativity to the situation, you'll come across as rude, boring, or simply clueless. Most everyday situations fall somewhere in between the party and the post office. We're all pretty good at sizing up the situation and picking the appropriate blend of script and improvisation.

Do we really want to say that the post office conversation is improvised? It seems like the script theory is more accurate in situations like the post office and the restaurant visit, where the improvisation zone is small. Now that we've seen the key role of improvisation in conversation, we can go back to the script, and get a better idea of where scripts really fit into everyday conversation.

BACK TO THE SCRIPT, PART 1:
USING SCRIPTED LINES IN CONVERSATION

In everyday situations like getting a haircut, we often use lines that we've heard other people use—We don't always make up completely new things to say. When the barber says "How's all the family?" no one would claim that he's being creative. These aren't really his own words, because thousands of people have said exactly that line in exactly that situation before. Like the barber, we often use catchphrases in conversation—phrases like "Could I talk to you for a minute?" or "Give me a break." Because a million people have said exactly the same sentence, we could think of these sentences as scripted lines. Linguists call these little bits of script *formulaic speech*. But using catchphrases still requires improvisational creativity; a catchphrase can send many different implicit messages, depending on the situation. In the following pages, I'll show several examples of the subtle, creative meanings that catchphrases can communicate. For example, Dagwood's barber uses catchphrases to send the message that this is a casual, friendly, relatively superficial conversation—his implicit message is that he is politely interested, but not being nosey. And in the same way, we often use catchphrases as a distancing mechanism, to indicate to the other person that we don't want to enter a truly creative, conversational performance. When we speak more spontaneously, improvising rather than using formulas, it sends the message that we are ready to enter into a more intimate conversation—fully focusing on our listener, our words personalized and created just for them.

A lot of small talk is formulaic, especially short interactions with people you don't know well—talking with the barber, or talking about the weather with a stranger in the elevator. Catchphrases and these short, conventional scripts are some of the hardest things to learn when we move to another country. We've learned the grammar of the language, and we may have a large vocabulary, but we don't yet know the hundreds of catchphrases that are used in everyday situations. Many foreign students in the United States have a common experience soon after arriving. A classmate passes by and asks, "How are you?" The new student interprets the question literally and provides a detailed answer, when he's expected to just complete the script with "Fine, thank you." When the classmate looks uninterested in his elaborate answer, he's offended, thinking that Americans don't say what they mean. The problem is that he hasn't yet learned this two-line script.

Catchphrases are lines that we all learned growing up, lines that we've all spoken. These catchphrases are second nature to us, since we live and breath our conversational culture every day. You are not the creator of these catchphrases, and when you say them, you're not really speaking your own words. For example, when someone says "Go ahead, make my day," you can't help but think of the Clint Eastwood's character in the movie *Dirty Harry*, and you might also recall President Reagan's famous repetition of the line. This basic idea was an important theme of the Russian literary theorist Mikhail Bakhtin. Bakhtin argued that even though each speaker intends his words to have a novel, personal meaning, those words have unavoidable connotations associated with past situations of use. A catchphrase demonstrates this point particularly well, because it's so obvious that the line has been spoken by others before. When we use a catchphrase, or say something with a stereotypical inflection or accent, everyone can't help but think of all of the other occasions on which they've heard the same thing. These connotations are like unavoidable baggage that the words bring with them from past situations of use; they're built into the catchphrases, the price we pay for using them. Bakhtin coined the term *dialogic* to describe this two-leveled nature of language; the two levels are the speaker's own meaning, and everyone's memory of how these words have been used in the past.[16]

Where do catchphrases come from? Like Clint Eastwood's famous line, many catchphrases originate in the popular culture of movies or TV shows. Popular culture also provides us with other kinds of conversational shorthand, such as styles of talking that remind everyone of other situations. When someone says "Wow, heavy, man," in a dazed tone, everyone thinks of a 60s-era stoner; if someone hunches his shoulders and speaks with an exaggerated German accent, it suggests a "mad scientist" character, recognizable from a multitude of late-night B movies.

Good improv actors are pop-culture experts, and improv actors assume that the audience will catch the references they make to popular TV shows or movies: bits and pieces of dialogue, familiar characters, or events from a famous sitcom episode or movie scene. Bernie Sahlins, a founder of The Second City theater in Chicago, explains that these pop culture references are a shorthand way of communicating quickly with your fellow actors and with the audience.[17] Improv actors know that each social group has its own distinctive speech style and catchphrases; a well-chosen catchphrase or a distinctive accent can implicitly tell us a great deal about a character: ethnic background, profession (lawyer or doctor), family role (father or son), status (an authority figure like a policemen or the boss), distinctive cultural stereotypes like cowboy, Southern redneck, or gay male. When the first actor steps to the front of the stage and starts to enact a Mad German Scientist character, a whole set of script possibilities is immediately suggested, and other possibilities get closed off. Actors use these styles of talking to communicate characters and situations, quickly and implicitly communicating to each other about the emerging drama.[18]

This kind of implicit communication is an example of what linguists call *indexicality,* from the Latin word for "point to" or "indicate." Your words are indexical when they indicate something about the situation that isn't in the literal meaning of the words. Using a well-known catchphrase or speech style is indexical, because it implicitly communicates so much about the situation; for example, if an actor starts talking in a Southern accent, he implicitly communicates to the audience that the setting for the scene is somewhere in the South, without ever having to say "Here we are in Ole' Mississippi." Some linguists estimate that as much as 90% of all of our spoken language is at least partially indexical—in other words, very little of what we say is completely context-free. Some of the most creative uses of language involve clever plays with indexicality, and we'll see many examples of creative indexicality throughout this book.[19]

In the above examples, choosing to use a catchphrase is a creative choice; for example, in everyday conversation people often use them just to get a laugh. It would be considered a little weird if someone spoke only in catchphrases and cliches. But there are some situations that require speakers to use catchphrases, such as high-pressure, performative jobs—a sportscaster, a radio DJ, an auctioneer. Even though these speakers use a lot of formulaic speech, their speech is still creative and improvisational. The Australian linguist Koenraad Kuiper, in his 1996 book *Smooth Talkers,* proposed an intriguing hypothesis: As the demands of the speaking situation increase, the speaker will use more and more scripted patterns, or catchphrases, during the performance. Kuiper called this *formulaic speech,* and proposes that "smooth talkers"—those with a unique fluency required in certain speech performance situations—draw on a large repertoire of formulas during their speaking. Kuiper tested his hypothesis by examining speech performance in two situations that demand high fluency: sports announcing and auctions. In each case, he examined a low-pressure context and a high-pressure one. For example, in sports announcing, he examined cricket announcing (slow, low pressure) and horse-race calling (fast, high pressure). And in auctions, he examined real-estate auctions and antique auctions at Sotheby's (low pressure), and tobacco auctions in North Carolina and wool auctions in Christchurch, New Zealand (high pressure). In auctions, for example, Kuiper's measure of "pressure" was the number of seconds it takes to make one sale. In both of the low-pressure auctions—real-estate and antiques—one sale typically took well over one minute. In contrast, the high-pressure auctions took only seconds; in wool auctions, one lot is sold every 10 seconds, and in tobacco auctions, a sale is made every five seconds—a dramatic contrast with the slower, refined pace at Sotheby's.[20]

Kuiper's hypothesis was supported: he found that all tobacco auctioneers used formulas; in fact, they did not use any freely created novel utterances! In the high-pressure situations, the speech was different from everyday speech because it depended on these formulaic phrases that had to be learned. High-pressure speakers drew from a stock set of standard phrases, unlike low-pressure speakers, who created sentences from scratch much as we do in everyday speech. And in high-pressure situations, the overall speech performance had a higher-level structure—with standard beginning, middle, and ends to the performance, and standard formulas for transitions between the sections.

Of course, these auctioneers don't just spout catchphrases like a robot—their creativity is still improvisational, because they have to respond immediately to all of the bidders, choosing exactly the right catchphrases at each moment. And like these skilled auctioneers, we also have to use creativity to choose when and where to use a catchphrase. Like an auctioneer, we still have to listen for the right moment in the conversation. For example, people in the early 1990s started adding a tag word, "NOT," after another comment that they disagreed with. The word is spoken with a flat emphasis, the same way every time. But it takes creative skill to use "NOT" appropriately—it doesn't always work. You have to *listen creatively* for the right moment to use this one-word catchphrase.

High-pressure speech situations often result in formulaic speech. But these aren't the only professions where scripted speech is required; sometimes, a situation can require formulaic speech, even though the speaker is not forced to respond quickly. Many professions are heavily dependent on specialized catchphrases that only have meaning for other experts in that area. For example, most of us have trouble understanding legal language—because of the many legal catchphrases that lawyers use, especially when they are in the courtroom. Defendants become understandably upset if they sense that the judge is simply spouting stock phrases at them; the outcome will affect their lives immensely, and they want to be treated like individuals. So why do judges keep using legalese? It's because judges have to balance the demands of two very different audiences: the laymen in the courtroom and the court record, which will be analyzed by other lawyers. Although the judge's job is to communicate with the defendants and the jury, they also know that their words will be written into the court record, and that anything they say could be used as grounds for an appeal. They are speaking not only to the laymen in the courtroom, but also, as they say, "to the record."

Even when they use legal catchphrases, some judges still try to give the impression that they are speaking spontaneously. The linguist Susan Philips analyzed the courtroom language of nine different judges, over the course of many different cases.[21] She found that all nine judges use the same formulaic speech—the same scripted lines—with every defendant. But most of the judges try to make the defendants think that they are speaking spontaneously, just for them. Even though they use the same scripted lines over and over, they use special speech techniques to make their speech sound more spontaneous: They pause, as if they are formulating their words; they pretend to make mistakes, starting their sentence again. Even though they used extremely formulaic speech, they managed to speak in such a way that they *sounded* unrehearsed and spontaneous. If you were in the courtroom for only one trial, you would get the impression that the judge was improvising; it's only when you listen to repeated trials that you see that they are using formulaic speech, but making it sound unrehearsed.

This example shows the extent of our cultural bias towards spontaneous, personalized, improvised speech. Although using scripted lines is completely natural, and everyone does it, it's still uncomfortable when it becomes so obvious—we all share an unspoken agreement that conversation will be spontaneous expression. When I'm retelling a story in front of someone who's already heard it, it's as if I've revealed a secret script that I've been using, violating our unspoken agreement to improvise anew each time.

Goffman, who thought that a great deal of our speech was scripted and ritualized, noted that we nonetheless try to hide this fact: "Performers tend to foster the impression that their current performance has something special and unique about it. The routine character of the performance is obscured and the spontaneous aspects of the situation are stressed."[22] Goffman was observing that all of us, not only auctioneers and lawyers, have our own personal scripts and catchphrases that we create ourselves, and that we use repeatedly.

A few months after moving to St. Louis, my friends all began to ask me how I liked the city—my new job, my new apartment, my city neighborhood. At first, I had to think a while to put my reactions into words. But after the fourth or fifth person asked me the same questions, without even meaning to, I had worked up a little script. There are only so many different ways to talk about a new job. I became conscious of speaking the same lines—in some cases the exact same sentences—about my new office, about the classic Gothic architecture of the campus, and about beautiful Forest Park, where I was walking my dog twice a day. Of course I wasn't repeating an entire prepared text each time, but I had developed what musicians call *licks*: distinctive, personalized solo phrases that a musician can use over and over again. When we recognize a musician's improvisational style, it's because their own licks act as signposts that almost cry out "Miles Davis" or "Jerry Garcia."

When you use a widely known catchphrase in conversation, everyone knows it. But when you use a personal lick with a new acquaintance, for all they know, you just improvised it on the spot. It's only your friends who know, and they begin to associate these licks with you. I had a friend once who frequently introduced his comments by saying "Let me tell ya somethin', Keith," but it took me several months of friendship before I realized how often he relied on this phrase. In the same way that a courtroom judge can make each defendant think that he's speaking only for them, talented conversationalists can maintain the appearance of spontaneous improvisation, even if they are using scripted lines.

You'll often notice close-knit subgroups forming their own idiosyncratic conversational shorthand. They create distinct catchphrases that they use to emphasize their own in-groupness and solidarity, and these catchphrases function almost like a secret code. This is common among groups as diverse as inner-city gangs and Ivy-league fraternities. When you use a catchphrase that's identified with your group, it has an indexical meaning—it communicates something about your shared context. It says something about who you are, what group you're with, and what your relationship is. Years later, you might use one of these catchphrases just to remind your old friend of the college days, and of the special bond that you share. If you're in a larger group, you know that only your old friends will pick up on the reference.

These are some of the ways that we use catchphrases creatively in conversation. Even though our talk may have some scripted sections, we are still improvising; choosing the right catchphrase, and using it at exactly the right time, requires creativity. Likewise, speaking a catchphrase in a spontaneous, natural way requires its own kind of verbal creativity—the way that an actor has to make every line sound spontaneous, even after many repeat performances. Catchphrases often carry a special, hidden meaning, that is not found in the literal meaning of the words; and their message is often targeted at specific listeners. Judges use formulaic speech "for the record"; your college friends might use some of your old private lingo to remind you of the good old days. In these many ways, creating conversations combine both scripts and improvisations.

BACK TO THE SCRIPT, PART 2: THEME AND VARIATIONS

Now we're beginning to see that the truth about conversation is more complex. Improvisation doesn't mean that anything goes, or that everything you say will be completely original; we often speak lines that have been spoken before, and our conversation often follows a familiar over-all structure, like Dagwood's exchange with his barber. The restaurant script is an overall structure; although there's a certain order of events that you have to follow, it's not as if you're reading from a script—you still get to perform "the restaurant play" your own way, creating your own lines. Improvisation within a structure is, in fact, harder and more creatively challenging than just saying any old thing you want, because you have to balance structure and creativity. The conversation analyst Emanuel A. Schegloff showed that many routines that seem highly scripted are actually improvised. Schegloff chose to analyze a segment of conversation that most of us think of as mechanical and routine—the first few standard sentences that we exchange at the beginning of a phone conversation. After observing hundreds of different phone calls, he had identified many variations of this "phone greeting script." Schegloff realized that although each one seemed scripted, the two par-ticipants had to collectively improvise their variation; each had a wide range of possibilities available. These exchanges were something like a game of chess, where the moves are limited, but a game is played nonetheless.[23]

Chess is pretty complicated, but most of us learn to improvise before we learn to read. Children's pretend play—the most silly and unimportant-seeming behavior—is where we learn how to improvise, and that's when we begin to participate in our first creating conversa-tions. That's why I spent a year, silently observing free play in a preschool classroom.

On one day, I watched a group of children sitting around the sandtable, enacting a scene from the movie *The Land Before Time*. Their play is similar to the movie—except that a teenage mutant ninja turtle appears instead of one of the regular characters. This doesn't faze the children at all. They weave the turtle's character into the drama to improvise a unique improvise a variation of the movie's script.

On occasion, children seem to be enacting a story from a single movie or TV show. However, it's much more common for them to blend themes, characters, and events from many different sources, working together to create a unique, improvised performance. They perform dra-mas with rescues, fires, explosions, earthquakes, bad guys and good guys, spaceships, and families of animals. When I saw preschool kids combining multiple scripts, creatively weaving in many symbols from pop culture, I thought of the French anthropologist, Claude Levi-Strauss, who famously compared a culture's myths and rituals to *brico-lage,* the French word for what a handyman does when he improvises a clever solution from whatever spare parts happen to be lying around.

Levi-Strauss used this humble metaphor to emphasize that culture is not always carefully planned by our wise ancestors. Rather, it's a combination of bits and pieces, forming a complex jumble, emerging from the small, daily creative acts of many individuals. Preschool children are bricoleurs, as they create mini-cultures in each new performance, by collecting bits and pieces from the adult culture.[24]

When children combine and embellish movie plots, is this still the same script, but with a minor variation? Or is it a uniquely new improvisation? William Corsaro, a sociologist who studies how children's play varies in different cultures, has studied how children embellish the *routines* of their preschool classroom.[25] A routine is a type of script, but it's a more general description of events than something like the restaurant script. Unlike the word-for-word connotations of "script," a preschool routine is a recognizable, repeatable game with a loose framework that the children collectively understand, and that has room for embellishment and improvisation.

Children's embellishments are often based on common emotional themes, such as fear of a bad guy. On one Friday morning in a preschool in Chicago, a *danger-escape* theme is the theme-with-variation. Kathy is playing again with her usual friends, Yung-soo and Rachel, and Jennie as well. This play starts out with Kathy announcing in a scary voice: "Santa Claus is coming!" The other girls scream. The only protection is for them all to go to bed. Eventually Santa Claus arrives, and the children open presents for just a few seconds before Kathy warns them of the next threat: "It's a bunny! Easter rabbit!" All of the girls hide underneath blankets, as Kathy enacts the evil Easter bunny, chanting in a deep voice, "I am the Easter bunny!" After the girls play out this variation of the theme, Yung-soo asks, "Now what comes after Easter?" Kathy immediately replies, "Uh oh. Here comes the Halloween people!" They all scream and hide once more.[26]

Like improv theater, these variations are improvised by the group. The danger-escape routine is woven together with two other routines: going to bed, and opening presents. Without a director, the children cooperatively improvise a novel performance. The script metaphor doesn't do justice to the richness and complexity of improvisational play; combining three themes to create a play performance is not a performance of any one single script.

Even in scripted theater—where the conversation is already scripted for the actors—they still have to *act*: to interpret the lines, adding personality and immediacy to the performance; to some degree, all performance is improvisational. Some actors get carried away, and embellish on their script or score during a performance; playwrights hate it when performers do this, because most playwrights are uncomfortable with the indeterminacy of performance; they don't trust the creativity of actors and musicians.

That's ironic, because today's theater has its roots in improv. Modern European theater is usually traced back to a popular Italian genre of improvisational performances—the *commedia dell'arte*. The commedia was founded almost 500 years ago in Italy, and thrived for the next 200 years, spreading throughout Europe and influencing playwrights in every language. Commedia theater companies didn't improvise the entire play from scratch—they started with a plot structure that all the actors memorized. Although the overall plot was decided in advance, commedia dell'arte performances still depended on the actor's improvisational creativity to create the dialogue.

Although the commedia dell'arte is often called the first improvisational theater, the performances were much more structured than Chicago-style improv. First of all, these ensembles worked from written plot summaries called *scenarios* that specified the characters of the play, an outline of the plot, the order of entrances and exits and the action for each scene, and summarized important conversations and monologues. Although there were many scenarios to remember, the same scenes, subplots, and plot mechanisms repeated over and over. There were only a limited number of sub-plots and themes: crises of young love, a lecherous old man, cruel masters, clever servants, greed, and sex. The scenarios always used the same stock characters, and each character was always performed by the same actor. This allowed the actor to refine his performance, and allowed him to develop portions of speeches and dialogue that worked well.

Second, there were standard sub-plots and pre-patterned dialogues between characters, called *generici*, that actors could choose to use at an appropriate point in the play. Finally, each actor memorized particularly successful monologues, called *lazzi*, that he could fall back on if necessary—something like a one-liner that is guaranteed to get a laugh. These multiple levels of structure allowed a commedia dell'arte ensemble to perform many different plays without having to memorize a lot of scripts. Compared to modern, Chicago-style improvisation, commedia dell'arte had a great deal of structure, and dramatically constrained the actors' possible actions. Nonetheless, this early theater had many of the key features of modern improvisation: The dialogue was not scripted, but was improvised anew in each performance; and the performance was collaborative, with the final performance emerging from the creative improvisations of many actors.

Why didn't they use scripts? No one is sure, but scholars have proposed several hypotheses. The commedia troupes were touring companies, and they would stay in a town as long as they were doing a good business; if they stayed 20 nights in a row, they would have to perform 20 different plays. Even the most talented actor would have trouble memorizing 20 different scripts; under this hypothesis, improvisation was the most efficient way to handle these demands, allowing the group to keep generating a "new" play each night. A second hypothesis is that scripts were not used because commedia drew on oral performance traditions. Comic theater has always been more improvisational than serious drama—the clown, the fool, and the buffoon are improvisational roles. Even though most of these Italian actors were literate, ensembles may have nonetheless retained the techniques of the oral tradition.[27]

The spirit of the commedia lives on in today's Chicago style of improv. Towards the beginning of the chapter, I pointed out that the first modern improv theater group, The Compass, was based on a set of children's theater games. Founded in the 1950s, this was the group that grew into the famous Second City Theater. But these cocky Chicago undergrads also knew about theater history, and their first performances were equally inspired by the scenarios that the commedia groups used. Like the commedia, the first Chicago improvs were based on plot outlines called *scene plays*. The scene play was a loose outline, with only the key plot events specified in advance. No dialogue was written in advance, and the specific path that the actors took through this plot was not predetermined. Every performance was different.[28]

The scene play is a kind of improvisation that has a little more structure than everyday life. It's like the restaurant script, because it specifies the basic events and the different possible sequences of events. Unlike today's improv theater, where the performance is created from scratch by the actors, a scene play also involves the creativity of a playwright and a director. The actors are expected to creatively embellish and fill out the "script" during the performance.

Most improv groups don't perform scene plays anymore, instead preferring the more unstructured types of improv that we learned about earlier. But a few years ago, one Chicago group started doing scene plays that were based on the conventional, predictable plots of TV sitcoms. This group, called Sitcom, will be our final example of how structure and improvisations combine in performance.

In the Fall of 1992, a new actor joined my improv theater group. I was intrigued when I found out that he was a graduate student in psychology. Like me, Dan Goldstein wanted to combine his interest in theater with his research in psychology. In his laboratory, he was developing computer models for social behavior, in the tradition of Schank and Abelson's script program. Drawing on the commedia, he devised a style of theater called *structured improvisation*. Together with another TV-generation student already in my group, he used the concept of structured improvisation to develop the show called *Sitcom*. It began when Goldstein developed a computer program that could model the typical plot twists and character relationships of the prototypical sitcom episode. To develop the program, Goldstein did rigorous and stressful research: "I watched a couple hundred sitcom episodes and read the plot synopses of even more."[29] Goldstein's computer plot structures are reminiscent of Schank and Abelson's scripts in their branching possibilities and in their overall narrative structure from a clear beginning to a satisfying ending. Goldstein's program maps out a narrative path that moves from Initiating Event and Conflict to Action and Resolution. In each of these broad event categories, Goldstein identified sub-categories and different versions of these events. Using these types of plot categories, Goldstein could identify the similar structures between an episode of Gilligan's Island and something that has probably happened to all of us who use a computer, the horrible realization that you have deleted an important file:

	Initiating Event	Conflict	Action	Resolution
	Enter Danger Indicator	*Believe There Is Danger*	*Take Action Against Danger*	*Danger Indicator Is False*
Gilligan's Island	Water-height measuring stick goes under water	Professor concludes island is sinking	Everyone relocates to dry part of island	Gilligan moved the measuring stick while fishing
Computer Disaster	Writer receives "disk error" message from computer	Writer fears that his book file is deleted	Writer calls editor to see if he still has last draft	Disk was not in the disk drive, after all

We often have the feeling that we can predict what's going to happen in a sitcom, sometimes even after the first five minutes. If an actor starts a show by complaining about a difficult project at work, we know the show will end up being about work, and that his project will be successfully completed by the end of the show. In entertainment copyright law, these predictable events are called *scenes à faire*: incidents, characters, or settings that are indispensable and standard in the treatment of a given topic. *Scenes à faire* are considered to be "boilerplates" that have no real author, and thus they can't be copyrighted.

Everyone who's grown up watching TV is an expert in sitcom plot structures. In fact, according to Hollywood legend, there are only seven stories underlying all movies and TV shows.[30] Professional sitcom writers consciously stick to these rules, knowing that TV executives, advertisers, and viewers have grown to expect them. Shows have an A plot and a subsidiary, or B plot, and sometimes a second subsidiary plot, the C plot. These plots are separated by the advertisements into a teaser and two acts; no character can leave the room without saying something funny; and a scene should end with a punch line that leads into the commercial.[31]

Goldstein took these sitcom structures to his fellow actors, and suggested that they could be used to improvise a 30-minute play. The idea was that the sitcom scenario would provide an overall structure, but the actors would improvise the exact plot events and dialogue. They decided to improvise commercials as well. The two commercial actors controlled the show's timing by controlling the show's lighting, cutting each scene after the agreed-upon time limit—and ideally, after a punch line.

Sitcom is an interesting combination of both structure and improvisation, an improvised performance that is guided by a rough outline. Is it scripted, or is it improvisation? Is each night a trivial variation, an embellishment of the basic script, or is it an entirely new performance each night? *Sitcom* forces us to ask, what counts as an original performance? What counts as improvisation? How much structure can a conversation have before we stop calling it improvisation?

IMPROVISED CONVERSATIONS: TOWARDS A NEW PERFORMANCE METAPHOR

I started this chapter by emphasizing two key facts about creating conversations: There is no script, and no director. That's why the chapter has focused on improvisational theater—the pure improvisations that actors generate without any script. These improvised dialogues are like creating conversations, because in both, there is no script and no director—like improv actors, we collaboratively create our everyday conversations.

But although our conversations are not scripted, improvisation doesn't mean that there is *no* structure at all; and we saw that there are two kinds of structures that we use in conversation. First of all, we often weave in licks, catchphrases, or pop culture references. These are like little pieces of script, raw material for our improvisations. Nonetheless, we saw that even when we combine bits of script into our conversations, we are still improvising. Second, some of our conversations are created within an overall framework—a story that we tell over and over, or a common situation like the restaurant or the post office—where the flow of the conversation is predetermined. But even in these situations, we are improvising, because we're embellishing on the overall framework.

If conversation is so creative and improvisational, why do we tend to underemphasize the creativity of conversation? I'll end this chapter by describing two common misconceptions about conversation that cause us to think it's not all that creative. These two misconceptions are related to the original theater metaphor—that conversation is like traditional theater, in that it has a script and a director. The first misconception derives from the idea that conversation—like theater—is scripted; this leads to what I call *script-think*: We assume that there is more structure to a conversation than there really was. After a conversation is over, we forget how unpredictable and improvised it really was. The second misconception derives from the idea that conversation is somehow directed, and I'll call this the *centralized mindset*. This misconception extends beyond conversation to all sorts of group phenomena: when we observe a group, we almost subconsciously assume that the group has a director, or that they're following a predetermined plan.

Getting Beyond Script-Think

We've seen that we use scripts during the improvisations of conversation. But why do we sometimes think that's all there is? Why do we ignore the creative, improvisation half of conversation? I call this *script-think*. Here are some examples of this bias.

While I was visiting improv groups in Chicago, I usually took along a friend, often someone who had never seen improv theater before. After the performance, I would ask them about what they thought. I always got the same response: They assumed that the actors were using a script, and only improvising small bits of dialogue. They thought that the performance they had just witnessed was a kind of magic trick—that the actors had a script up their sleeves. My friends were always surprised, and a little disbelieving, when I told them that *nothing* about the performance had been scripted. I could testify to that because I had seen the same group so many times before.

Why did my friends have this reaction, even though I told them ahead of time that the performance was going to be completely improvised? I think it's just hard for us to accept that an actor could work without a script. The script theory caught on because it's so natural for us to think this way about our own lives. I saw a classic example of script-think in the *New York Times* during the closing days of the 1996 Presidential campaign. Clinton had a 20-point lead in the polls, but the headline cautioned "The Script Is Still Being Written."[32] This headline shows how easy it is to fall into script-think. Even when life is improvised and unpredictable, we still persist in thinking of it as a script. This headline implies that life is scripted, and we simply don't yet know the script. It's as if the script is already there somehow, pointing ahead into the future, and we just can't tell what our lines will be.

Script-think influences the way we think about theater, too; for example, we think that "the play" is what's in the script, the written words of dialogue. When we see a performance, we think of it as "a version" of the (written) play. In European theater, the written script dominates our performance tradition; by the 19th century, the *commedia* improvisations—popular for over 200 years—had been replaced by scripted comedies. It's interesting that this happened during the same 200-year period that literacy was becoming more widespread throughout Europe; it suggests that there may be a connection between literacy and script-think.

The psychologist David Olson has analyzed the ways that our writing system changes the way we think about language. For example, he compared our phonetic writing system—with each letter representing one sound—to cultures with ideographic and syllabic writing systems, and discovered that aspects of language *not* represented in the script are almost impossible to bring into consciousness. Once individuals become literate, and learn a written script for their spoken language, it's almost impossible for them to imagine how anyone thought about language *before* writing was invented.[33]

Those aspects of language that the printed word can't represent—including pauses, emphases, pitch contours, and even the speaker's intentions—can vary from performance to performance, and we think of those aspects of a performance as "interpretation." But of course, a script alone is never a play—because theater is a performance art, not just another kind of literature. Still, script-think leads many people to think that plays are a type of literature—theater experts are often found in English literature departments.

Script-think is a tendency to assume that there is more structure behind events than was really there. Especially after the fact, it's easy to think that a sequence of events was more predictable than it really was at the time: Hindsight is 20/20 vision. After a conversation is over, it's hard to remember how many different ways it could have gone. In the improv skit with the shifty passenger and the bus driver, it's easy to forget that it could have gone in a hundred other directions. When we think back on a conversation, or describe it to someone else, we talk as if the conversation had only one way that it could go—as if we were only "writing the script." Many thinkers of the modern era have suggested that this is a natural human tendency; that we often see more structure in life than is really there, we often assume that what actually happened had to happen.[34]

The tension between script and improvisation is found throughout our lives, not only in conversations. Our drive to be creative is often opposed by fixed structures—our job, our neighborhood, our social class or education level, by the conventions of how things have always been done. By focusing on the structure of our lives, we end up neglecting the creativity and freedom that we are all capable of. Structure is static and stable; improvisations are free-flowing and open-ended.

This idea of *structure* is one of the most important themes of social science research, and the tension between social structure and individual creativity is one of the most important contemporary issues in social theory. The types of issues that arise are often similar to the tension between script and improvisation. The school of thought called *structuralism* has played a major role in the last 80 years in linguistics, psychology, anthropology, and sociology. Scientists known as structuralists conduct research with the goal of determining the conventional structures that guide social life.[35] For example, when linguists study everyday conversation, they write about the scripts we use—for example, the "greeting script" where I say "How are you," and you say "Fine, how are you?" Part of the job of an anthropologist in describing a society or a culture is to identify the set of scripts and structures that is shared by all of the members of the society; the "restaurant script" is an example from our own culture.[36]

I often compare the concept of "structure" to a script. The script is not the same thing as the play, and is not the same thing as a performance of a play. You need a director to interpret the script, to choose costumes and accents for the characters, to decide on the pacing and tempo of the lines of dialogue. And you need actors to bring the characters to life—to suffuse dramatic roles with emotion and meaning. There's no way that any script could specify all of this information. Instead, the most a playwright can do is to specify the plot and the dialogue. The script is only the outline of the play. Each performance, even in a single run, with the same cast and the same stage and director, will be a little different, because there is some indeterminacy in every performance.

And of course, everyday discourse is much more improvised than scripted theater. How could an improvised conversation be represented using something as static as a script or a structure? Many social scientists have moved beyond structuralism for this reason: our daily conversations are not exact imitations of any script, and our daily lives do not exactly follow the structure of anybody's social theory. Researchers who explore these issues are often called *post-structuralists*, because they are concerned with those aspects of social life that structuralism doesn't explain: individual creativity, variation across performances, and change over time. Post-structuralists focus on the balance between structure and improvisation; for example, improvisation was a central concept for two influential French social theorists; in his influential 1972 critique of structuralism, *Outline of a Theory of Practice*, Pierre Bourdieu[37] focused on "regulated improvisation" (which he also called *habitus*), and in a similarly influential 1974 book, *The Practice of Everyday Life*, Michel de Certeau's[38] central concepts were improvisation, strategy, and contingency. Following Bourdieu, many post-structuralists refer to improvisation as "practice," in the sense of the word related to "practical knowledge" or "everyday practices."

These theorists are nonetheless careful to point out that we aren't making up everything about the social world from scratch in each conversation; there is structure guiding the practice of everyday life. In this chapter, we've seen that even though everyday discourse is improvised, we nonetheless use scripted elements—catchphrases, speech styles, and overall routines. That's why structuralism is half-right—it describes the scripted bits, those aspects of social life that tend to stay the same from day to day. But structuralism doesn't explain the improvisations—the ways that we embellish, modify, and merge different lines and scripts in a single conversation. And it's not a very effective way to explain how something unpredictable could happen, or how important the unintended consequences of an action can be.

Getting Beyond The Centralized Mindset

There's a second common misconception about conversation that's closely related to script-think. We've seen that creating conversations—like all improvisations—are not directed by anyone. Instead, the performance emerges from the actions of everyone, collaborating and working together. Because the performance emerges from everyone's actions, you can't predict what's going to happen next; you have no idea what everyone else will do. You can't even predict what *you* will do next, because that also depends on what everyone else does.

Conversation is only one example of a more general characteristic of group behavior: *emergence*. We see emergence whenever a group has no director guiding them. For example, how many times have you run into a traffic jam on the Interstate? If you commute to work, this could be a daily occurrence for you. But if it only happens occasionally, if traffic slows to a crawl, you're likely to wonder why. "There must have been an accident," you mutter, thinking about how you're going to be late for that meeting. Fifteen or 30 minutes later, as traffic starts to flow again, you're surprised when you don't see any visible cause for the delay—no tow trucks, no flares on the shoulder. It's frustrating to realize that many traffic jams are completely random. They don't have any obvious cause—they simply result from the actions of hundreds of drivers, each reacting to the cars in front of them. Traffic delays like this *emerge* from the actions of hundreds of drivers.

The world is filled with emergent phenomena. When you see a flock of birds, you assume that the bird in front is leading, and that the other birds are following. In fact, this isn't the case—most bird flocks don't have leaders at all. Rather, the orderly "V" shape that crosses the sky emerges from all of the birds acting together, each responding only to the ones nearby. Like an improvisational performance, the flock is organized without an organizer.

Emergence has become a hot topic in several scientific fields, including biology, computer science, and psychology. A computer scientist at MIT, Mitch Resnick, points out that our "centralized mindset" almost invariably leads us to assume that complex group behavior results from a central controller. It's the same mindset that makes improv audiences assume that the group secretly has a script, or that makes you assume that a traffic jam has a cause. But why would Resnick, a computer scientist, be criticizing the centralized mindset? Isn't a computer program just like a centralized script? Well, that was true in the old days. But today, Resnick is one of a growing group of computer scientists who are experimenting with new ways of designing decentralized computer systems that are based on emergent designs. Resnick believes that these emergent systems are more likely to display intelligent behavior. He points out that at a biological level, human intelligence is also emergent—arising from the interactions of millions of neurons. Resnick and others are trying to mimic these emergent processes with a new type of computer design, called a *connectionist* computer, named after the millions of connections among the neurons. These computer scientists are building computers that are collections of hundreds, or even thousands, of small microprocessors, and experimenting with ways to make these networks of small computers behave in smart ways. This recent work in computer science makes it seem as if human intelligence results from an internal, subconscious conversation. Just like improv scenes emerge from interactions between actors, intelligence emerges from interactions in the brain.[39]

Conversations are also emergent phenomena, a type of emergence that I call *collaborative emergence*. When a conversation has emergent properties, we can't analyze it using a psychological method that simply analyzes the mental states and goals of all of the participants. In fact, a recent mathematical study of group decision making has proved that group behavior is emergent and unpredictable, even if you know the views of all of the participants.[40] That's why we need an interdisciplinary approach to study creating conversations—an approach that draws on not only psychology, but also fields that study group behavior, fields like anthropology, organizational dynamics, and sociology.[41]

* * * * * * * *

In this chapter, we've seen that we need a new performance metaphor, because conversations are improvised performances with no script and no director. To see how creative we are in conversation, we need to focus on collaboration, improvisation, and emergence. To understand the performance of everyday life, we have to be careful not to think it's more predictable than it really is. We have to stop thinking that we are writing scripts—and start focusing on the flow of free improvisation.

Chapter 2

Dialogues

Creating conversations are different from conventional theater performance—we're not reading from a script and no one is directing us. Instead, creating conversations are like improvisational theater, where the actors collaborate to spontaneously create their dialogue in front of a live audience. In Chapter 1 we learned about improv theater and some of the rules that actors are taught; in this chapter, we'll begin to focus more closely on how we collaboratively improvise a conversation. We all know that a lot of what goes on in conversation is beneath the surface—never spoken out loud—even though everyone knows what's going on. Conversation researchers have begun to study this hidden, unstated level of conversation, and they are beginning to uncover the unwritten rules that allow us to collaboratively create conversation.

In this chapter, I'll share the findings of conversation researchers, discovered through years of tedious and time-consuming research that involves sifting through hours of conversation. I'll describe some of the techniques that we all use—subconsciously and instinctively—that make conversation work. Because these techniques are hidden beneath the surface, we don't usually think about them, and we are only dimly aware that we are using them. Some of the most creative aspects of conversations are found in this hidden, implicit level.

These researchers have also discovered that these unwritten rules tell us about more than just how conversation works. It turns out that they also tell us important things about our most fundamental beliefs about social life—like how we think people should relate to one another, and how we think about individual rights and responsibilities. Researchers have found that many of these unwritten rules vary from one culture to another, and they vary in ways that are consistent with the worldview of the culture. As we explore how conversation works, we'll also examine which rules are universal and which rules are different in every culture.

HOW CONVERSATION WORKS, PART 1: THE FOURTH WALL

Most improv theater groups follow a strange-sounding rule: "Don't cross the fourth wall." If you think of the stage as a room with four walls, the first three walls are the back and the two sides of the stage; the "fourth wall," of course, doesn't exist, because the fourth side of the stage opens out onto the audience. The *fourth wall* is an old theater metaphor that actors use to refer to the invisible boundary between the stage and the audience.

The fourth wall was rarely crossed in Western theater until the influential, revolutionary work of an Italian playwright, Luigi Pirandello (1867-1936), an innovator whose influence is still being felt. Pirandello wrote plays in which the actors frequently crossed the fourth wall. His famous play *Six Characters in Search of an Author*, first performed in 1921, destroyed the fourth wall. Pirandello's stage directions begin:

> When the audience arrives in the theater, the curtain is raised; and the stage, as normally in the daytime, is without wings or scenery and almost completely dark and empty. From the beginning we are to receive the impression of an unrehearsed performance. . .

> As soon as the houselights dim, the TECHNICIAN is seen entering at the door on stage. He is wearing a blue shirt, and a tool bag hangs from his belt. . . . He kneels down to hammer some nails in. At the sound of the hammering, the STAGE MANAGER comes running from the door that leads to the dressing rooms.[1]

The stage manager is bothered by the hammering. He shouts "The director will be here any moment for the rehearsal!" The actors then begin to arrive to rehearse for a play-within-a-play that is by Pirandello, "The Game of Role Playing." While the actors are improvising the typical pre-rehearsal small talk, others arrive: the Prompter, the Director, and his Secretary.

Pirandello's dialogue contains frequent references to aspects of the theater environment that are not on stage, that are not supposed to be exposed to the audience: the stagehands, the audience, the playwright. Shortly after the director begins the rehearsal, six unusual people arrive unexpectedly at the theater. These, Pirandello indicates in his script, are the *characters*; he suggested that they wear masks, to distinguish them from the actors already on stage. They announce "We're here in search of an author." The director responds, "There's no author here at all. It's not a new play we're rehearsing." In the ensuing discussion, the audience finds out that the characters have a drama in mind, but that they are incapable of writing the script; they need an author to bring their drama to life. The remainder of the play involves a series of intriguing exchanges between characters, actors, and the director, dialogue that explores the concept of a play, the distinction between the staged reality of the theater and everyday life, and what role the script and the author play in the creation of a performance. Although the characters require an author to bring their performance to life, it turns out that they already know the drama they want to perform. They don't really need a creative author, but rather an author as a spokesperson. The characters have a series of arguments with the director about their roles, the writer's role, and the director's role in creating a play. For example, the director agrees to write the script, but once it's complete, he wants his own actors to perform it—he plans to dispense with these six mysterious characters after he has written their play. The characters object, stating what they think is obvious: "We are the characters!" The central tensions of Pirandello's play explore the nature of performance itself. Who is the creator of the play? Is it the characters, the director, or the author? What defines the play? Is it the written script, or the drama that the characters already contain within themselves?

In today's TV world, Pirandello's influence is everywhere— tongue-in-cheek ad campaigns that include the ad's creators, or refer to the marketing reasons behind the ad. This frame-breaking technique was made popular largely through David Letterman's late night talk show. In his first few seasons on NBC in the early 1980s, Letterman broke the television-studio equivalent of the fourth wall frequently. Letterman had a camera go back into the producer's glass-walled room, and he interviewed his producer, Hal, about the show. He invited his production staff onto the stage and made some of them stars in their own right. He frequently led a camera backstage to explore some aspect of the studio. He joked with the man holding the cue cards, rather than trying to hide the fact that he was using cue cards.

Crossing the fourth wall has long been an accepted technique in contemporary theater. In the 1938 production of Thornton Wilder's classic, *Our Town,* a character called the Stage Manager chats with the audience about the characters, and also occasionally steps into the play to perform a small role. And in avant-garde performance art, it's practically a cliché to confuse the performer/audience distinction. For example, in a performance in New York in the Fall of 1996, audience members were locked in cages, raised on cables above the floor, and the actors walked among the cages observing them and taking notes—a rather heavy-handed way of making it obvious that the usual performer/spectator roles are being reversed.[2]

Since the 1960s, such performances have taken place in small, obscure theaters, without much commercial success. But by 1997, the *Times* reported that "participatory theater" had become so popular that it had become mainstream. The granddaddy of this genre, opening in 1987 in New York, is *Tony 'n' Tina's Wedding,* a show that recreates a church wedding and reception where the audience participates in the wedding as guests. These performances are like scene plays—partially improvised within an overall predetermined structure. In spite of commercial success, participatory theater doesn't get much respect from the theater community; many critics and theater purists still think that it isn't *real* theater.

Although crossing the fourth wall has been a successful and innovative development in contemporary theater, it doesn't work in improv, and actors are taught not to do it. Instead, they have to stay in character, and engage only in dialogue with the other actors. If an actor begins to direct the action explicitly, or to describe a scene to the audience, the collaborative nature of the improvisation is compromised. That's why actors are taught "Don't write the script." Beginning actors are often uncomfortable with the unpredictability of group improvisation, and their lack of control over the flow of the action. A beginner's way to deal with this uncertainty is to spell out an entire scenario, speaking almost like a director: "You're my mother and you're upset that I've eaten all the cookies, aren't you?" or "Look at that evil monster that's coming our way and wants to eat us because we discovered his cave!" This is almost like "crossing the fourth wall," because in such lines the actor is directing the action explicitly, practically taking on the director's role.

Another lesson that helps to keep actors from writing the script is the rule "Show, don't tell"—if you want to introduce something new into the dramatic frame, just do it, don't tell us about it. Stepping out of frame destroys the flow of improvisation, because once an actor steps out of character, there is a temptation to start speaking as a director, controlling the other actors, and undermining one of the central goals of improv, which is for the drama to emerge from the collaborative dialogue of the actors, together.

It would also become less true to life, because in our everyday conversations, we almost never step out of character, and we rarely step out of the conversation itself. The sociologist Erving Goffman referred to the social setting of a conversation as a *frame*.[3] Imagine something like an invisible stage, surrounding the participants in the conversation. On rare occasions, if something goes very wrong in a conversation, one of the participants may *break frame*, step *outside* of the conversational frame to comment on it: "How dare you talk to me that way!" Or demanding an apology: "Take it back!" In these cases we step out of our role as a character in this conversation, and take on something like a director's role.

The fact that we can all recognize a broken frame makes it clear that our conversations occur in a frame. We are acting, in a sense, on stage. Because the fourth wall is crossed so rarely, we can proceed in every life without having to think very hard about the stage we are on, the frame we are in. But in these rare moments when the frame falls apart, or when we have to suddenly switch to a different frame, we are instantly made aware of the staged qualities of our daily conversations.

Most of the time, we don't cross the fourth wall during a conversation. For example, we rarely change topics by saying something like "Now let's segue to a new topic." But once a conversation is over, it's OK to talk about it—because now you're outside of the frame of that conversation, and talking about it doesn't count as "breaking frame." For example, we have many ways to describe strange topic shifts in a conversation. When someone says something that doesn't seem to fit into the conversation at all, we call it a *non sequitur*. If a person makes an unexpected comment that shifts the topic radically, but isn't as radical as a non sequitur, we might say that the comment came "out of the blue," or "out of nowhere." It's not as crazy as a non sequitur, because we can understand why the topic has been raised. When someone changes the topic smoothly, we call it a *segue*. Or we can say that we're "shifting gears."

All of these are ways of talking about talk, what the linguist Deborah Schiffrin has called *metatalk*. We often metatalk when we're repeating a conversation to a friend: "And then out of the blue, he said . . ." But if you metatalk during a conversation, you would be breaking frame. Good improvisers work together without using this kind of explicit metatalk—they don't cross the fourth wall. Unless we break frame, our metatalk is *implicit*—hidden in our words, woven into our dialogue.[4]

Two other theorists used similar terms to refer to metatalk. The cybernetician Gregory Bateson first wrote about this phenomenon in the 1950s, calling it *metacommunication*, and used the concept to describe how children jointly manage a play session. He emphasized the importance of both explicit and implicit metacommunication. In the 1970s, the linguistic anthropologist Michael Silverstein coined the term *metapragmatics* to refer to both implicit and explicit metatalk; Silverstein is the only theorist who has attempted to develop a theory of implicit metatalk, and much of this chapter draws on his writings.[5]

In rare cases, we use explicit metatalk during conversation; for example, we might say "I don't want to talk about that right now." But most of the time, we shift topics, start and end conversations, without having to stop in the middle and step out of frame to talk about what we're doing. So how do we create conversation, if we stay in frame? How do we do something as simple as changing the topic, without saying "Let's talk about something else"? How do we send these metatalk messages implicitly?

For example, instead of saying "I don't want to talk about that right now," we can pointedly change the subject to the weather, or last night's game. In most conversations, when we shift topic, no one has to talk about it. These implicit messages are a subtle, indirect type of metatalk. Implicit metatalk is a kind of verbal shorthand that allows the conversation to keep flowing, the hidden glue that allows us to improvise our conversations. But we usually aren't aware that we are doing it. Like improvisational actors on stage, we're more creative if we don't write the script in our heads, if we don't try to consciously plan these transitions ahead of time. If we stopped to *think* about it, it would interfere with our ability to *do* it. There's just too much going on for us to juggle it all in our conscious mind.

Implicit metatalk shows us that there is more to conversation than what is explicitly stated on the surface. But in the United States, speakers think that we should strive to avoid these hidden meanings—that conversation works best if everyone says exactly what they mean.[6] I call this belief about conversation the Horton theory, after Dr. Seuss's character Horton the elephant, who keeps repeating "I meant what I said, and I said what I meant." This assumption—that it's always better to speak clearly and to say exactly what you mean—carries with it some other, more subtle implications: that clarity of speech reflects clarity of thought, and that indirect, metaphorical, or implicit styles of speaking indicate confusion, deception, or stupidity. However, these beliefs are not culturally universal; they represent a distinctly European cultural ideology about language, and are even more extreme in English-speaking countries than on the European continent, as we'll see later in this chapter. Because of these cultural beliefs of English speakers, it's not surprising that such assumptions underlie many Anglo-American theories about language use; for example, Grice's theory of *conversational implicature*[7] claims that speakers follow "maxims of conversation" such as:

- Make your statement as informative as is required for the current purposes of the conversation
- Avoid obscurity
- Avoid ambiguity
- Be brief

Horton's theory can't be the whole story, even for European speakers—many of the messages that we send in conversation are implicit, unstated metatalk messages. If we always said exactly what we meant, we would constantly interrupt our conversations in the middle to metatalk. Of course, we don't do this; implicit metatalk is an essential and unavoidable part of conversation. Not only is it hidden in your words, but it's highly dependent on the exact moment that your words are spoken, who is in the room, who spoke just before you, what has been said in the last 20 minutes. In other words, the metatalk meaning depends on more than just the *words*—it also depends on the *context*.

In creating conversations, there are many transitions and shifts that have to be collectively managed—changes in topics, in tone, rhythm, volume, or tempo of speech; accepting new participants to the conversation, or acknowledging when someone is leaving. When our conversation changes smoothly without breaking frame, it's not the responsibility of any one person—everyone in the conversation participates in these transitions, and everyone has to be on board. For example, the decision to shift topics is a collective decision; one person suggests a new topic, but the others have to agree to go along with it.

No one ever taught us these rules. So how did we learn to do this implicit metatalk? Like so much about creating conversation, we learn it without being taught—we learn it ourselves, from our classmates and friends, during preschool fantasy play.

Because I was performing with a theater group when I first went into a preschool classroom, I couldn't help noticing how much like improvisational theater it was—the children spoke with exaggerated, dramatic voices, and voiced the lines that a mom, or an astronaut, would speak. The one thing that stood out was that a group of children would both enact and direct the play drama at the same time. For example, I often saw children step out of their play character to speak as a director. A child who is pretending to be the Superhero might pause, and say in his normal voice, "Pretend those are the bad guys." They use the director voice to metatalk about their play characters, and to add a new twist to their play drama. This is like the explicit metatalk that we use in our everyday conversations when we break frame.

But that wasn't the most creative technique that the children used to improvise their play drama—children have an amazing bag of verbal tricks they use to create the play world.[8] For example, children frequently combine their character's voice with the director's voice, in the same utterance. For example, the Superhero who wants to introduce some bad guys into the drama might stay in character, and shout "Watch out for those bad guys!" This is an amazing creative skill, because it requires children to both metatalk and "talk" at the same time. It's *implicit* metatalk, because the Superhero is communicating his director's wishes without saying it explicitly. This type of talk makes play much more improvisational, because children can negotiate the drama without stepping out of character and disrupting the flow of the play.

For example, Jennifer and Jennie are good friends who play together almost every day. This morning, Jennifer is wiggling a plastic horse and speaking as the horse, and Jennie is speaking as a slightly smaller zebra. These two plastic animals perform their drama on a stage that the girls have created, a building made of wooden blocks in the middle of the floor. They've already agreed that Jennifer's horse is the mother of Jennie's zebra. Suddenly, Jennie moves her baby zebra from the carpet, up to the top of the block building, and screams in a high-pitched voice that is almost a whisper:

(1)   Jennie   Momma! Help!
(2)   I can't get down!
(3)   Help!
(4)   It's too scary!

Any mother would want to help when her child is in trouble—that's why Jennie's implicit proposal is so clever. But Jennifer's horse doesn't budge—she keeps it down on the carpet. Without looking at Jennie, Jennifer wiggles her horse and says in an angry, deep voice, "I'm not gonna get you down."

Jennifer and Jennie have both stayed in character; neither of them stepped out of character to speak as a director. But that didn't keep them from negotiating a whole series of complex changes to their play drama. When Jennifer pretends to be a scared baby zebra, stuck on top of a building, she is also suggesting that Jennifer's horse—the mother—come to rescue her. Jennifer is willing to accept that Jennie is stuck up on the building, but she can't be bothered to get her character involved in a rescue. Of course, saying "No" when your child is in trouble isn't consistent with the mother character. So Jennifer's implicit response is quite creative; by using an angry tone of voice, she's implying that her daughter, the zebra, has done something wrong, and that it's her own fault that she's stuck on the building.

I spent several months in a preschool classroom, just to try to get a handle on all of the different metatalk techniques that children use to improvise the play drama. When I counted up all of my observations, I found that over half of their metatalk is implicit—it's hidden in the dialogue itself, just like adults improvise changes in topic without breaking frame.

By the end of my time in the preschool, I began to realize how this kind of play allows children to practice the skills needed for everyday conversation. Just like Jennifer and Jennie, we rarely step out of character to explicitly metatalk about our conversation. These are cases when we explicitly take on the role of a director, and say things like, "Oh, sorry to interrupt, but I just remembered what I was going to tell you," or "I don't like the way you said that to me." But this is rare; we usually try to avoid explicit metatalk, because stepping out of frame like this always stops the flow of the conversation abruptly. Improv actors also know that this will stop the drama cold—thus the rule "Don't cross the fourth wall." If you step out of character, it destroys the dramatic illusion being created for the audience. And if a conversation is interrupted too frequently with explicit metatalk, it won't flow like good improvisation.

It's difficult for children to improvise conversation using implicit metatalk—preschool children can't always figure out how to communicate their play goals this way. That's why they have a whole range of strategies for improvising their play drama. They use many different kinds of metatalk, both in-character and out-of-character, both explicit and implicit. It's nature's way of helping them rehearse for the adult world of creating conversations.

Conversations about Conversations

Because implicit metatalk is the norm, those cases where we choose to be explicit are particularly interesting. When do we break frame and explicitly metatalk?

Most of the time when we talk about talk, we are telling a friend about a conversation that we just had. If you're asked to describe what it was like to talk to someone, you have plenty of words to choose from. You can say it was "difficult" or "stilted," to indicate that the conversation didn't flow very smoothly. If a person doesn't talk very much, I might say "Talking to him was like pulling teeth." What I mean is that I had to do all of the talking, and nothing could get him to participate more actively. Since we're talking *about* conversation, this is a kind of metatalk.

When we want to get past these broad judgments and tell someone what really happened in a conversation, we'll often repeat the dialogue. Of course, it's almost impossible to get the words *exactly* right, so we paraphrase the lines. Repeating a conversation always involves embellishment and improvisation, and this gives us room for creativity. There are many subtle ways that we can alter what was said—the tone of voice, the exact wording that was used—to make a point more clear, to fill in our audience on some important background detail, or to put our own spin on the conversation that we're repeating.

Paraphrasing the words of another person, but in "your own words," is an example of what Bakhtin called *double-voiced discourse.*[9] The words that you speak are, in a very real sense, the words of both you and the original speaker. Of course, they can't be your own words, because after all, you're reporting what someone else said; but at the same time, they are *partly* your words, because you are choosing to represent these words in a particular way, to accomplish your conversational goals. Often in conversation, a person will restate something you just said, giving it a slightly different spin that might not be exactly what you meant. Radio talk show hosts are particularly skilled at paraphrasing guest's comments, either to clarify for the listening audience, or in some cases, to make the speaker look bad or to get an argument going.[10] Teachers are also skilled at paraphrasing their student's comments to connect to a theme of the lesson or to another student's comment, a technique that has been called *revoicing.*[11]

Our paraphrases might be perfectly innocent. But you have to be careful when someone repeats a conversation to you; sometimes a person will embellish a little too much, repeating the conversation in a way that serves his own goals. It could be because they just heard what they wanted to hear, or they might be taking the comment out of context on purpose, to make the speaker look bad. But if you call them on it, they can always say "*I* didn't say it, I was just telling you what *she* said." Because it's impossible to repeat a conversation word for word, you have to permit some degree of paraphrasing.

When is it fair to accuse someone of taking your words out of context? Quoting you "out of context" means that the person repeating what you said has not provided enough background on the conversation to give the real meaning of what you said. But it has additional connotations: It suggests that the person repeating your words has left out some important details about the conversation *on purpose,* to try to make you look bad. It suggests that if they had only been careful to include this missing information, your words would seem innocent and understandable. Of course, this is a judgment call. What would it take to provide your listeners with the full context every time you were repeating a conversation? No one can remember every detail of a conversation, every creative twist to the improvised flow. Repeating a conversation requires many skills—a good memory for conversations, an ability to detect people's intentions behind their words. It also requires the ability to understand how your audience will hear the version you're telling them. And you can't simply *lie* about what happened—you have to repeat the conversation in a way that is at least plausibly connected to reality. That way, if someone calls you on it later, you can say "Well, I'm just telling you what he said!"

Paraphrasing provides us with a creative opportunity to report a conversation in a way that satisfies our conversational goals. This kind of explicit metatalk—also called *reported speech*—is an example of how we creatively use language to communicate meanings on many levels.[12] It's not fair to focus only on the literal meanings of what someone says when we're repeating a conversation. That's because this kind of meaning is so dependent on the surrounding context: who is telling the story, what you already know about this person's relationship with the person whose talk they are reporting, the tone of voice that they use when they say what that person said, and perhaps most importantly of all, the overall flow of the conversation up to that point. The creative options expand as conversations flow and develop. A creative conversationalist has much more to work with after a tone has been established, a few topics covered, and everyone gets familiar with how each the others are feeling. Things can get messy and murky after a setting has been established for the speakers. This is what we mean by "context," and it's always there when we talk. The context allows an increasingly elaborate improvisation to develop, and almost no words can be understood without some understanding of the context.

That's why it's often hard for someone to join in a conversation that's been going strong for a while. Because you've already established an elaborate context, it's easier to maintain the implicit metatalk that keeps everything going. Everyone's been talking and chatting for a few minutes, and you don't have to keep saying what you're talking about. Because you've all been in it from the beginning, you all know what the topic is. And because the topic has already shifted a few times, you also know the history of the conversation—not only what's going on right now, but what you were talking about five or ten minutes ago. If one of you wants to go back to one of these topics, the transition will be smooth because you all remember that earlier portion of the conversation.

This all gets thrown off when a new person joins the group. This can happen at a party, when a friend arrives late and walks up to your group after you've been talking for half an hour; or when your group is in a car, and one person has gotten out for a few minutes to fill up the tank, missing part of the conversation. Sometimes we don't have to tell this new person everything—we know they'll be able to figure out just by listening for a few minutes. But in other conversations, we feel the need to give the new person some background. One of us will summarize the part of the conversation that the new person has missed, filling him in on the topic. And sometimes we might fill someone in, even if we don't think it's really necessary, just as a polite gesture to make that person feel more welcome in the conversation.

Filling in is an example of explicit metatalk. It's like reported speech, but it's a special case, because we're taking time out to summarize a conversation while it's still going on, to help someone join in for the rest of the conversation.[13]

Because we can all do it without thinking, it's easy to forget how complicated a skill this is. It's interesting that we all usually agree on whether or not metatalk is required. We all seem to have a shared intuition about how complicated the conversation is, and how difficult it will be for the new person to figure out what's going on. It takes a deep understanding of conversation just to decide whether or not filling in is even necessary. Think about the differences between filling in at a party, and filling in for our friend who was pumping gas. At a party, we summarize from scratch: we know the new person hasn't heard any of our conversation. At the gas station, we know we only have to summarize that portion of the conversation which the driver has missed; we can take advantage of our shared knowledge of the conversation up to the point when the driver left the car.

The fact that we can fill in when necessary shows that we always have a mental image of the conversational frame. And when we're asked to fill in, we may realize for the first time that our version of the frame isn't identical to everyone else's; a friend may interrupt our filling in to clarify or correct our version of the frame. These occasions show us that conversation can continue even if everyone has a slightly different mental image of the conversational frame. The way that speakers coordinate their mental frames is often studied under the topic of *intersubjectivity*. Preschool children, for example, have to work hard to learn this frame-coordinating skill, as the developmental psychologist Artin Goncu has documented.[14] In a 1996 book, *The Culture of Education*, the prominent psychologist Jerome Bruner proposed that intersubjectivity is the biggest unresolved issue in psychology today.[15]

Filling in is an example of a general principle: We're most likely to do explicit metatalk at the beginnings and the endings of conversations. To join a conversation, we have to pay particularly close attention to its flow, and wait for an opportunity to join in. To leave a conversation, we usually have to make some sort of explicit statement explaining why we're going. These are simple examples of the creative management of conversation. Conversation analysts have discovered that a great deal of interesting social negotiation is played out in these beginnings and endings, which researchers sometimes call *openings* and *closings*.

During an improv theater performance, the actors who are not actively participating in the current scene stand or sit at the back or sides of the stage; they don't want to interfere with the ongoing performance. But at the same time, they have to be close enough to the action to hear the dialogue, so they can detect when it would be appropriate to enter the performance as a new character. When an actor decides to join an ongoing scene, he or she will walk on and speak a line of dialogue, or begin miming an action. The actors who are already on stage must then adjust their performances and redirect the emerging plot to incorporate this new character. At no point does any actor step out of character to discuss the change or to direct the performance; everything is done in character. The "No denial" rule applies: The new actor must be incorporated into the ongoing improvisation. The option to reject the new actor and continue as before is not allowed.

During a long-form improv performance, which typically lasts 30 minutes, the actors create one scene after another, and each scene is usually less than a minute long. There is no stage direction; no director stands in the wings and tells the actors when it's time to enter for the next scene. An actor cuts from one scene and starts another just by walking to the front of the stage—"upstaging" the last scene. The actors who are already there have to end their scene and leave the stage so that the next scene can start. Like everything else about improvisational theater, these entrances and exits are collaboratively, spontaneously determined.

Actors are so good at improvising these entrances and exits that my friends often think it's all been planned in advance. Although many of us are good at it, joining and leaving conversations is not a trivial skill. Self-help books for shy people always have chapters on "How to start a conversation" and "How to close a conversation." Like many other conversational skills that we take for granted, skillful entrances and exits have to be learned. I discovered this when I began to study children's play conversations in the preschool. Imagine yourself at the age of three, four, or five, starting the new year at a new preschool. If you don't want to spend all of your time playing alone or doing crafts at the worktables, you have to learn how to join a play group. This is really hard for children, especially because children can be so much more brutal when they reject each other. To engage in play, a child has to overcome the fear of rejection and make the attempt. Here's an example of what can happen when a child is rejected:

Muhammed and John have been playing with Legos in the Lego area since 9:05. At 9:15, Bernie attempts to join them, since his friend Sam is late this morning.

(1)	Bernie	Can I play with you?
(2)		Can I play with you?
(3)		Can I play with you?
(4)	Muhammed	No!
(5)	Bernie	You need some animals?
(6)	Muhammed	No!
(7)		Then I won't be your friend again. Right, John?
(8)	John	Right
(9)	Bernie	Those are animals, so can I play with you? (Bernie offers toy animals "in trade" for being allowed entry, but to no avail.)
(10)	(Bernie is ignored.)	

A few seconds after this, Bernie is saved by the timely arrival of Sam, a frequent playmate. Bernie and Sam leave for the doll corner and begin playing.

Children's entry attempts are rejected about 50% of the time.[16] This high percentage of rejection, even in classrooms where the children know each other, shows how hard it is to accomplish play entry successfully. The writer and preschool teacher Vivian Paley wrote an entire book, You Can't Say You Can't Play,[17] about the year when she instituted a new classroom rule: All children's play entry attempts must be accepted. The children had trouble adjusting to this rule, and she had only partial success. Even though rejection is never pleasant, perhaps the possibility of rejection forces children to learn how to negotiate and form social groups.

As adults, our attempts to enter conversation are often easy and natural, and don't require much thought. It's only in unusual situations that we have to think about how to approach a person or a group. For example, at a lecture, when a prominent speaker completes a talk, interested members of the audience may approach the speaker with a specific entry strategy in mind, knowing that famous people are often too busy to talk to every fan. And in everyday life, many conversations begin with a little script, variations on "How're ya doin?—Fine, how are you?" There are many different kinds of entrance and exit strategies, and some of them require more creativity than others. But even the everyday, easy entrances require a kind of social skill that has to be learned. It's another example of how often the conversational abilities that we take for granted are complex, creative, and improvisational.[18]

HOW CONVERSATION WORKS, PART 2:
TAKING TURNS

Even before they start talking, two of the first things children learn are to *share* and to *take turns*. These are moral and social principles that we think it's important for children to learn. And we all believe that children who share and who take turns with their peers will grow into more popular, happier adults.

In fact, we have to take turns in conversation as well, because only one person can talk at a time. Of course, sometimes we slip up and talk at the same time, and when the discussion heats up we might interrupt each other a lot. But generally, we believe that conversation works better if we take turns—this way, everybody gets to talk, and only one person talks at a time.[19]

Classic boardgames like *Monopoly* have a very specific turn order. In the simplest games, you just go around the table; other games complicate things by allowing challenges that can modify the order of turns. The rules surrounding turn-taking are just about the most fundamental rules of any game. But in creating conversations, there are no rules about who gets the next turn. If these rules are so fundamental to board games, how does everyday conversation get along without them? Without explicit rules, how do we figure out when to switch turns? What's worse, in conversation we don't even know what counts as a "turn." You can choose to say just one word, or you can talk for five minutes, depending on the conversation and who you're talking to.

We all subconsciously know these unwritten rules about how conversations work. For example, if you're talking with a friend, you know your turn comes when she stops and ends her turn. But if you're talking with two or more friends, you all have a more complex task: when your turn is over, who gets the next turn? We also know that if we're talking to two or more people, we can implicitly select the person who gets to talk next, by asking them a question or saying something we know they want to respond to. We also feel that everyone should get a chance to talk; if someone hasn't spoken for a few minutes, they somehow have more of a right to the next turn.

Some formal situations—such as a business meeting or a debate—specify the order of turns, the length of turns, and who has more right to speak than everyone else. But in creating conversations, turn-taking is collaboratively improvised. The ways that we improvise turn-taking have some interesting implications. For example, when one speaker stops talking, the first person to jump into the gap and start talking gets the next turn. This gives everyone an incentive to jump the gun, to start talking at the slightest gap in a person's turn. One implication of this is that the larger the group, the shorter the turns will be, because everyone has more of an incentive to jump in quickly. That's why if we're in a group of people who love to talk, it can be difficult to get a word in edgewise—someone will jump in as soon as you pause to take a breath. In this kind of group, each conversational turn is like a possession, and they don't want to give it up. The only thing that keeps some people from talking all the time, turning a dialogue into a monologue, is the preschool lesson of sharing: We believe that everyone should get a turn and that no one should talk too much.

Deciding who gets to talk and when to take turns is always collaborative. Like everything else about creating conversations, turn-taking is a group effort; everyone collaboratively improvises these transitions among speakers.

Some People are More Equal Than Others

When conversation isn't shared, it's often because the speakers aren't equal in status. If you're talking to your boss, even if it's just small talk in the elevator, you'll let her turn go on as long as she likes. In a group with your boss, when your coworker finishes a turn, you'll probably pause a second to give your boss the opportunity to take the next turn.

Interruptions vary with status, as well. Your boss has more freedom to decide when to interrupt and end your turn. But if your boss is talking, you pretty much have to wait until that turn is finished.[20]

Does conversational creativity change when we aren't all equals? If one person has absolute authority, they might take control and determine the flow of the entire interaction—like an autocratic manager running a business meeting. But such an extreme case is rare, at least in everyday conversations in the United States. Because of our egalitarian ethic, even when participants have different statuses the higher-status person doesn't usually get to single-handedly direct the conversational performance. Everyone who speaks plays a role, contributing to the final performance. Even in a rigidly hierarchical context, some inferior-status speakers might be more creative conversationalists, and they have more influence over the conversation than their status would suggest.

In fact, very few of our conversations occur among people of exactly the same status. Think of talking to your parents, or to your doctor about a medical problem, or engaging in dinner-time conversation with your children. Nonetheless, these conversations are not directed and created by one high-status participant. All but the most extreme of these unequal situations involve collaboration, because you can't have a conversation without the participation of everyone.

Cultural Differences

Not every culture values talk as much as Americans. Whereas we talk about having the right to speak and getting our turn in conversation, other language communities place a higher value on silence. In America, we assign a value to talk and we assume that higher-status individuals will talk more. But many other cultures have different attitudes. The conversation researcher Deborah Tannen, best known for her books on gender and language, points out that many cultures place a higher value on silence in some situations. For example, Japanese speakers prefer not to talk in confrontational situations.[21] Many Scandinavian cultures are stereotypically silent and slow to talk, relative to other Americans. In Finland, proverbs about conversation indicate how much they value silence:

> Listen a lot, speak a little.
> One word is enough to make a lot of trouble.
> A fool speaks a lot, a wise man thinks instead.
> One word is as good as nine.

American language researchers have only recently begun to study cultures that place more value on silence than we do. Learning about these cultures can make you think twice about the unwritten rules for turn-taking that we all take for granted. For example, in a conversation among Americans, silences are a little embarrassing. Someone will always start talking, or else it will seem as if something is wrong—as if we aren't getting along very well. But in Denmark, people interpret silence very differently. They think a pause in conversation symbolizes that everyone is satisfied and feeling good about things. The silence underscores the genuineness of your feelings. Different approaches to turn-taking and to silence can cause problems when people with different norms talk together. Scandinavians, known around the world as taciturn, often joke among themselves that the farther north you go, the less people talk. The people in the extreme north of Sweden are the least talkative. They say that the need for honesty and sincerity increases as the climate gets more forbidding; they think that silence signifies honesty and sincerity.[22]

Although Americans talk more than Scandinavians, America isn't the most talkative culture in the world, either. After all, there are countries where people tend to talk at the same time and to interrupt each other a lot more than we do—they don't follow the same rules of turn-taking that we all implicitly share. It's often said that an English visitor to a Latin country has to learn how to listen to several people speaking at the same time.[23] Many linguists have studied cultures where the American turn-taking style doesn't apply. Although we often think of speech overlaps as rude or impolite, in these cultures, it's acceptable and expected for more than one person to talk at the same time.

The reason turn-taking is so important to us is because we believe that only one person should talk at a time. You probably think this is obvious: If people want to understand each other, you can only have one person talking at once, right? Interruptions and overlaps make conversations less effective, because they are breakdowns in turn-taking. But not even all Americans share these beliefs about conversation. For example, Deborah Tannen compared English speakers in New York City and California.[24] She found a much higher frequency of interruption in the New York families than in the Californian families, and found that the Californians who watched the videotapes of the New York families thought they were being rude to each other. In contrast, when New Yorkers were shown videotapes of other New York families, they made a radically different judgment: They said the families were emotionally involved, connected, and concerned with each other. New Yorkers thought that interruption was a sign that you were really listening, and that you cared. Tannen called this a *high involvement* style of conversation, and contrasted it with the *high considerateness* of the "one at a time" speakers in California. In both styles, the flow of the conversation is collaboratively coordinated; but depending on your style, you use different unwritten rules to guide the conversation.

Another one of my favorite studies shows just how different these rules can be. The anthropologist Karl Reisman studied conversation patterns in a small village in Antigua, an island in the Caribbean. In three predominantly male genres of talk—boasting, cursing, and argument—it's common for all of the participants to talk at the same time; there are no pauses, and there is no turn-taking. For example, this often happens after a cricket game, when the men are all discussing what happened during the game. To American ears, the Antiguan "conversations" appear almost anarchic. If a new person joins the group, although he will be greeted, he will not be formally acknowledged as a conversational participant. Instead, he just starts speaking whenever he feels ready. Sometimes people are heard, sometimes not; there is no guarantee that anyone will really hear what you're saying. Using a musical metaphor, Reisman called this *contrapuntal* conversation.[25]

Think about what your conversation would be like if everyone was talking at once. When you first join in, you don't have to find out what the "topic" is before you start talking. There is no requirement to relate your subject to that of other members of the group; in fact, there may be multiple competing topics vying for dominance in the conversation. And any one of the speakers can step out of the conversation to make an aside—for example, greeting friends who walk by, coming back to the main topic several minutes later—with no apologies necessary. And to increase the chances of being heard, men will repeat the same argument over and over, with different embellishments and emphases each time. In contrapuntal conversation, you'll hear a lot of repetition and variation of theme.

Because this simultaneous speech is very difficult for an American to follow, or for a scientist to transcribe for analysis, Reisman had to spend a lot of time listening closely. With increasing familiarity, he began to realize that the speakers were listening, simultaneously, to all of the other voices. Like a good improviser, the Antiguan conversationalist listens to the group mind, attending to multiple speakers at once.

The message in all of this is that we need to be careful about using our own intuitions about how conversation works and careful about assuming they are universal characteristics of all language use. Language, society, and culture are intimately related, in complex and poorly understood ways. Different cultures have different conventions for how the performances of everyday life should be played, how the improvised dialogues of everyday conversation are created. We aren't consciously aware of these unwritten rules until someone violates them. If you came across a group of Antiguans in the street, you'd probably perceive the conversation as a little disturbing, not only because it's hard for us to follow, but because it violates many of our own norms about how conversation is supposed to work. Rather than think of it as an equally valid way of organizing conversation, we are likely to view it in almost moral terms. We think that interruption is rude and impolite, so the Antiguans must be rude. Or we might come up with a rational explanation for our discomfort: It's inefficient for them to talk at the same time, because they won't communicate as effectively. This judgment also has an insulting tone to it: the Antiguans must be ignorant and stupid.

Reisman, however, argues that this contrapuntal conversation requires even more intelligence, verbal skill, and social awareness than the "one at a time" style. And he also suggests that this conversational style tells us some interesting facts about the Antiguan's unwritten views about conversation—for example, that the impulse to speak is seen as coming from within, and not from the structures of the conversational group one finds oneself in. Contrapuntal conversation indicates the value that Antiguans place on the spontaneous expression of feeling.

It's amazing how a subtle difference in conversational practice can lead one group to make moral judgments about another group. Just like Tannen's study of New Yorkers and Californians, the group that interrupts and overlaps more thinks that they're being more expressive and more involved; the quieter group thinks they are rude. The group that pauses and lets only one person talk at a time thinks that they're being polite and efficient; the more talkative group thinks these "polite" people are disengaged and inexpressive.

When we realize that there are many different ways to manage the creative improvisations of everyday conversation, and that all are equally creative and equally effective for their contexts, we can better understand differences in cultures. We can avoid making the mistake of thinking that a style of talking is really based on some moral or personal quality of the speaker. No style is better or worse; they're just different ways of creating conversations.

COLLABORATIVE CREATIVITY

Although the ground rules change from country to country, all conversations are improvised and creative. Anthropologists have studied just about every world language, and no matter where you go, people are creative in conversations, and no language is any more creative than any other. Some things are different from one language to another—each culture has its own unique set of metatalk techniques, and each culture has its own rules for taking turns and sharing. But no matter what language you speak, you still have to collaboratively improvise to resolve the same issues: what is going on, what you're talking about, who is participating in the conversation, what role everybody is playing, and when you change everything to a different topic.

We all have the potential to be creative in conversation. But some talented artists are exceptionally creative with words—poets, novelists, and speechwriters. How are creating conversations like these other forms of linguistic creativity? Of course, the poet works alone and has control over his own words, and doesn't have to improvise because he can revise as many times as he likes. In conversation, we have to improvise, without a chance to revise; and we create collaboratively, because we need other speakers before we can have a conversation. Nonetheless, we can learn some things about creating conversations by looking at what they share with the most artistic use of language—poetry.

Conversation researchers have identified many similarities between poetic language and everyday conversation; in fact, even preschool children use poetic devices to help them negotiate changes to the play drama. The most common poetic technique that children use is *parallelism,* when two lines work together, just like in a rhyming couplet.

In play couplets, children use the first line to propose a play change out of character, and then use the second line to enact the play change in character, as *if* the change had already taken place. Or a child might reverse these two lines: acting out the play change first, and then using the second line to restate the change out of character. Here's a short exchange that includes one example of each of these techniques. Jennifer and Kathy are playing at the sand table. Jennifer has a duck she calls "Littlefoot."[26]

(1)	Kathy	Pretend there was a earthquake right now.	
(2)		Dum, dum, dum	Enacting the earthquake
(3)	Jennifer	Littlefoot! Littlefoot!	
(4)		Are you with your mommy?	
(5)		Littlefoot, are you with your mommy?	
(6)		Pretend the Dad was calling them.	

Lines (1) and (2) are parallel. Line (1) proposes that an earthquake will happen, and then line (2) is an on-stage performance of the earthquake's soundtrack. Jennifer responds by speaking as the daddy toy, calling to his daughter Littlefoot, in lines (3) through (5). Line (6) is parallel to these, making the same suggestion, but this time out of character. I think that at (6), Jennifer realized that her performance could be misinterpreted, that she did not specify her proposed play change clearly enough. So Jennifer steps out of character to clarify, restating her proposal, a parallel repetition of lines (3) through (5). This play example combines four different types of metatalk in an intriguing poetic structure:

out-of-frame	(Kathy)
in-frame	(Kathy)
in-frame	(Jennifer)
out-of-frame	(Jennifer)

Poetically parallel repetition can make a child more effective at communicating her play goals. Jennifer's choice to start out with in-frame speech is poetic, because it follows on Kathy's in-frame enactment of the earthquake: "Dum, dum, dum." Poetic uses of language are often effective ways to accomplish metatalk goals. Jennifer takes advantage of her poetic skill to more effectively introduce her new play idea: "Pretend the Dad was calling them." In my research, I've discovered that children are constantly practicing this "poetic metatalk" in their pretend play conversation.

This example from children's play demonstrates one of the distinctive properties of poetic language—you can't get the full meaning by analyzing a single line, because the structure of the entire poem often carries its own hidden meanings. In the same way, we can't understand conversational creativity by looking at any single turn of the conversation—it's a series of turns, spoken by different people. Like the above play transcript, all coherent conversations have a poetic structure; "poetic" because people will interpret what you say within the context of what everyone else said just before you, and what others will say after you. How you are interpreted depends on the structure of the whole conversation. (This is why it's so easy to take things out of context.) Because the "lines" of a "conversational poem" are spoken by different people, we could say that creating conversations are *collaboratively poetic*—poems improvised by all of us together. Conversational poetry is created across turns, by multiple speakers, with each person's turn repeating and elaborating on the grammatical structure of the prior speaker's turn.

There are many parallels between poetry and conversation. In fact, that's why the field of language study called *poetics* is not really the study of poetry—when you try to study poetry you soon discover that there's no easy way to describe how poetic language is different from any other type of language. This observation was first made by a group of linguists working in Prague just before World War II. These linguists, so influential that they are commonly referred to as the "Prague School," compared artistic language and everyday language, and discovered that everyday language is often just as creative as a poem or a play.[27] The problem of defining "poetry" has only gotten worse since then, because contemporary poets and novelists love to mix genres, inventing the "prose poem" and the "poetic novel." For all of these reasons, the field of poetics has turned to an examination of some pretty basic questions: What is poetry? What does it mean to use language poetically?

Because of the ways that literary genres have been blurred, our definition of poetry has to be pretty broad. Poetics researchers have come up with the following working definition, initially proposed by the most influential of the Prague-school linguists, Roman Jakobson: Any use of language where the meaning depends not only on the words used, but also on the structure of the words, is a poetic use of language. This definition easily takes care of traditional poetry, where the conventional structures of iambic pentameter and the sonnet form contribute to the overall impact of the poem, and are essential in interpreting the poem. But it's broad enough to potentially also include modern free verse.

This broad definition also allows us to make the connection to everyday conversation. In the above four-line transcript from children's play, we see that the parallelism across lines reinforces the goals of the children—the structure of the conversation carries part of the meaning, above and beyond the exact words spoken. That's why conversational poetics is an example of implicit metatalk—when the way you say something carries a hidden meaning. The important thing to note here is that the implicit metatalk only functions within the context of the four-line sequence; it's not possible to identify a single utterance that "contains" the metatalk message. The implicit metatalk message is collaboratively, poetically created.

A conversation is more poetic, in this metatalk sense of "poetic," when everyone's words are connected to everyone else's, when each person's turn is more closely related to the prior flow of the conversation. In these poetic conversations, it's impossible to understand a person's words outside of that context. The words don't stand alone—their meaning is dependent on the context.

Now let's expand our scope outward and upward, beyond the single conversation. We've seen that conversational creativity emerges over time through collaborative improvisation. Let's move to a longer-term perspective, bigger than a single conversation—to look at how language and conversation develop through history.

Who Creates a Language?

In fact, language itself is a collaborative creation, emerging from an entire people. Who's responsible for inventing the English language? Of course, that's a meaningless question—no single person invented the English language, or the Japanese language, or any other language. But English hasn't been around forever—so it must have been created somehow. How can we ever know how a language gets created, as we can't travel back in time? It turns out that we can, in a way—because new languages are forming even today.

New languages often form when people who speak different languages are thrown together, and have to communicate. This has often been the case throughout history, especially among traders, who have been mediating cross-cultural contacts for thousands of years. Traders have always made their money by traveling between cultures, picking up languages as they go. In our modern world, with widespread travel, immigration, and television and radio spreading European languages around the globe, it's more and more rare that you can't find a translator, or someone who speaks English. But over the course of history, without a well-established world language or modern communication technology, it has been common that people have to figure out their own ways to communicate.

With the onset of European immigration and colonialism entire language communities came into contact with each other. In many cases, the European language won out, and the colonized natives were forced, economically or otherwise, to learn that language. But in many parts of the world, the balance of linguistic power was more even, and neither language dominated. When neither language can dominate the other, what often emerges is a halfway blend between languages that is called a *pidgin*, a *trade language*, or a *creole*.[28]

Trade languages tend to fade out of existence as the trader becomes fluent in the native language. Such languages remain fluid, changing weekly or monthly; they are simple, being used only for basic business transactions. In these situations, the European language does not always dominate—for example, in the American Northwest, the Chinook Jargon (about 1,100 root words) used Nootka and Chinook grammar, although the vocabulary was mostly English.

Creole languages are much more complete than trade languages, and have more stability. Unlike trade languages, they result from the political domination of one people by another, rather than an equal balance of power. For example, many creoles emerged from contact with a small European colony. The European settlers had to trade with the locals to acquire necessary supplies, but they were clearly in a dominant role, able to force their language on the local people. Nonetheless, in many cases they found it was more effective if they spoke a modified version of their language with the locals during the early years of contact. The local people gradually picked up the European language, and local dialects formed, with words and idioms from their own language blended in.

In these contact situations, people don't spend a lot of time worrying about the structure of the language or the direction of the change—they just do whatever works. Over time, each person successively refines the hybrid language over repeated encounters with others.

So who creates these hybrid new languages? Of course, no one is *the* creator of a creole. These new languages emerge over a long period of time, from thousands of individual conversations. Languages form and develop in an improvisational, collaborative, flowing pattern. Language change emerges from the creative conversations of everyone in the community. Generations come and go, but language flows on, dependent on no one and yet dependent on everyone. The formation of a creole language is in this way similar to how older languages, such as English or Chinese, formed. In fact, the English that is now a world language has its roots in a contact language that developed after the French invaded and colonized England in the 11th century.

Language creation is another example of *emergence* in conversation. Recall from Chapter 1 that novel patterns can emerge from group interaction, even when there is no single person controlling or directing the group. Conversations are emergent because they are collaborative improvisations, with no script and no director. And language itself is emergent—because so many people are involved in language creation, no one person has any real control over it. It's unpredictable, and emerges from the actions of thousands of people. Like improv, language itself is unpredictable, collective, emergent—collaboratively created.

Who Created Conversation?

We've seen how a language is an emergent, collaborative creation. But what about the culturally unique ways of improvising conversation— how did these emerge? How do the Scandinavians and the Antiguans develop such different ways of creating conversations? These rules for creating conversations also emerge, collaboratively, from the collective behavior of an entire language community.

Historians have recently begun to explore the roots of modern conversational practice. They've found that the unwritten rules of conversation—turn-taking and metatalk both—change over time, although they change extremely slowly, perhaps even more slowly than a language's grammar and vocabulary.

Peter Burke, a historian at the University of Cambridge, has studied the "art of polite conversation" by reading "how-to" books that were published for aspiring members of society in 16th-century Italy, 17th-century France, and 18th-century Britain.[29] These little manuals were like the Emily Post of the time. In the 16th century, people began to think of polite conversation as a social art. In fact, most of these manuals were called "The Art of Conversation."

These manuals describe several different styles of conversation—styles that we can recognize 400 years later. Conversations could be competitive—with each speaker trying to outshine the others—or cooperative; conversation occurred among peers, but also across status levels in the rigid social hierarchy. The rulebooks helped aspiring gentlemen to be more effective conversationalists. But you were expected to be spontaneous—these books cautioned that if you were going to script your lines in advance, you should stutter and hesitate to make everyone *think* you were improvising.

The rules for proper conversation were different in every European country. You might be considered an elegant gentleman in Milan, but an oaf when traveling to Paris. This is why many books were written for travelers to foreign countries, describing how conversation there was different from your own country.

As long ago as the 16th century, the Italian language had eight different terms for different varieties of small talk. But it was in 17th-century France that the art of conversation really took off. Books about "elegant conversation" were everywhere. These books focused on conversations between three or more people, semi-formal encounters that were halfway between the intimacy of a family dinner and the formality of speaking in public. Social institutions such as the Parisian salon and the London men's clubs were founded during this time, increasing the number of situations in which gentlemen were forced to engage in polite conversation and increasing the social anxiety of the book-buying public. Typical rules of conversation found in these books include:

1. Don't talk too much. Listen, don't monopolize the conversation.
2. Accommodate your conversation to those present—relate it to the group you are in.
3. It's uncivil to speak about yourself all the time.
4. Don't interrupt.
5. The need for at least apparent spontaneity in conversation is stressed in all of these manuals. Some of them even recommend intentional hesitation and occasional clumsiness in order to preserve the illusion of spontaneity.
6. The most frequent theme: Avoid forms of speech that are too direct, too pedantic, too technical. Avoid direct questions, imperatives.

The main difference between the Italian and French manuals, on the one hand, and the British ones, on the other, is that the British emphasize informality in conversation, and that all speakers should be treated as equals. French visitors to England often said the British were too direct, or worse, that they were just rude or unsophisticated. Of course, we've taken this informal egalitarianism to its logical extreme in the United States, where just about all of our conversations are supposed to be casual, and we're supposed to treat everyone like an equal, regardless of status.

It's funny how the differences among countries from 200 years ago still seem to be true of England, France, and Italy today. On the continent, the English and the Americans are still thought to be overly direct and straightforward. If you've traveled to a foreign country, you know that learning the grammar and vocabulary of a language doesn't make you fluent. The rules for creating conversation are just as hard to learn as the rules for grammar. In fact, because they're unwritten and subconscious, you can't just learn them in class, like you can with grammar and vocabulary.

These rules are surprisingly similar to the handbooks of today—the "how to" books for shy people, with advice on "how to start a conversation," how to "keep the conversation going," and Larry King's *How to Talk to Anyone, Anytime, Anywhere.*[30] Although these rules were originally written for speakers of Italian and French 400 years ago, we can still recognize them in our own conversational style. It shows that the techniques of creating conversation change extremely slowly, even more slowly than slang, vocabulary, and accents.

Using Collaborative Creativity

Like many aspects of our culture, language and conversation are not created by any one person, but are collaborative creations, emerging from millions of conversations over hundreds of years. Collaborative emergence is a uniquely powerful and creative force.

We've all had the experience of something unexpected emerging from conversation. Your friend's last comment might remind you of something you wanted to tell her, or remind you of a piece of information that you need that she might have. You may discover that you both have a common interest that you didn't know about, leading to a plan to do something together in the future.

Many unexpected things can emerge from creating conversations. In fact, these collaborative conversations can even lead to big insights. In a research project with Mike Csikszentmihalyi at the University of Chicago, we examined the everyday work habits and creative processes of exceptional artists and scientists. When we asked them to tell us about their most important insights, we expected them to tell us stories about having an "Aha" moment in the shower or walking on the beach. We always think that creative insight happens in a private moment. Instead, we were surprised to find that most of these creative individuals depended on creative conversations for their insights, during collaboration, brainstorming, and team meetings.[31]

What's the connection between conversation and creative insight? When you're engaged in creative conversation with people who are working on the same problems or creating in the same medium, you can become inspired. These creating conversations can lead to unexpected and valuable new ideas. That's because creating conversations are unpredictable—new ideas emerge as we talk. The unexpected ideas that emerge from creating conversations come from the creativity of everyone, just like an improv skit is created by the entire ensemble.

For example, many Nobel prize scientists told Csikszentmihalyi about how conversations with colleagues was essential to their creative innovations. The physicist Freeman Dyson told him that "Science is a very gregarious business; it's essentially the difference between having this door open and having it shut. If I'm doing science, I have the door open. You want to be all the time talking with people—it's only by interacting with other people in the building that you get anything interesting done; it's essentially a communal enterprise."

Especially in the early stages of the creative process, when people are looking for the right spark—the connection that will make it all clear—they seek out conversational partners for brainstorming. John Reed, the CEO of CitiCorp, told us: "When I'm trying to get my mind around something new, I seek out people and talk to them." His first instinct is to pick up the phone for a conversation. Hazel Henderson, the economist and activist, said "I develop a lot of my ideas in dialogue. It's very exciting, the sparks, and dynamic interaction, and very much newer things, new ways of looking at things, that come out of those conversations."

This is very different from our usual understanding of the moment of insight, the brilliant idea that suddenly pops into conscious awareness. In the classic story, it happens in the bathtub: the Greek scientist Archimedes, who gets into a bathtub and then realizes that an object floating in water would displace an amount of water equal to its weight, and shouts "Eureka!" a word that we still use to mean "Aha! That's it!"

Researchers are finding that many of these "Aha" moments come to us when we're engaged in creating conversations. In improv theater, the actors can't plan their lines ahead of time—they don't know what they're going to say until they say it. Consequently, an "aha" moment can happen in every line of the play. The rules of improvisation result in a stage dialogue that is both unpredictable, and is created collaboratively by all of the actors. Looking at the spontaneous creativity that can emerge during improvisational theater, we can better understand how conversation can lead to creative insights. During an improvisation, a scene is created that no one of the actors alone could have come up with—that's why we say that it *emerges* from the actors working together. It's like this with other types of creativity as well. During a laboratory conversation, ideas can emerge that none of the scientists would have thought of on their own. During a brainstorming session at work, the solution to that sticky problem may become obvious, even though everyone in the room has already spent an unproductive week thinking about it.

Psychologists who study creativity have traditionally focused on individual mental processes; our cultural myths about creativity are all about isolated individuals: the lone genius, staying up late in the laboratory, or the tortured, isolated artist, who can't even tear himself away from his studio long enough to try to sell his paintings. But psychologists have gradually come to realize that these stereotypic myths don't represent the reality of creativity. Collaboration is becoming an increasingly important issue for both creativity researchers and conversation researchers.

* * * * * * * *

Recall Horton the elephant, who keeps repeating "I meant what I said, and I said what I meant." If we acted like Horton, we would always say exactly what we meant—for example, we'd go into that business meeting with all of our lines already written out. If conversation really worked this way, nothing original or unexpected could ever emerge. But the fact is, we have to improvise our everyday conversations, and we have to do it in collaboration with everyone. At the end of the conversation, we have created a performance together, using only our words to improvise. The final conversation emerges from the moment-to-moment flow from one speaker to another, and it's a social creation.

Collaboration is what makes conversation so uniquely creative. In this chapter, we've seen some of the techniques that we use to collaboratively create conversation, and some of the creative results of those collaborations—which include even language itself. In the next chapter, we'll continue to explore the collaborations of conversation, by looking at our co-creators—the audience for our words. In a sense, the audience collaborates in what we say, even as we are forming the words.

Chapter 3

Audiences

Our everyday talk is spoken for an audience—the people listening to our words. In most conversations, without thinking about it, you modify your talk to match the audience. You talk differently with four people listening than with only one listening; you talk differently to an old friend than to a first date. Your audience influences how formal you will be, how long you expect to talk before being interrupted, and what you'll be careful *not* to say. In creating conversations, our audience is a silent collaborator, and their influence can always be seen in our words.

In the last chapter, we learned about *turn-taking*—and we saw that although we usually assume that only one person can speak at a time, there are many situations where this isn't true. When your audience is interrupting, or when several people are talking at once, it's easy to see that the conversation is not a solo performance—it's collaborative. The Antiguan "making noise" genre of contrapuntal conversation is perhaps at a collaborative extreme, because there is no turn-taking; everyone talks in parallel. But this conversational genre can help us think about the parallelism of our own conversations. When we're talking, we're always looking at the people listening to us, checking to make sure they are still listening and still interested, looking for any signs of confusion or enthusiasm, as they quietly murmur "Hmm..." or "Uh..." during our words. Listeners communicate a lot of this information non-verbally, with their eyes or their posture.[1] Conversation researchers refer to this as *back channel communication*,[2] and effective conversationalists can intuitively monitor these messages, to calibrate their ongoing talk.

We process this feedback subconsciously, and often don't even realize how it's influencing the way that we talk. To explore these subtle cues, the linguist Charles Goodwin videotaped conversational groups, making sure to get both the speaker and the listener on camera. He noticed that both speakers and hearers use their gaze—who they are looking at—to communicate important nonverbal information, and speakers construct their words based on where they see the listener looking. For example, speakers often stop their sentence once they get the listener's attention, and start over again.

Goodwin developed a novel way to transcribe the gaze of both the speaker and the listeners.[3] The following transcript shows a mother talking to her two children; she wants to suggest that they move closer to the teacher so they can hear better, but when she starts speaking, Brian is not looking at her. At the X, Brian turns to look at his mother, and notice how she interrupts herself and restarts her suggestion:

Barbara: Brian, you're gonna have—you kids'll *have* to go down *closer*
Brian: X_____

The horizontal line after the X indicates that Brian is looking at Barbara. Although Barbara is the only one talking, Brian's gaze contributes to the way she forms her words—when he turns to look at her, she starts again, this time addressing both children. Goodwin also noticed that speakers sometimes stop in mid-sentence, waiting for the listener to look at them; in the following example, each dash in parentheses represents a pause of one-tenth of a second:

Mike: Speaking of pornographic movies, I heard (---------) a while
Carney: X_____

Mike pauses because he's not sure if Carney is paying attention; he continues after Carney turns to look at him. Needless to say, this type of analysis requires incredible attention to detail, advanced video equipment, and extremely patient researchers—perhaps that's why these collaborative behaviors were not analyzed until the 1970s, when researchers first had access to video equipment.

The ways that we use catchphrases are also influenced by our audience. For example, in Chapter 1 we saw that some courtroom judges alter their use of stock legal phrases for the benefit of their audience. They hesitate or pause to say "um" so that the person on trial would get the impression that they were speaking spontaneously. In some situations, speakers use catchphrases to make it easier for the audience to understand them. For example, New Zealand radio and television weather forecasts are highly structured, both in overall outline—with geographic regions and different types of weather always presented in the same order—and in the set of catchphrases that are repeatedly used. Unlike the catchphrases used by sportscasters, these structures don't exist to aid the speaker; the forecasts are composed in advance and then read on the air. Rather, the formulas are for the benefit of the audience—they make it easier for the listener to process the information, because they listen to the weather every day and thus learn the order of the broadcast, the standard formulas that are used, and can process the forecast with only minimal attention.[4]

Although these may seem like minor, trivial influences on speech, they demonstrate that even a silent listener influences what is said. Listeners can have an even more significant effect by murmuring assent or objection, or providing brief back channel comments like "uh huh" or "Oh wow!" Listeners can communicate interactional messages even with subtle differences in the timing of these comments, as Goodwin documented in another close study of audiotapes. If a back channel comment like "Oh wow!" comes while the speaker is talking, it simply indicates an evaluation of what the speaker is saying. However, if the comment comes just as the speaker is coming to the end of a sentence, it indicates something extra: that the listener wants the speaker to continue telling the story. Without this "continuer" as feedback, the speaker might pause to give the listener a chance to take a turn, or to ask a question.[5]

But in our common-sense ideas about conversation, the audience doesn't matter. For example, Horton's theory of conversation—we say what we mean, and we mean what we say—doesn't leave any room for audience influence. Horton's theory is closely related to another common-sense theory about how conversation works—some linguists call it the *conduit metaphor* or the *football metaphor*.[6] In the football view of conversation, the speaker has a thought, and forms a sentence to communicate that thought. By speaking the sentence, the thought is "passed" to the "receiver," the listener, who "receives" the sentence and decodes its meaning.

The football metaphor has several unfortunate implications, and all of them lead us away from the collaborative dimensions of conversation. The metaphor implies that we know what we want to say before we start talking, we always say pretty much what we mean, and that the only job for the listener is to pay attention and to try to understand what we meant. Many linguists—used to thinking of language in terms of the syntactic structures and the meanings of sentences, rather than as a social, collaborative phenomenon—implicitly assume the football metaphor when they turn to the study of conversation; an example is Grice's theory of conversational implicature (page 48). The football metaphor focuses on the speaker and ignores the role of the audience.

This chapter continues the collaboration theme introduced in Chapter 2—we'll see how often the listener contributes creatively to what the speaker says. We'll see examples of how talk changes for the following audiences:

- Talking to a friend's dog
- Talking in a public place where you know you're being over-heard by strangers
- Talking in a public place, where you're being overheard by someone that you want to impress
- Writing a private letter to a friend, versus writing in a friend's yearbook, knowing that others will read what you write
- Writing an email to the office

There are some situations where we become more aware of our audience—for example, when we talk in public, or in semi-public places like the office hallway, where there are other people nearby. Conversations become even more creative when there are people who can overhear our words even though we're not talking to them. Although we're not addressing our comments directly toward these bystanders, we often watch what we say because they might be listening. In these situations, we become more aware that our conversation is a creative performance. In focusing on public conversation, I am following in Goffman's footsteps; his conversational examples were almost all taken from public situations, and he identified many different types of audiences for speech: not only participants in the conversation, but also bystanders and overhearers. In public conversation, you have less control over your audience, and you consequently have to be more creative.[7]

In focusing on how conversation changes for different audiences, many of the examples in this chapter are illustrations of Bakhtin's concept of *addressivity*, the observation that speech is always influenced by who it's addressed to, its audience.[8] Because all spoken language has an audience, that audience's influence can always be found in the words. Bakhtin was a literary critic, not a linguist, and developed this concept primarily to analyze the 19th-century novels of Dostoyevsky and others. He believed that written words also had the quality of addressivity, in the sense that the novelist writes with a mental image of who his eventual audience will be. We'll return to this theme—that even written language is a collaboration with its audience—at the end of the chapter.

In the following pages, I'll discuss some particularly creative examples of how we improvise our conversations for different kinds of audiences—both when we are consciously aware of the audience, as well as some less obvious cases where our creativity is unconscious and unplanned. These examples reveal some of the unwritten rules about conversation, and help us to see how different audiences influence the ways that we talk. We'll see that conversation is much more complex than a simple exchange of information—it's nothing like playing catch with a football.

CREATING THE AUDIENCE

I began to notice an interesting type of conversation soon after I got my dog. He's a golden retriever named Monk (after the jazz pianist Thelonius Monk). At the time, I lived in downtown Chicago, and every day I walked Monk on the city streets and in the nearby park on Lake Michigan. I soon met all of the other dog owners in the neighborhood. Here's a typical sidewalk conversation between me and another dog owner. She is bending down, petting Monk, and looking into his face during the following dialogue:

Dog owner:	You're so cute! How old are you?
Me:	He's 3 months.
Dog owner:	Wow, 3 months. What's your name?
Me:	"Monk."

At no point does she turn to face me. She's looking at Monk, and acting as if she is talking to Monk. And my dog is wagging his tail as if she is talking to him. But clearly, I am also an audience—she obviously expects me to answer her questions. In this case, it's almost as if I am speaking *for* Monk, taking the voice of my dog, to answer the question that was put to him. I call this *dog talk*.

A different sidewalk encounter occurred a few years later, when Monk and I lived in New York City. On the busy sidewalk, another dog owner was walking her dog toward us from the other end of the block. As they began to pass us, Monk, in his usual friendly way, went over to "greet" the other dog. They seemed to be getting along fine, but the owner was clearly nervous. After a few seconds, she said to her dog, "I think you're tired. I think you're ready to go back inside," and then she pulled her dog on down the block. As in the first example, at no point did she look at me, or speak any words to me.

In this case, the owner seemed to be talking to her dog, and, at least on the surface, her words did not even acknowledge that I was there. By talking to her dog, she calmed the dog while indicating it was time to go. But she clearly meant for me to overhear what she was saying to her dog. What was she trying to say to me? Did she mean "My dog's tired now, and we're going to go back inside"? Or did she mean something more like "I'm nervous about your big dog and I don't want my dog playing with him"? Or was it "It's New York City, and I don't talk to strange men on the sidewalk?" Her statement to me was indirect, and her words were directed at two different audiences, both me and her dog. This woman chose a creative strategy for accomplishing several goals. She didn't have to be rude; she didn't have to express any concern directly, which may have offended me. She managed to avoid getting into a conversation with a stranger—a common goal on a New York City sidewalk. Because she had not, technically, spoken to me, she did not give me the conversational opportunity to respond. In this sense, I was not a participant, because I was not expected to respond. In my Chicago example, I was expected to respond and I could be said to be the intended, but indirect, audience for the remark. This New York example places me in a different role. Even without officially starting a conversation with me, she has communicated with me.

This example shows how people can creatively accomplish their goals in conversation, using talk in such a way that it chooses its own audience. Your words can selectively include or exclude people from a conversation. For example, some people are particularly good at large parties. They can play the room, moving from one conversational group to another, weaving in and out of conversations effortlessly. Politicians at public events are also required to move quickly from one person to another. In these situations, the politician can't be direct and say, "I've talked to you long enough, time to move on"; people will go to great lengths to avoid this kind of direct metatalk. One of the most effective ways to leave a conversation is to say something that you know will be overheard by another person who is nearby, as a way of making the transition into a conversation with that person. In large, crowded settings, our talk often has this dual quality—being directed to one person but intending to be overheard by another.

The New Yorker who I never met has creatively defined me as *not* being the audience. She can do this because it's not always obvious who is included in a conversation. In theater, there is an unbreakable fourth wall separating the performers from the audience; in conversation, the fourth wall is fluid and permeable. There is no physical stage separating the participants in a conversation from the audience. This makes the creative challenges that much more demanding, and provides even more opportunities for everyday creativity. Because there is no obvious fourth wall, we often have the opportunity to create it with our words.

The dog walker's strategy is an example of a more general conversational technique: *indirection.* Indirection is when you use language to communicate something more than the literal meaning of the words. The branch of linguistics called *pragmatics* studies several different kinds of indirection. For example, ironic statements are indirect: You might say "I love the winter," but your tone of voice, and the fact that you arrived an hour late at work because of the overnight snowstorm, makes it clear that winter makes you miserable. To analyze examples like this, linguists make a distinction between *speaker meaning* and *sentence meaning.* Indirect speech demonstrates that language is much more than just grammar and word meanings.[9]

Another type of indirection is when you apologize to someone without stating it explicitly. For example, if you get stuck in a traffic jam and your passenger is going to be late, you might say "I shouldn't have chosen this road" as a way of indirectly apologizing to your friend. Like an ironic statement, your apology is not found in the "sentence meaning," but it's still perfectly clear to your passenger that you mean to apologize. Linguists call this an *indirect speech act,* because the "act" is the apology, and it's not stated directly.[10]

Dog talk is an example of yet a third kind of indirection: *indirect addressing.* This phenomena has been studied primarily by sociologists like Goffman and the conversation analysts, rather than by linguists. In indirect addressing, your words seem to be addressed to one person (or a dog), but underneath the surface, they are implicitly addressed to someone else standing nearby. This strategy is pretty common—especially with insults like the following example.

Two men are walking down the sidewalk in their clean, suburban neighborhood. They pass by a home that everyone agrees is an eyesore: The grass is never cut, and various items of junk are scattered randomly in the yard. Today, the owner—who neither of the men like—is sitting in the front yard enjoying the sun. Neither of the men looks over or says hello; but one of the men says loudly to the other: "I like this neighborhood because everyone is so careful to take care of their property." His friend, picking up on the real audience for the comment, responds "I'm sure that no one wants their home to be an eyesore."

Conversational creativity also has its dark side; some people use it to come up with clever insults, or to spread rumors. One of the most effective ways to do this is by intentionally being overheard—most of the time we know when someone is nearby and can overhear what we say. You can be clever and phrase your remarks in such a way that they indirectly send a message to the overhearer. Many subtle insults and snide remarks are done this way. It's an effective way to insult some-one—first of all, because you can always say "That's not really what I meant," and second, because the target of the insult isn't a participant in the conversation.

This indirect insult strategy has been widely documented among African-Americans. The anthropologist Marcyliena Morgan has done some interesting work on the use of two types of indirect insults among African-American women; my suburban sidewalk insult is an example of what Morgan calls *pointed indirectness*.[11] Perhaps the first study of this kind of indirectness was done by Lawrence Fisher in Barbados, where it's called *remark dropping*. Fisher used the following example of remark dropping:

> A woman chose to wear an overly bright shape of lipstick to a party.
> She overheard a woman say, "Oh, I thought your mouth was burst"
> to a man whose lips were in perfect order.

The target of such an insult doesn't have a good way to respond. One Barbadian told Fisher "If I drop a remark to you and you challenge me, I would just say, 'Who told you I was referrin' to you? You must be hearin' things.'"[12] If our suburban man jumps up and says "How dare you insult my yard," the two walkers can act surprised and deny everything: "Why would you think we were talking about you? We were just having a pleasant conversation about our wonderful neighborhood." In fact, any response at all becomes a form of self-incrimination. A target of this kind of insult can only remain quiet and pretend not to overhear—he is creatively excluded from the conversation.

OVERHEARERS

We've just seen two examples of how speakers can creatively define who is not a participant, by speaking so that they will be overheard and indirectly communicating that the overhearer is not included in the conversation. This is only one example of the many creative ways that we speak for the benefit of overhearers. In contrast to the above examples, we sometimes use our words to encourage an overhearer to join our conversation; or we might modify our speech to impress a nearby person, or because there are certain things we don't want them to know. These conversational performances show us how often our words have multiple layers of meaning, and how much creativity we need to speak on all of these levels at once.

We sometimes perform our conversations to impress overhearers, even though we act as if we don't realize they are listening. For example, in an episode of *Friends*, the cast was talking in a coffeeshop at lunchtime. Phoebe, the ditzy blond, was waiting for a lunch date with a cute guy she had just met, and she was telling her friends about how great this guy was. When she saw through the coffeeshop window that he was about to enter the store, she excitedly said to her friends, "When he walks in, act like I just said something really funny and interesting!" The man enters just as she finishes making this request, and the others all laugh appreciatively, on cue, as Phoebe gives them a smile of thanks. Phoebe's date sees a group of people laughing at Phoebe's witty comment. But we laugh, because we see Phoebe's calculated performance and how quickly her friends agree to collaborate with her in the deception.

This is what friends are for—in social settings, friends are supposed to help make you look good. When you go to the bar, or the party, your conversations with your friends change. Because other people are nearby, you have an audience for your conversation. You can't do this alone; you have to go with a group of friends, to provide each other with opportunities to perform. Like Phoebe's little deception, these conversations are performed for people who can see you, but often can't overhear you. You want to appear to be engaged in interesting, active conversation with your friends. Maybe none of you even care what is being said. Your friends all realize what's going on, and you all actively participate in this conversational performance.

Many of our conversations are semi-public performances, where our talk is affected by an indirect, non-participating audience. Last Fall, I was sitting on a crowded university shuttle van, going home at the end of the day. In the seat in front of me were two women, who were speaking clearly. Because the van isn't very big, myself and the eight other passengers could hear everything they said. It was clear from their conversation that they had just met. Because the bus ride took 20 minutes, we all learned quite a bit about these two women: One of them had just graduated from Washington University, the other, much older, had a daughter who was considering coming here for college. We learned their political affiliations (liberal), their attitudes about religion (unhappy about living in the Bible Belt), and what the younger woman's plans were after graduation.

These women obviously knew that the other passengers could hear everything they said. Think about what these women might have said if they were alone in an office or in a car—it could have been very different. Although they didn't know any of us on the bus, they had a general sense of who their audience was. They knew they were on a University shuttle and that their religious and political views probably wouldn't offend anyone. On a city bus, where the overhearers might have been bible fundamentalists, these women would have spoken more cautiously. We all make subtle adjustments like this in our public conversations, modifying what we say to be appropriate to our audiences.

Even though everyone on the shuttle could hear their conversation, we were not participating in it, and we didn't have the right to join in the conversation. However, there are occasions like this where people can jump in—if the topic veers in their direction. For example, if the girl had mentioned her home town in Maine, another Mainer on the shuttle would not be out of line to say, "I couldn't help but overhear you—I'm from Maine, too!" In an odd, peripheral way, we are all participants in these public conversations, simply by being in the audience.

Even in small groups where you are technically a part of the conversation, two other people might engage in a private exchange that you clearly are not meant to join; still, your presence will make them watch what they say. Last year I drove to a wedding in Minneapolis, where I had known both the bride and groom for many years. Because most of the guests had flown in from out of town, they had scheduled a brunch on Sunday as a final event before they all went to the airport. All of the good-byes had been said, and the now-married couple was driving me, the last guest, to my car about 10 minutes away. I was riding in the back seat as they began to go through the typical post-party synopsis: who had changed over the years and how, who got along with whom, what had gone wrong during the party. I was not a speaker in this conversation, and in fact I could not be, was not expected to be. But they knew I was there, overhearing their talk, and of course their talk was influenced by my presence as an audience. Although I was not addressed directly, I was a silent audience.

In these examples, we've seen that there are many different kinds of overhearers—Goffman called them *bystanders*—with different statuses vis-à-vis the conversational performance:

- Walking my dog, I was an excluded overhearer;
- Phoebe's date is an intended overhearer, although he doesn't know it;
- On the shuttle bus, we could all overhear but had no right to join in;
- In the backseat of my friends' car, I could have joined in, although the conversation would have to have gone in a certain direction before it would have been appropriate.

Because a bystander's participant status is not always clear, he has to do a little work if he wants to join in the conversation—first, to figure out what his status is, then to choose the proper strategy to gain access to the conversation.

Overhearers are a cross-cultural universal—no matter what language you speak, this kind of audience requires a special creativity. In fact, in one of the native cultures of Australia, everyone learns two languages, and a different one has to be used depending on who is overhearing. These aboriginal cultures are perhaps best known in America for their abstract, dream-inspired paintings, which have become quite expensive, as art dealers and galleries have begun to represent some of the most talented Aboriginal painters. But they are known to linguistic anthropologists for another unique reason: The special "mother-in-law" language that men and women are required to use when speaking in the presence of their in-laws.

Why is it called "mother-in-law" language? If you're a man, you have to speak this special language anytime your mother-in-law is within hearing range. For example, if you're in the center of the village talking to your best friend, and you see your mother-in-law approaching, you have to immediately switch your conversation into this completely different language. There's no double standard here: If you're a woman, you have to use this language if your father-in-law is nearby.

Since both men and women use the language, the point is not to keep your conversation a secret. Your mother-in-law can still understand your conversation. It's something like the conversation my recently married friends had in the front seat of the car while they drove me home—I could understand everything they said, but I also knew they were modifying the way they talked because I was in the back seat, listening. In both cases, there is a silent audience that affects how people talk.

If your in-laws can understand you anyway, what's the point of switching languages? In this society, you are not allowed to talk at all with your in-laws. They are *taboo* relatives—you can never approach them or look at them directly. The language switch is a way of reinforcing this avoidance relationship.

It gets more complicated. You are only *required* to use this mother-in-law language with in-laws of the opposite sex. A man absolutely has to use it around his mother-in-law, and his mother-in-law has to use it around him. But it's optional with his father-in-law. A man will typically switch to mother-in-law language in the presence of his father-in-law, as a sign of respect; but the father-in-law can choose whether or not to use it.

Children have to learn two separate languages: the everyday language, and the mother-in-law language. Because children were traditionally promised to marriage at an early age, they already have a full set of taboo relatives while they are growing up, and they grow up speaking both languages in their appropriate contexts.

Mother-in-law language is a fascinating case of how a silent audience can change a conversation. You don't have to participate in a conversation to have an effect on how it unfolds. The mother-in-law is not a participant in the conversation; in fact, she cannot be, because one simply doesn't speak with a taboo relative. But her presence as a potential overhearer forces the men to switch languages.

As with many of the world's most unique languages, this language is dying out. Linguists are working hard to document such languages while the last remaining speakers are still alive. In 1970, the linguist Robert M. W. Dixon visited one of the most isolated Aboriginal societies, in the Cairns rain forest on the Northern coast of Australia. Even in this remote location, he found less than 30 speakers of the traditional language, and they were all very old. Almost everyone was speaking English. Even in 1970, these 30 elders were no longer using the mother-in-law language—although they knew it, and remembered using it in their youth. When they die, the mother-in-law language may be lost to history.[13]

Closer to home, there are many situations where people can hear your conversation without being participants. A TV talk show is a good example of how an audience can influence the conversation even though they can't join in. The host and the guest sit on the TV stage and engage in conversation. The stage set looks like a room in a home, with plush armchairs or perhaps a couch. We expect that these conversations will be intimate and natural, almost as if the guest had just dropped in on a Sunday afternoon. But as relaxed as they may be, the host and the guest know there is an audience. Clearly, the conversation will be quite different than if they were at home in the living room. Guests on a talk show are faced with a complex balancing act: They must appear to be having a natural, intimate conversation, while at the same time carefully creating their talk to make it entertaining for the viewing audience.[14]

Have you ever seen a bad interview on Letterman or Leno, where the guest was so awkward it was painful to watch? The conversation didn't flow smoothly. The next time this happens, notice how much of the metatalk becomes explicit, and how much more of the dialogue is focused on metatalk—on just negotiating what they'll talk about. In our everyday conversations, we sometimes stop the conversation to metatalk explicitly. But as we saw in Chapter 2, most of the time we do this implicitly, without having to talk about it directly. A good talk-show host is experienced at smoothly metatalking, while speaking to both the guest and the TV listener; but not every guest has this skill.

Metatalk becomes a lot more difficult when you have an audi-ence—you have to be even more creative than usual because you know the audience is watching; your metatalk has to be polite and implicit. If you do something awkward, or say something that doesn't quite sound right, you know the audience will pick it up. If you don't want to talk about something embarrassing, you can't just say "I don't want to talk about that"; that would break a rule of the talk-show genre—you're expected to answer questions, after all. In fact, a denial like this can sometimes make the studio audience start booing or snickering.

In a successful, entertaining talk-show interview, both the host and the guest know how to do their metatalk so that it doesn't interfere with the flow of the interview. They're both talented at creative metatalk that works not only in the conversation itself, but as entertainment for the TV audience. Bad guests usually can't figure out how to talk in the presence of a TV audience. This is symbolized by their posture and where they look. They look only at the host, never look at the camera, and turn their body towards the host in a way that seems to close off the audience.

PERFORMING FOR MULTIPLE AUDIENCES

We've seen some examples of how we creatively use language to select who the audience is, and to speak indirectly to people who aren't even in the conversation. Speaking for non-participating audiences requires a special creativity, because you seem to be talking to one audience, but everyone knows that your words secretly reach out to another audience. This is similar to another common conversational situation—speaking to more than one *participating* audience. Many of our everyday conversa-tions include three or more people, and we often want to communicate something slightly different to each of them. There are many conversa-tions where we have to say things that work on a different level for each person in the group. And if you have to speak indirectly to nearby over-hearers at the same time, the creative demands become mind-boggling.

When there are multiple audiences, we manage a complex bal-ancing act—we say things that are appropriate for everyone who's lis-tening. Creative speakers are skilled at accomplishing multiple goals with the same words; here's an example of what I mean.

Just after lunch in my office, I walked across campus to get cof-fee at the campus food court. As I walked back to my office across the quadrangle, a group of high school boys approached me, carrying duffel bags. Just behind them, there were three adult men who were clearly their chaperones. Seeing my coffee, one of the boys said "The food court's that way?" in what I took to be a somewhat disrespectful tone, but I brushed it off and politely said yes, it's that way, and down the stairs in the basement. As the boys turned towards the food court, the three men passed by. They had overheard our exchange. One of them asked with exaggerated deference, "Is the food court this way, Sir?"

We both knew that he had heard my directions the first time. The purpose of his question was not to request information; he was implicitly apologizing for the boy's rudeness, acknowledging that he had also perceived the tone to be somewhat disrespectful. Even more fascinating was the way that the man spoke loudly and distinctly, so that the boy could overhear his question. With this one question, he spoke to two audiences—apologizing to me, while reprimanding the boy. And he made it clear to me that he was reprimanding the boy.

When I thought about it afterwards, I was amazed at the creativity and effectiveness of this question. No one can be this creative all of the time in conversation. But most of us have had moments of such conversational brilliance, coming up with the perfect thing to say in a split-second.

The surface meaning of the question is irrelevant—the man has already heard my directions to the food court. The apology is hidden in the words—he has not said "I apologize for my student's rudeness." The reprimand is also hidden—he has not said "How dare you be rude to this man!" Unlike Horton the elephant, this man did not "say what he meant." In fact, in our most creative conversations, we are often indirect and implicit, with the real social meaning hidden in the words.

An apology is a type of *speech act*, a social action that people accomplish using speech. When you apologize, "saying something" serves the function of "doing something." If you're very explicit when you apologize, you may even say "I apologize." This kind of explicit speech act is self-referential, because at the same time that you are apologizing, you are *saying that* you are apologizing. That's why linguists call this an *explicit speech act*.

The food court apology is an *indirect speech act*, since you can't find the apology anywhere in the literal meaning of the words. Literally, it's a completely different speech act, a *request for information*; but I know that more is going on, because I know that the man already heard my first answer. Speech act theory[15] has been fairly successful at analyzing explicit speech acts, and is now the predominant model for the computer-to-computer communication of *agent communication languages*;[16] nonetheless, it's widely believed to provide an inadequate account of indirect speech acts. Fortunately for network designers, computers tend to communicate in a football style—sending explicit informative messages—rather than engaging in the implicit, indexical metatalk that is so important in human conversation.

Also problematic for speech act theory is that this man spoke with the intention of being overheard by two different people—both me and the boy. In a way, he accomplished two different speech acts: an "apology" to me, and a "reprimand" to the boy. As with this apology-reprimand, we often use the same words to send different meanings to multiple audiences; in our most creative conversations, we can send different messages to everyone in the group.[17]

A few years ago, when I left a job for another city, I got a going-away card from my group at work. About 10 people had written brief wishes of good luck—the usual comments for this sort of card. But as I read, I realized that as each person writes, they know that all of the other card-writers will see their remarks! Of course, everyone sees the remarks of the first writer, and no one sees the remarks of the last writer. And what's the first thing that you do when you are handed a card like this? You read what everyone else has written, of course. I've had this experience too—I write differently depending on whether I'm one of the first or one of the last to write.

A similar thing happens with high-school yearbooks. Students trade yearbooks and write to each other about all the good times they've had. But these notes can't be very intimate, because they all show their friends what their other friends have written. These are very public writings![18]

In both cases, you're supposed to write as if you're writing to one person, the owner of the yearbook or the recipient of the card. But of course, you won't write anything private. Woven subtly into our writing, we are also writing to everyone else that we know will be reading our comments; we are writing for multiple audiences.

Think about the last time you wrote a postcard to a close friend or a family member. You know that anyone can read it—the mailman, a housemate of your friend, another family member. As you write, your writing is influenced by these potential audiences. Even if the mailman doesn't read the postcard that you've sent to your spouse, you'll still write as if he might read it. So compared to a sealed letter, you'll use a less personal tone. Of course, your spouse knows this too, and doesn't get offended at the distant tone.

I have an old friend who only sends postcards, never letters. Even after years of corresponding, I always get a postcard in exchange for my most recent letter. She admits that it's because if she wrote a sealed letter her friends would expect her to be more intimate. She's more comfortable with the breezy, distanced style that is expected on a postcard.

In the presence of multiple audiences, speakers have a more challenging creative task. At the beginning of the chapter, we saw an example from Charles Goodwin's research: a mother trying to manage her two children. Goodwin found that speakers usually watch all of the listeners, trying to make sure that each of them is still following along. If one person looks puzzled, or bored, a speaker will notice this and alter his or her speech.

Doctors and psychologists who work with children often have to counsel the children while the parents are in the room. These professionals have to manage a complex balancing act: They have to reach both the child and the mother, and each audience may be listening for very different things. Using Goodwin's method, the British researcher Christian Heath analyzed a series of doctor-patient conversations, including this one between a social worker (S), her client (E), and the client's mother (M). The odd punctuation marks that are scattered throughout the transcript are technical tools that researchers use to indicate facts of speaking that don't translate well to the printed word: pauses, shifts in volume, overlapping speech. For example, a colon indicates that the prior word is drawn out; "hhhh" is an audible intake of breath; numbers in parentheses indicate the length of a pause, in seconds.[19]

S: and: I: w:ill
        (0.3)
M: Um::
S: See him an tell him about this: interview: that=
S: =we've had
M: Yes
S: together:: hhhhhh I think he: will be able to:
        prescri:be something   [hhhh
M: [yes
S: which Elizabeth: (0.6) Elizabeth: (0.3) you'll have to ta::ke hhh
        (0.3) regularly without let up

Where is Elizabeth in this transcript? She is a participating audience for this talk, but her participation is non-verbal. In fact, the social worker has been trying to get Elizabeth to talk (and to get the mother to talk less) throughout the entire session. She has been balancing two audiences the whole time—trying to be polite to the mother, and to communicate important information—while at the same time, trying to get the mother to leave some space for Elizabeth to talk, and trying to encourage Elizabeth to speak for herself. The social worker finally succeeds in the final line of this transcript, but we can only see what is really going on when we add each participant's body language, as I've done below. Everything in the following detailed transcript happens simultaneously, in a three-part collaborative construction, although only the social worker is talking. Elizabeth has been looking down at the floor through the entire session, until the "X," when she raises her eyes towards the social worker. Note that the horizontal lines indicate a gaze towards another person; the social worker looks at Elizabeth during her speech, while the mother starts out looking at the social worker.

```
        S nods at E              S "kicks" E's leg
        S looking at E_____

S:    hhh which Elizabeth: - - - - - - Elizabeth: - - - you'll have to
E:                                X_____
M:    M looking at S              (M turns to E)_____
```

Recall that each dash represents a pause of one-tenth of a second. The social worker pauses almost a full second when she first fails to get Elizabeth's gaze; then she repeats her name, this time practically kicking her in the leg! Note also that the mother doesn't turn to Elizabeth until after she sees the kick, even though the social worker starts this turn by raising her voice (indicated by underlining) and nodding towards Elizabeth. The social worker does this not only to get Elizabeth's attention, but also to signal to the mother that she should be quiet this time.

The football metaphor of conversation is clearly too simplistic. If we analyze only the spoken word, we would say it's the social worker's turn, and we would analyze her speech in terms of her goals and intentions—neglecting the ways that the mother and daughter influence the interaction. But when we look more closely, we see a three-part collaboration—with everyone acting in parallel, not always waiting her turn.

INVISIBLE AUDIENCES

Sigmund Freud has been one of the most influential thinkers of this century, in spite of the controversy surrounding his ideas. In the past few years some historians have claimed that Freud was a fraud who faked his data and only became famous because he was good at PR. But even Freud's most vocal critics still grant the truth of some of his therapeutic innovations.

One of Freud's least controversial ideas is the theory of *transference*. Transference occurs in a conversation when you start reliving interaction patterns from a past relationship. An example of transference would be if you started treating your boyfriend like your father. If your father was a controlling, dominant figure, you may react to your boyfriend as if he is controlling and dominant, even though he may not in fact be this way. You might hear "control" in even the most innocent of comments. You have transferred your past relationship with your father to your present relationship with your boyfriend. What makes this so destructive in relationships is that you're usually not aware that you're doing it.

If you are transferring during an argument with your boyfriend, he might be the only other person in the room, but he's not the only audience—at some level, you are also speaking to your father—he is an invisible audience for your words. Of course, you are speaking to both your boyfriend and your father, in a complicated and confusing mixture. This complex blend of audiences makes it difficult to know what's real about the current relationship.[20]

If you are transferring—reacting to your boyfriend as if he was your father—then what kind of audience are you for your boyfriend's words? Unfortunately, you're not completely listening. At some level, you'll hear him as if you are your childhood self. Like a bad improv actor "writing the script in your head," you aren't improvising in the moment. The transferred interaction pattern—a child with a controlling father—is a kind of script that we keep enacting, a script that prevents us from responding to the unique creative demands of the conversation. The goal of the therapist is to get us to stop following this dysfunctional script and to start improvising new, spontaneous relationships, by truly creating conversations.

When we're transferring, it's as if we have two audiences—the person who is in front of us and an invisible audience, the memory of a past relationship. Sometimes we talk when no one is in the room. Most of us think aloud at times, or talk to ourselves. And it's not uncommon for surviving spouses to silently speak to their deceased mates—as we sometimes do when we visit the grave of a loved one.[21]

There's a fascinating variation of this kind of talk found in rural Japan:

> Bursting through the unlocked front door of his friend's house, Saio Akita turned left into the living room and bypassed other family members to chat with his buddy, offer him a drink, and ask for some help.
>
> "Hi there," Mr. Akita said casually to his friend. "It's a beautiful day, isn't it? How are you? Let me take a look at you."
>
> The friend, Isekichi Tsujimoto, did not reply. He died last November.[22]

It's a simple matter of protocol, Mr. Akita later explained: You always say hello first to the oldest person present, even if he is no longer physically present. The rest of the family, sitting nearby, found his actions completely proper and ordinary.

This practice is common in many parts of Japan. Deceased elders remain a respected presence in the house, and they are regularly consulted on important matters. Family members may even give them a daily rundown on the local news, or offer them food and drink.

Some Japanese claim that the dead participate in these conversations, speaking in response when they are addressed. Miyoko Suzuki says of her deceased husband, "He became gentler than when he was alive. He doesn't say harsh things the way he used to." She says that she hears responses in her head and tells a story about how her husband helped direct her to a lost wallet.

After the above examples about how multiple audiences influence speech, we can't help but wonder to what extent this sort of talk is indirectly influenced by the other family members who are in the room. After all, it's not a private conversation with the deceased. Would it be fair to say that these survivors are the intended audience for the remarks? I doubt that Mr. Akita would agree with this—he believes he's talking to his dead friend. But still, an American thinks, how can this talk be genuinely directed to a person who is dead? Mr. Akita, and the family, might counter that he is indeed, in the room, although he's not capable of actively participating in the conversation. It's too simplistic for us to say that the real audience is the rest of the family, when the speaker himself doesn't see it that way.

It's not uncommon, even in America, for surviving spouses to speak to their deceased mates, although we might be more likely to do it silently. But this can help us understand how a friend could be talking to a deceased friend; the only difference is that it's out loud, and there are other people overhearing. Along with mother-in-law language, this example is another demonstration that different cultures create conversations differently; some of the most intriguing differences reflect how we deal with multiple audiences.

CROSSING THE FOURTH WALL

In many of the above examples, a special creativity is required because the boundary between overhearers and participants—the fourth wall—is rarely obvious. For example, think back to the semi-public conversation in the university shuttle van. Even though we overhearers are not really participants in the conversation, there are times when it becomes appropriate to jump in—if one of them mentions our home town, or if it becomes apparent that they need directions. You can quickly go from being an overhearer to being a participant, if you know how to jump in without being offensive.

Our everyday conversations are like performances without a fourth wall. We can join and leave whenever we want, or we can move from being a silent listener to an active participant. And we manage the audience-performer boundary differently in different kinds of performance. At one extreme—theater—the boundary is absolutely fixed. At the other extreme—everyday conversation—it's flexible. When we look at different kinds of performance, we see a whole range of variations on these extremes. For example, in America, we expect rituals to be different from everyday conversation. In our religious rituals, the roles are specified and the participants are assigned their roles in advance. We have a fairly sharp "fourth wall" in American rituals; in fact, most of our churches reflect this architecturally, with the ritual roles performed on a stage at the front, and the audience—the congregation—watching rather than participating.

But in many non-Western cultures, performances do not have the rigid fourth wall of European theater. These unwritten rules about the audience-performer boundary say a lot about the beliefs and attitudes of a culture. Like many of the unwritten rules of conversation, these rules are some of the hardest to understand, as non-Native Americans discover when they first visit a Native American Indian culture. For example, the anthropologist Susan Philips studied how participation and the audience are structured in traditional rituals at the Warm Springs Reservation in Central Oregon. Approximately 1,500 descendants of three Warm Springs tribes—Sahaptin, Wasco Chinook, and Paiute—live on the reservation.[23]

Like many reservations, Warm Springs allows non-Native Americans to visit and observe some traditional rituals. Because the non-Native American visitors want to make sure they see the entire ritual performance, they make sure to arrive on time, or perhaps they even arrive early. But sometimes an hour or more can pass beyond the "starting time," and the non-Native American can't tell if the performance has started yet—although something seems to be happening. The Native Americans explain this confusion by saying "We're on Indian time," but this seems to send the message that Native Americans don't care about being punctual. Philips realized that something different was going on, when she realized that the starting time confusion was connected to another confusion among non-Native American visitors—they have trouble telling which activities are part of the performance or who is participating in it.

Although it's sometimes frustrating for these non-Native American visitors, it's not the case that Native Americans just don't care about starting on time. Instead, the confusion results from how our European culture defines the "fourth wall" in a performance—we expect a sharp boundary between the performance and everything else. We expect the performance location to be clearly defined—on a stage. We want to know who is an actor and who isn't. And we expect the performance to have a clear beginning and ending.

But in Warm Springs rituals, it's common for people to move in and out of the ritual while it is continuing. People can be in the performance one minute, and in the audience the next. Because of this, people who want to participate know that it doesn't matter if they arrive "late," because they can join at any time. Participation is optional, and doesn't have to be planned in advance. In contrast, non-Native Americans expect that the full cast will be assembled before the performance begins, and that the actors will maintain their performance roles until the performance is over.

Of all the world's cultures, European performance genres are at one extreme: they tend to have a very firm fourth wall, and to make clear who is performing and who is watching. This is true both of European religious rituals, and of European artistic theater. But even in America, we find several religious denominations that explicitly attempt to break out of this pattern: The Christian Scientists have a lay reader instead of a minister, and the Quakers have no authority figure at their "meetings." A Quaker meeting—their equivalent of a church service— does not have any one individual in charge, because of the Quaker's aversion to authority figures. Instead, members of the congregation speak prayers as they are moved to do so. Ideally, the meeting is an emergent, improvisational collaboration, with a spiritual purpose: the Quakers believe that the spirit of God will emerge from this undirected group process.

The Warm Springs example shows that not all rituals have a sharply defined fourth wall, but there are some cross-cultural universals. For example, in most of the world's cultures, the more sacred the event is, the more fixed the fourth-wall boundary is; religious ceremonies are more like stage performance than everyday conversation. During a Warm Springs ritual performance, the rules about when you can enter and leave are more circumscribed than with ordinary conversations. Each culture has its own spectrum of formality—from ritual to everyday—and on that spectrum, rituals are always at one extreme, with the most clearly defined fourth wall, and with more rules about entrances and exits. More impro-visational performances, because they also tend to be the most informal, are the ones that have the most permeable fourth wall.[24]

The rules that guide conversational interaction are subtle, so deeply ingrained, that it's hard to see them. Most of us can't verbalize these rules, because the rules are implicit—they seem to be natural, common sense. That's why it's helpful to look at how other cultures create conversations. Because everyday conversation is a kind of performance, with ground rules that vary from one country to another, it's hard to learn the implicit rules that guide conversation in another language. It's a different kind of learning from just learning the words and the grammar—we have to learn the rules for creating conversations.

Like non-Native American visitors to Warm Springs, we take our unwritten assumptions about performance for granted, and when another culture does it differently, we find the new rules disturbing and hard to get used to. It's the natural, common-sense quality of conversational rules that makes it so disturbing when we find ourselves in a situation when our own rules aren't being followed.

In this chapter, we've seen the creative demands posed by audiences in everyday discourse. Speakers have to speak to multiple audiences, and to keep track of where the fourth wall is. Perhaps more than anyone else, classroom teachers have to creatively manage these audience demands—this is one of the reasons that teaching is such a difficult job. In fact, the most effective teaching strategies—those that use a more active, participatory style of teaching, rather than lecturing—make the most creative demands on teachers. In participatory classrooms, the teacher is not the only person "on stage," and the fourth wall starts to break down—as it does every day in the cutting-edge classrooms of the Paideia group.

In one Paideia school, a junior-high school class is discussing a text from Plutarch's *Lives,* the "Life of Lycurgus." This biography describes a period in Spartan history with a rigid authoritarian social structure within the city and a sharp difference in status between Spartan citizens and the much more numerous slaves, or helots, who farmed the land for them. The two team-teachers are using a teaching method where they and the students take on roles from the book, and then role-play as the characters. They improvise dialogues in the classroom in an attempt to get the students to confront the universal issues of the text.

This is a city school and the students are mostly black. The two team-teachers are both white. The students clearly identify with the slaves in the text and take on the roles of the slaves in the classroom dialogue. So far, so good: Their identification with these ancient slaves could be used to bring out the universal themes of the text. In fact, the goal of this "participant example" teaching method is exactly this—to help the students identify with the universal themes in these classic books.

But instead, something goes wrong. The teachers, without even realizing it, slip back into the teacher role, speaking in the voice of the Spartan slave owner while they assert their traditional authority over the classroom. Although they are playing a role from the book, they still have the responsibility to maintain discipline in the classroom, and they want to cover certain topics during the class. They keep slipping back and forth between the Spartan role and the teacher role. In response, the black students act out the role of the helots—and it's not clear when they are role-playing as a helot slave, or when they are just resisting the teacher's authority, as students do every day. Plutarch's text becomes a kind of script that ends up reinforcing the power and race relations of the classroom. The *content* of the text becomes what they are *doing*. But they don't realize what's going on, and a chance to teach a valuable lesson is missed.

To use our theatrical metaphor, the teachers and students did not carefully maintain the fourth wall. Because they are both the performers and the audience, the boundary is fuzzy; it's hard to tell which dialogue is part of Plutarch's *Lives*, and which dialogue is normal classroom maintenance.

This classroom is using a role-playing method of teaching that's designed to make the classics of the Western tradition relevant to today's students. This technique was developed by the Paideia group, founded by the philosopher and educator Mortimer Adler. Classrooms that follow the Paideia philosophy often use this interactive method of teaching. The two team teachers take on roles from the text being studied—in this case, a Greek biography—and one or more students are assigned other roles from the text. The teachers and students then improvise a dialogue, acting as the characters. While role playing, the teachers try to force the students into situations where they have to confront the same issues that faced these Greek characters.

My colleague Stanton Wortham, a linguist and education researcher, has studied several Paideia classrooms. He's found that the fourth-wall confusion that happened in the above classroom is not unusual.[25] At the same time that the teachers and students are enacting the historical characters, they are also playing the expected roles of "teacher" and "student." For example, Wortham never observed the teachers taking on the role of the lower-status character in a book, with the students taking on the authority role; the role-playing relationships always end up reinforcing the authority of the teacher.

These dual roles, and the absence of a clear fourth wall, make it confusing which comments are addressed to the historical character and which are spoken to the real-world student or teacher. Who is the audience for the teacher's words? It's not always obvious in a Paideia session. Are they speaking "in character" to the on-stage Greek slaves, or are they talking to a class of students? This confusion can't be avoided when you role-play like this—in fact, it's the potential strength of the Paideia method. But it's asking a lot of teachers to require them to manage this complex performance situation! Even professional actors sometimes find this difficult.

When teachers enact two roles at once in a classroom—one is on-stage and performed, the other is the everyday teacher role—they have to be careful to make clear who the audience for their words is. Are they speaking to the students? Or are they speaking to the Greek slaves? To do this effectively, the teachers have to spend a lot more time doing metatalk—stepping out of character to talk about the ongoing performance. We've already seen how rare this metatalk is in our everyday lives, so it's not surprising that teachers have to work at it.

There are many everyday conversations where our audience isn't so clear. Often these are situations where the roles we are expected to be performing are ambiguous. For example, suppose you are in a business meeting, but you're good friends with one of your colleagues. Perhaps the two of you have been out to dinner the night before. You have two different kinds of relationship with this person: You are both friends and colleagues, and needless to say, you have different kinds of conversations at work than you do at dinner. When you say something to your friend during the meeting, you could be speaking to him in two different audience roles—you could be speaking to a friend, or to a colleague. Just like the Paideia classroom, the person that you're talking to could be more than one kind of audience.

These situations—where the audience for your words is ambiguous—require conversational creativity. You can choose to use this ambiguity in clever ways, or you can make it clear which audience you are talking to. But whichever you choose, it's always more effective to do it subtly, without having to say explicitly which audience you are talking to.

MEDIATED CONVERSATIONS

We've all grown up surrounded by the written word. Many of us learn to read while we're still in nursery school, and we learn how to write in the first grade. It's impossible for us to imagine what life would be like without knowing how to read and write. Without literacy, if you wanted to learn from a famous teacher, you had to go to them and see them in person. But once the written word is introduced into a society, a creative verbal act no longer needs to be performed in the presence of the audience. The creator has the option of writing it down and distributing it to others, who can read it at their convenience. The written text expands the potential audience considerably, and it has a major influence on how performances are learned and passed on. For example, you can learn how to participate in a play or a ritual by staying at home and studying the script; you don't have to keep going back until you memorize what you see and hear.

We take literacy for granted, and we sometimes think that European cultures are practically defined by writing. We're all taught about old books like *Beowulf* (10th century) and *Chaucer's Tales* (14th century) that have been around forever. But just because books were being written doesn't mean most people could read them. It wasn't until about 1800 that over 50% of the men in England could even sign their name (although requiring minimal reading ability, this is a common historical measure of literacy). And it was probably another 100 years before the majority of English speakers could read books and newspapers. If you don't know how to read, the only way to learn is by participating in conversations and performances.

But even without knowing how to read, we can imagine that there must have been many creative verbal artists—people who could tell a great story, generals who could inspire their troops with a speech, or priests who could give a sermon that could convert men to Christianity. Of course, if a society has no writing, no one would even think of writing it down ahead of time—composing the story or speech—and then memorizing it before a performance. The idea that a verbal performance would have a *text* or a *script* is a recent development. Unscripted performance is much more common in human history.

However, verbal performances that continue to be repeated tend to take on a recognizable form, even if they have never been written down. Rituals, prayers, and stories that we think of as part of a nation's folklore probably began as improvised performances and then gradually became more and more structured through repeated performances. Anthropologists refer to this historical development as *ritualization* or *formalization*. The most formalized rituals and musical performances can be almost as firmly fixed as if they were written down.[26]

Thus, even without written scripts, a people can have an *oral culture*—a set of stories, rituals, and other creative verbal genres that all members of the culture know. Unlike literary culture, oral culture is performed in public, as part of meaningful cultural events. At such events, the audience is an essential part of the performance. When the story or the ritual is known by many people in the audience, they have expectations of the speaker, since they know how the performance is supposed to happen.

Here's where literacy often changes things.[27] Once the text is written down, the audience begins to think that there is one, correct way to perform the story or the ritual. This is an example of the "script-think" of Chapter 1. In contrast, even the most traditional oral genres provide the performers with opportunities for creative improvisation. European folklore remained mostly oral for centuries until people began to write it down in the 19th century. For example, *Grimm's Fairy Tales* are a collection of traditional folk stories that had existed for centuries, before they were collected and transcribed by two brother-scholars.

Before literacy, all communication required speech. Literacy freed communication from speech, allowing people to communicate with each other without engaging in spoken conversation. For example, people could hold extended conversations through letters, conversations *mediated* by the written word. As linguist Michael Mulkay points out, letters are similar to everyday conversation in several ways—they use direct, personal forms of address, and they require you to respond to the other person's last letter, so that there's a back-and-forth exchange that's something like a turn-taking pattern. But there's also a critical difference: A letter is not improvised, but rather is composed in private.[28]

Electronic mail is a new kind of mediated conversation. People exchange texts, just like writing letters; but, because email is so much faster, you can engage in several exchanges in just a few minutes, rather than over days or weeks. Because of this speed, emails are compositions with some of the immediacy of conversation. Electronic mail conversations change the relationship between speaker and audience, because they affect so many of the phenomena that we've discussed in this chapter—back channeling, multiple audiences, participant structures, and bystanders.[29]

I've been using email since 1979, starting with the precursor of the Internet, the ARPAnet. Until the early 1990s, only University researchers used this technology. With the invention of the Web, it's become part of popular culture, and email takes up more and more of my time each day. It's free for many of my friends and colleagues, because their company or university pays for the expenses. Some of my friends have gotten in the habit of sending messages, short or long, for just about any reason or purpose. Sometimes my email exchanges continue for days, creating an interesting kind of slow-motion conversation.

More so than letters, email takes conversation into the realm of the written word, creating conversations that are a series of compositions. For example, sometimes a friend and I exchange three or four messages in a day, as we bounce ideas off of one another, and keep elaborating on each message. Also in email, it's possible to have multiple audiences and bystanders. If you want to send a message to several people, you can put all of their email addresses in the "To" line. If you want yet another person to "overhear" the message—although it's not really "to" them—you can put their address on the "Cc" line. And unlike a conversation, you can send a copy to someone without the other recipients knowing about it, using the "Bcc" field, adding another element of creativity.

This interactivity reminds me of conversation—but it's a conversation that combines both composition and improvisation. You respond to your partner in the same way that you respond to someone in any other conversation; but an email program gives you a chance to revise your words before you send it off, and you can compose your message more carefully. Like all conversations, email exchanges are collective, emergent, and directorless. But unlike improvised performance, you have the chance to revise and compose along the way.

Email conversations require literacy, and email has some of the characteristics of written communication: There is less immediacy, less responsiveness, less direct involvement of the audience you are "talking" to, no possibility of being interrupted. Email conversations fit right into the football metaphor of conversation, and it's not surprising that we use them primarily to exchange information. With email, we are more like Horton the elephant—we are more likely to "say what we mean." Email doesn't require the same degree of implicit metatalk skills and audience collaboration as spoken conversation, and I think this is why many shy people and introverts are drawn to email—the creative demands are not as challenging.

This lack of audience collaboration is part of the reason that many on-line newsgroups are filled with often unenlightening exchanges of disconnected opinions. I predict that electronic communication will begin to incorporate more immediacy and more improvisation, and become more like spoken conversation. Several researchers are developing software and discussion practices that encourage collaborative conversation; for example, AOL chat rooms, and Internet MUDs and MOOs, allow several people to "talk" at once, providing some of the improvisational flow of conversation. Even newer technologies are in the works that will further increase the collaborativeness and immediacy of electronic communication.[30]

Several influential modern theorists have argued that all written language—not just letters and emails, but even novels and historical records—communicates to the reader in the same way that a speaker talks to a listener in conversation. In the last several decades, these theories have been influential in disciplines that focus on written documents, including history and literature. The French historian Michel Foucault is associated with the idea that all written documents are conversations over time; he used the term *discourse* to refer to all interaction through language, whether verbal or written.[31] The German literary critic, Wolfgang Iser, argued that novels do not have fixed meanings, but instead have to be creatively "composed" or "performed" by the reader. Iser's *reader response* theory shifted the critic's perspective away from a focus on the author's creativity and towards a consideration of the creative role played by the audience.[32] In part because of the influence of theories such as Foucault's and Iser's, many contemporary social theorists argue that spoken and written communication aren't really that different.

From this perspective, all modern communication technologies—radio, television, movies—are forms of mediated conversations. Some media studies researchers have proposed replacing the term "mass communication" with *mediated communication*.[33] These researchers argue that conversation is the most fundamental form of communication, even though it's not "mediated" by technology. Of course, mediated communication is different from conversation; but these researchers emphasize that we can't analyze media products using the football metaphor because the audience plays a role in creating the meaning of the message—whether a movie, a TV show, or a radio news report. For example, communication researchers in the field of *audience study* have empirically demonstrated that different audiences construct different interpretations of TV shows.[34]

Modern technology has also resulted in *mediated performance,* when an audio or video recording of a live performance becomes a fixed, unchanging product. It wasn't that long ago that if you wanted to hear improvised music, you had to be in the right city and go to the right clubs. It wasn't until the 20th century that we had the technology to record verbal or musical performance that was improvised, or traditional folk songs that were never written down. The blues musicians from the Mississippi River Delta passed on their traditional lyrics, song forms, and guitar techniques without the benefit of music books or tape recorders, and they only began to be recorded after World War I. By the time folklore researchers showed up with their pens or tape recorders, the stories and the music had been evolving and developing for generations. Today, young blues and jazz musicians can hear the music in their own homes; they have access to CDs and videotapes—not only the classic performances from decades ago, but also last year's hot new album.

But a recording can never be the same as a live performance. When you're there in the club, the performance has a *presence* that a recording doesn't have. This presence results from the unpredictability of performance, and the fact that we are watching the creative process in action. When a performance is recorded, it becomes an unchanging product. The second time you watch a tape of an improv theater performance, you know what's going to happen next. The second time, the performance loses some of its indeterminacy and immediacy.

Although these technologies are new, the issues they raise are old ones for aesthetic philosophers. There's a long tradition of aesthetic philosophy that compares fixed arts, like painting, to the performances of theater and music.[35] In the 1920s and 1930s, R. G. Collingwood argued that all art is a form of communication, and like conversation, all art reflects the role of the audience. In an influential 1968 essay, Richard Wollheim explored the same connections in an attempt to identify the "art object" underlying a performance, using the linguistic theory of *types* and *tokens*. Perhaps most influential today is the aesthetic theory of the American philosopher John Dewey, first published in 1934 but still widely read. Dewey observed that a painting doesn't appear on the canvas all at once, and it can't be viewed simultaneously, either. Creating a painting involves a creative process through time, with errors, corrections, and new insights during the process. Likewise, viewing a painting takes some time; the viewer chooses what to focus on first, then his eye begins to move towards other aspects of the painting. Dewey described both the act of painting and the act of viewing a painting as an *experience*; for Dewey, these "experiences" are not significantly different from the experience of watching a stage play or listening to a band. Dewey's claim was that when we focus on the end result of creativity—for example, a painting in a gallery—it's harder to see the connection with performance creativity. To see the common roots of artistic and performance creativity, we have to step back from these products to the creative processes that generate them.

At the peak of his fame, Pablo Picasso agreed to allow himself to be filmed as he painted. I show this movie, *The Mystery of Picasso*,[36] in my college class on the psychology of creativity, and we get a rare chance to see the creative process in action. The film starts with the camera directed at one side of an etched glass plate, while Picasso sketches on the opposite side. You can't see Picasso through the etched glass, but you can clearly see the marks of the pen. The first few curves and lines seem random, but as the minutes pass by, the lines come together to form a landscape. The final sketch is perfectly composed; Picasso must have had the entire image in his mind before he began the first line.

Later in the film, Picasso sits before a blank canvas with a full set of paints. The camera then focuses on the canvas and we see what his painting looked like after five minutes. After a few seconds, this image fades into a photo of the painting after 10 minutes. We see the painting's evolution through stop-motion photography. Although the entire session lasted five hours, in the movie the painting goes by in 15 minutes. It's clear that this time Picasso doesn't have an image worked out in advance—that's obvious, because as we watch, the entire structure and theme of the painting change three or four times. He improvises in front of the camera, while an audience watches. He paints out entire sections of earlier work, changing a woman's foot to a horse, later changing the horse to a boat dock. Since I'm not a painter, this film gave me a rare chance to see the creative process that led Picasso to this final product. I felt as if I was inside Picasso's head, experiencing the act of creation. I can never look at a painting in the same way again, knowing that I'm seeing only the endpoint of the creative process. Watching this movie, we are Picasso's audience. The museum visitor who looks at a painting sees the painter's creativity only indirectly, through the finished painting.

In an improvisational performance, the creative process of the actors is the product—nothing is left when the performance ends. In improvisational theater, the audience gets to see everything—the entire creative process, mistakes and all. The audience sees the collaborative group mind, as if they were looking into the brain of a creative genius. The audience's relation to the creative process is *immediate*—there is no delay. But Picasso's creative process results in a creative product, and the audience for a painting usually doesn't get to see the "performance" of the painting, as we do in the movie of Picasso while he's painting. Instead, all that we see in the museum is the finished product: the painting. In the movie, we see the immediacy of Picasso's creativity, but in a gallery, our experience of Picasso's creativity is *mediated* by the painting.

Nonetheless, a painter creates for the eventual audience, no less than a theater performance is performed for an audience. The painter's communication with the audience is a type of mediated conversation. Although mediated conversations are not the same as everyday conversation, we can gain insights into artistic creativity by thinking about writing and recording as messages in a long-running mediated conversation. At first, this might sound ridiculous; after all, in our everyday conversations, our audience is standing in front of us, listening and responding to what we say. They are the audience for our words, but they are also participants in the conversational performance that we create together. But when we're listening to a recording or looking at a painting, the artist is long finished; how can we have any influence on the creative process? We influence it indirectly, because no artist creates without thinking about the eventual audience.

In 1938, the philosopher R. G. Collingwood argued that the audience for a work of art can be considered co-creators, collaborators, in that work:

The work of artistic creation is not a work performed in any exclusive or complete fashion in the mind of the person whom we call the artist. That idea is a delusion bred of individualistic psychology. . . . This activity is a corporate activity belonging not to any one human being but to a community. It is performed not only by the man whom we individualistically call the artist, but partly by all the other artists of whom we speak as "influencing" him, where we really mean collaborating with him. It is performed not only by this corporate body of artists, but (in the case of the arts of performance) by executants . . . and . . . there must be an audience, whose function is therefore not a merely receptive one, but collaborative too. The artist stands thus in collaborative relations with an entire community.[37]

Despite Collingwood's observation, the study of creativity remained under the sway of "individualistic psychology" for over 40 more years. It wasn't until the 1980s that creativity researchers began to consider the collaborative role of the audience, and now it's an active topic for two of the biggest names in the field, Mike Csikszentmihalyi[38] and Howard Gardner.[39] They are both advocates of a *systems model* that acknowledges the important creative role played by the audience. Postmodern literary theorists—often drawing on the ideas of Foucault and Iser—came around to this viewpoint about 10 years earlier, arguing that novels are so closely tied in with the artistic conversation of their time that it's wrong to focus only on the artist as the solitary creator.

If art is a mediated conversation, the audience influences the artistic process, like the audience at a concert influences the flow of the performance, and like we modify our words depending on who we are talking to. For example, jazz musicians often say that their playing is a dialogue with the jazz tradition, a tradition that they know only through recordings. And the history of art is like conversation, in which the artists and audience communicate with each other through artworks. These are mediated, long-term conversations that extend over time, the conversations of art—where instead of words, painters communicate with their paintings, and musicians with their albums.

* * * * * * * *

If conversation really worked like a game of football—if we each had time to plan our words carefully, and then say them without interruption—it would be a lot less improvisational and a lot less collaborative. The football metaphor doesn't do justice to the creativity of conversation, because it implies that you speak almost in a vacuum, deciding what to say and then saying it, as if you were giving a lecture or reading from a script that you've written in your head.

We saw in Chapter 1 that our tendency towards script-think often leads us to think about conversation as if it were written down.

Script-think goes hand in hand with the football metaphor, because when we read a dialogue from a novel or a play, it looks as if only one person is talking at a time. That's because the printed page can't show us all of the constant interaction between speakers and their audiences. In this chapter, we've seen some of the elaborate notation systems that researchers have to use to represent this kind of nonverbal interaction.

Collaboration is especially visible in creating conversations, when our audience is participating in the performance. But all creativity is collaborative—even the creativity of mediated conversations such as email, writing, and painting. Our explorations of creating conversations can give us insights about all of human creativity—because although we can't all paint like Picasso, we can all understand conversation. Conversational creativity is not a rare gift—it's part of being human.

Chapter 4

Rehearsals

Although theater groups perform in public, they rehearse in private. But we don't get to rehearse for conversation in private—to become a creative conversationalist, you have to get out in the world and converse with other people. That's why each conversation is a rehearsal for the next—the next argument, the next party, or the next business meeting. Just like an improv group, our conversations evolve and change through repeated rehearsals. The ability to improvise can't be learned overnight and can't be learned from a book. It requires repeated practice over an extended period of time—the more you do it, the better you are.

In this chapter, we'll see that creating conversations are their own rehearsals, and can result in three kinds of change over time. First, we'll see how our personal histories with language affect each new conversational performance. How do we learn in conversation? What do we learn that we take into the next conversation? How do we grow through creating conversations? We often find ourselves in situations that are familiar, where we can re-use bits and pieces of dialogue—the catchphrases and personal licks of Chapter 1. In these familiar situations, our prior experiences affect how we create conversation. But of course, no two conversations are exactly alike; we can't just memorize the successful lines from one great conversation and expect them to work in the next conversation. In the rehearsals of conversation, we learn catchphrases and we also learn how to improvise with them.

Second, because conversations are always collaborative, and because we often have conversations with the same group of people over and over, these conversations function as rehearsals for our social group—along with our friends, we develop a kind of ensemble creativity. I'll explore this idea by showing you how improv groups get better through rehearsal improvisations.

Third, we'll see how creating conversations often result in *unwritten scripts* that get better over time and that eventually take on a life of their own. These are like the scripts of Chapter 1—the catchphrases and restaurant scripts that we all learn and share. For example, a good joke or an urban legend is like a script; even though it isn't written down, it stays essentially the same no matter who is telling it. To explore this theme, I'll describe some innovative theater groups that are using improvisation to help them develop scripts; and I'll show how unwritten scripts are developed over time among many kinds of groups, including preschool children, adults, and musicians.

In these three ways, creating conversations are like theater rehearsals, with some paradoxical twists: The rehearsal takes place in public, during conversational performance; and because there is no script and no final production, there is no endpoint, no final goal to these everyday rehearsals—creating conversations continue throughout our lives, always improvised anew, and always building on each other.

LEARNING TO IMPROVISE

How does a child learn how to participate in all of the complexities of social life? This is a central research topic for developmental psychologists, who study how a child's knowledge of the world changes from birth through adulthood. Children are born with very little knowledge of the world, but by the time they are in first grade, they're almost like little adults in their ability to learn, to converse, and to engage in friendships. This development is incredibly complex, and one of the major discoveries of modern developmental psychology is that children don't just passively absorb this kind of information—instead, they are active, creative participants in their own development. This discovery is usually associated with the Swiss psychologist Jean Piaget; his theory is often called *constructivist*, referring to his claim that children "construct" their own knowledge, through exploration and interaction with the world.[1] Although contemporary research has moved far beyond Piaget's original ideas, most developmental psychologists today are constructivists, and almost all preschool and primary school teachers are trained in this model.

From the constructivist viewpoint, children don't learn social skills by being explicitly taught how to act by their parents, or by just watching and absorbing behaviors; they learn by actively and creatively engaging in conversations with their parents and peers. For example, psychologists have discovered that the fantasy conversations of pretend play are essential for the normal development of a wide range of social, cognitive, and language skills, and they attribute this to the fact that children's play is incredibly creative and improvisational. We've seen that the essence of all conversation is creative improvisation; in play, children rehearse the ability to improvise. The improvisational skills required in play are the same skills that children will need in primary school, as they develop friends and social groups by participating in creating conversations.

A few years ago, I visited a preschool classroom to watch children's play improvisations. I chose a school that was located in a pleasant suburban neighborhood. My first visit was on a warm fall day, and as a I walked up to the house, I heard the familiar sounds of children playing in the yard behind the house.

After the outdoor play period, the children returned inside for their morning play period. I was overwhelmed by the chaos. At the time, I was young and single and hadn't spent any time with children—consequently, children always intimidated me. Twenty-four children, aged 3, 4, and 5, were all playing at once, and it seemed as if they were all talking at once, too. The teachers believed in the value of play, so they were standing to the side rather than controlling the children's activities. Later, the head teacher told me that some parents take a while to adjust to this idea; some parents are surprised that the children spend so much time in free play. Shouldn't they be practicing some useful skill? Working at a computer?

But preschool teachers know that children at play are learning something much more important than computer programming. They are rehearsing for the performance of everyday life. They take on the roles of other family members, like mommy, daddy, and big sister or occupational roles, like a cook or a racecar driver, or fantasy roles, like a spaceman or a dinosaur. They enact dramatic scenes with their playmates, often imitating scenes they have observed among adults.

On the first day I had difficulty making sense of anything—the noise of multiple conversations, some children walking around in groups, while other groups huddled together, intent on their play. That day, I started taking notes:[2]

The children's play ebbs and flows in the room, almost like traffic or an ocean—it moves really quickly—kids come and go constantly, alone, or hand in hand, or a whole group may suddenly decide to move to a new room. Most of the dialogue today seems related to the "spaceship" made of blocks. The dialogue sounds staged already—spoken clearly and distinctly, almost unnatural—

Child 1:	Let's go to the stairs!
	Countdown—10, 9, 8, 7, 6, 5, 4, 3, 2, 1, BLASTOFF!
Child 2:	We can't go to the stairs the sun is too hot
	It will burn you
Child 1:	That's why we have to go to the moon!
Child 2:	The sun is coming towards us now!

This creative play conversation is wild and improvised, and it reminded me of the spontaneous dialogues of improvisational theater. But children's play dialogues are not exactly like improv theater. For example, improvisational actors are quite good at maintaining the boundary between the world of the stage and the off-stage reality—the fourth wall. They also have to distinguish between their on-stage characters, and the relationships they have with each other off-stage. In contrast, children blend the boundary between play and social reality all the time, and their social relationships sometimes have a big effect on their play. The children cross the fourth wall so smoothly that it's almost as if they don't notice the difference between play and reality. For example, when Eddy, who rarely plays with the girls in this classroom, tries to join a group of girls playing in the doll corner, they immediately assign him a role:

(1)	Eddy	Who can I be?
(2)		Who can I be?
(3)	Kathy	You could be, the, King, or the princess
(4)		cause these are just visitors.
(5)	Eddy	I wanna be the King.
(6)	Kathy	Alright, you can be the King.
(7)	Eddy	Who are you?
(8)	Kathy	I'm a hopping, I'm a hopping Queen.
(9)		Yung-soo is the princess.

Although Eddy and Kathy are discussing their play characters, their negotiation reflects their relationship history. Eddy is rarely in the doll corner, and rarely joins Kathy in play. When Eddy asks who he can be, Kathy gives him two choices, and both of them are "visitors." This play status is a reflection of the real-world fact that Eddy does not often come to the doll corner.

Children at play often pretend to be fantasy characters—like the King, Queen, and Princess. That's why psychologists call it *role play*.[3] Some role play seems like a rehearsal for the roles they will have to play as adults—by pretending to be a father or a mother, they seem to be learning how to become fathers and mothers. But how *exactly* do these play rehearsals help children practice for adult roles? That's a surprisingly difficult question. For example, most children stop doing pretend play by first or second grade, yet they don't become parents until much later. So how could this early play really function as a rehearsal for an adult role 20 years later? Also, a lot of children's play has nothing to do with real life. Children enact roles that they have never encountered in person, like astronauts, or roles that exist only in fantasy, like dinosaurs or Teenage Mutant Ninja Turtles. They certainly aren't rehearsing to be turtles in adult life!

So, if children aren't rehearsing for adult roles, what are they rehearsing? Another possibility is that they are rehearsing the *scripts* of adult life.[4] For example, by playing a restaurant game, they are rehearsing for the scripted adult activity of eating out in a restaurant. Even if children are pretending to be characters that don't exist in real life, like turtles or dinosaurs, they could be rehearsing scripts that *do* exist in real life, scripts about threats, danger, escape, struggle, and defense. But this can't be the whole story, either. The most interesting thing about children's play is how unpredictable and creative it is. Most of the time, they aren't following a script—they're improvising a new drama each time.

These two theories about play rehearsals—that they are rehearsals of adult roles or of scripts from adult life—both enjoyed periods of popularity among psychologists. Both of them assume that children are imitating what they have observed in their everyday lives— they imitate their mother's behavior, or they re-enact going to a restaurant the night before. But these theories don't explain the creativity of children at play, when they improvise new dramas, characters, and scripts that have never been performed before. They are not only imitating adults, but altering and extending social life in their play rehearsals, and in this process, making the performance their own.

By creatively improvising their play drama, children are learning the creative skills that are essential for everyday social life. Rather than learning roles or scripts, children at play are learning how to improvise in conversations with others and how to collaborate with other children to create a conversational performance. Although the chaos of the classroom overwhelmed me on that first day, I came to realize that play has to be random and chaotic. Play is important because it is unscripted—it allows the child to practice improvisation. Children need to improvise with others, because the conversations they will have as adults are also creatively, collaboratively improvised.

Improvisational learning doesn't end in childhood; adults continue to learn to be better conversationalists, as they participate in more and more conversations. We recognize this increasing experience as maturity, or as an intangible social ease that teenagers rarely have.

Improv actors have to rehearse to improve their skills, as well. But some people find it confusing that improvisational artists need to rehearse at all. You're supposed to be making it up on stage, saying whatever comes into your head, right? We often think that improvisation is the opposite of skilled expertise. When we use the word "improvise" in everyday life, we're usually referring to a situation where the rule book doesn't apply, when we have to toss our book learning out the window.

But I've spent enough time with jazz musicians and with improvising actors to know that as you practice more, you become a better improviser. And I've played enough jazz piano myself to realize the truth of this. Jazz musicians talk about rehearsing as a way of working on their "chops," their musical skills. Most musicians have to practice constantly. There's an old jazz saying that emphasizes the importance of practice: "If you miss one day, only you can tell. If you miss two days, only your wife can tell. And if you miss a week, everybody can tell."

This seems like a paradox: How could discipline and practice result in more creative and flowing improvisations? To explore this question, the musicologist Paul Berliner spent 10 years studying how jazz musicians learn their craft. In his amazing book, *Thinking in Jazz: The Infinite Art of Improvisation*,[5] he describes how young musicians start out by imitating a famous jazz figure. For example, a trumpet player might spend months listening to a single Miles Davis album, playing along with Miles's solos until he has memorized them, note for note. Eventually, the young musician can play like Miles. At some point, after years of copying other musicians, the best musicians start to develop their own voice. They begin to move out from under the influence of their idols, and play their own music. It's almost as if learning how to improvise requires first going through a period of structure and discipline.

Countering the myth that jazz musicians play whatever comes into their heads, Berliner's research demonstrates that many years of discipline and practice are required before a musician can improvise creatively. It may seem contradictory, but practice and rehearsal are essential for improvisational ability.

Improvisational actors also have to rehearse to develop their performance creativity—theater improvisation also requires years of rehearsal and practice. This is true not only for music and theater, but for any profession that requires you to improvise—including teaching, sales, or contract negotiation. In the real world, structures, plans, and formulas never come out the way you expect. That's why improvisation is such a powerful technique for learning: Improvisation can't be learned from a book. That's why rehearsals are so important—they allow you to learn by doing, to practice the quick reactions and the listening skills that you need in group improvisation.

You have to improvise to learn how to improvise—there's no shortcut. And in fact, even performing from a script requires a kind of improvisational ability, because actors have to creatively interpret their lines. Rehearsal improvisations are helpful for all actors—this is the core insight of the famous Stanislavsky method of actor training, which Lee Strasberg drew on to develop his teaching technique, called simply "The Method," and taught for more than 30 years at the Actor's Studio in New York. Method actors—such as Harvey Keitel, Marlin Brando, and Al Pacino—are known for their ability to play a wide range of characters. Dustin Hoffman, for example, has played radically different types of roles, ranging from a woman (*Tootsie*) to an autistic adult (*Rainman*). This ability—to convincingly act many different parts—is typical of actors that have been trained at the Actor's Studio. The Method emphasizes that the actor must enter the lives of the characters he portrays, as thoroughly as possible, in order to understand their emotions and perspectives. It's a familiar cliché: we imagine the acting coach urging his students: "*Feel* the anger! *Express* your anger!"

Although today this is a cliché, a hundred years ago plays were performed very differently. For example, no audience expected actors to speak in a normal tone of voice—actors were expected to speak "dramatically." By today's standards, the dialogue must have sounded awkward and staged. The person responsible for changing all of this was the Russian actor Konstantin Stanislavsky. Born in 1863, he developed a new theater method, and then founded the world-famous Moscow Art Theater in 1898 to teach it. He explored new acting techniques that would result in a stage performance that would seem more natural and true to life, and the New York Actor's Studio was an American version of these techniques. Influenced by the psychology of the turn of the century— when Freud's new theory of the unconscious was the latest thing— Stanislavsky taught his actors to emphasize the feelings, moods, and expressions of a character, so that the performance would seem more authentic. Above all, the actors should act natural, and not appear to be "acting." Stanislavsky called this new technique *psychological realism*.[6]

Stanislavsky was one of those people whose impact on history was so profound that it's impossible to imagine what the world was like before. His method—so innovative at the time—is now the standard in acting classes. And many directors use the improvisational core of Stanislavsky's original technique—*character improvisation*, where actors improvise a monologue in character during rehearsal. Sometimes, two actors improvise a scene together, creating an alternative dialogue for a scene that is scripted in the play.

Stanislavsky's innovations freed the actor to be much more creative in interpreting a part. For the first time, actors began to be thought of as creative artists. In his Moscow Art Theater, Stanislavsky told his actors not to worry too much about the lines in the script; the most important thing was the inner psychology of the character. If, by following the inner voice of the character, you messed up a few lines or rephrased them slightly, that was OK. The Chicago actors that invented improv theater in the 1950s had all been exposed to Stanislavsky's ideas; modern improv theater was made possible by this new focus on the personal creativity of the actor.

GROUP LEARNING IN REHEARSAL

Few people realize how much work goes into a theater production. The work starts at home, with each actor memorizing his lines. After all the actors have memorized their lines, there are still weeks of rehearsal ahead. Why can't the performance start right away, once the actors have memorized their lines? It's because a play requires a kind of *group learning*—like all emergent social performances, a play is more than the sum of its parts. In group rehearsals, the cast works out the blocking, the physical movement of the actors on stage, and their entrances and exits from the stage. Group rehearsals also give the ensemble the chance to refine their timing, the pacing of the dialogue and the speed at which each actor's lines follow the previous actor's line. After all these basics are in place—the lines are memorized, the entrances and exits fixed—the group spends the final weeks on the artistry of their interpretation, practicing intensity and development, the buildup and release of tension, the balance of the overall work.

How long does all this take? A two-hour play takes about 100 hours of rehearsal to prepare, months of work that is frequently tedious and repetitive. Any actor can tell you about the endless hours they spend in rehearsals, often bored to death while two other actors work on a scene. In the typical theater production, the cast spends ten times as long in rehearsal as they do on stage.[7]

There is such a thing as *too much* rehearsal—critics call some plays "over-rehearsed," when the life and spontaneity are gone. The pianist Keith Jarrett says that he cannot rehearse in advance of an improv concert, because hearing himself play will interfere with his musical voice. He says "I have the need not to hear piano music before I improvise on the piano. So what does that mean? It means I can't practice. So what does that mean? Sometimes, it's been a month or two that I have not touched the piano and then I go and do a concert."[8]

Because I played piano with an improv group for two years, I spent a lot of time at rehearsals. When I told my friends that I was going to an improv group rehearsal, someone would always joke, "Why do you need to rehearse for improvisation?" It might have been a joke—or perhaps slyly implying that we must secretly be working on a script—but I realized that the question had a serious dimension to it. Why, indeed? In fact, one improv group in Chicago, the Improv Institute, had a policy of never rehearsing, and the two actors who owned the theater brought in a different set of fellow actors every night. They agreed with my friend: Why rehearse? Instead, they were more worried about the possibility that structure and repetitiveness would creep in if they kept performing with the same people. Without rehearsals, and without any opportunity to become more familiar with the personal quirks and patterns of other actors, they believed that the performances would be more spontaneous, more unpredictable, more fresh.

But unlike the Improv Institute, most improv groups, both in jazz and theater, are committed to the idea of *ensemble* comedy. The cast rehearses together to learn each other's rhythms and to develop trust among the group members. They don't rehearse to work on a script, or to develop portions of dialogue that will be used in a later performance, because that's not the way improv is done (even though this is what my friends suspected we were doing). In all my years of watching improv, I never saw any group use even a small chunk of dialogue more than once, neither from rehearsal to a performance, nor from one night's performance to another.

So what are the actors getting out of the rehearsal? They're learning the *process* of group improvisation—how to listen to each other, how to get into the odd mindset of not thinking ahead. They're also learning to become an ensemble: how to create collaboratively with the group. Every actor is different, and through rehearsals, the actors become comfortable with each other's styles. They learn the rhythms and attitudes that are unique to each performer.

Even theater groups that don't improvise on stage use group improvisation in their rehearsals. Like Stanislavsky's method, these rehearsal improvisations are not meant for an audience, but are for the actors themselves. The difference is that whereas Stanislavsky used improv to train individual actors, these groups use rehearsals as a technique for group learning. Some innovative directors even use rehearsal improvisations to create the script itself.

For example, the British director Mike Leigh is famous for using improvisation to develop scripts and characters. An award-winning director of 14 feature films, his 1996 film *Secrets & Lies* won two awards at Cannes, Best Actor and Best Director. This wasn't a fluke—his prior film, *Naked*, won the same two awards at Cannes. Improvisation is the key to Leigh's unique directing style. During his long career, Leigh has created over 20 award-winning movies, television films, and plays that begin with no script. Instead, he begins with an intuition, or a scene with a certain atmosphere, or a situation—really, just the seed of an idea.

Starting only with this seed, scenes and dialogues are worked out in close collaboration with his actors in months of rehearsals and improvisations, like a crystal forming and growing around the original seed idea. In the initial improvisations, Leigh works closely with the main actors, collaboratively creating each character's personality and his or her personal history. As the overall plot emerges from these improvisations, Leigh begins to create a rough plot outline—but he keeps it to himself.

After developing the characters, the next step is to have the actors improvise scenes that Leigh is beginning to sketch out. But the actors don't know what is "supposed" to happen in the scene, or where it fits in the overall scheme of the movie. When they are first thrust into a scene with another actor, their dialogue is as spontaneous as it would be in real life. For example, in the five months of rehearsals for *Secrets & Lies*, Leigh was the only one who knew all of the characters' secrets. He says "I shot three quarters of the damn movie with the crew under strict instructions not to reveal anything to the actors." But there is no improvisation when shooting: Leigh has written out a script and the actors memorize their lines before the final scene is filmed. Still, the actors don't know how it all fits together until they sit in the screening room and see the final edit of the film.[9]

Mike Leigh has taken Stanislavsky's psychological realism to a new extreme. Stanislavsky started with a script and used his method as a way of rehearsing a play. But Leigh starts with rough characters and then uses the actor's performance of a character, in rehearsal, to refine the character. And he uses the actors' improvised dialogues to develop the script.

Why would a director use improvisation to develop a script, when it takes so much longer and costs so much more than simply buying a script from a playwright? Leigh believes that improvised scenes are more true to life than any script, that improvisation can create dialogues that are more realistic than anything a playwright could invent.

Leigh's technique isn't just for independent art-house films—it also forms the cornerstone of the most successful improv group, Chicago's Second City Theater, and its famous spin-off, *Saturday Night Live*. *Saturday Night Live* may be the most influential TV comedy show of all time. The show, appearing every Saturday night since October 11, 1975, inaugurated a new genre of comedy: a series of short, five-minute sketches, using actors drawn from a small ensemble of comedians. Many of the show's riffs entered pop culture—like the tag line that ends every opening skit: "Live from New York, it's Saturday Night!"

Most people don't know how misleading this line is; *Saturday Night Live* is not native to New York, but was inspired by the Second City theater of Chicago. The world-famous Second City had its humble beginning on December 16, 1959, in a small club on the North Side of Chicago. By the mid-1970s, it had a national reputation, and the owners had opened theaters in several other cities. Most of the original *Saturday Night Live* cast came from the Chicago and Toronto ensembles. Some of the most famous of the 1970s TV skits were Chicago inside jokes, like the fast-food restaurant where you could get whatever you wanted as long as it was a hamburger and fries—and "No Coke, Pepsi." The real restaurant, the Billy Goat, is still serving lunch every day on Michigan Avenue in downtown Chicago.

Second City evolved from The Compass Players, founded by a group of students at the University of Chicago that included future stars like Elaine May, Ed Asner, and Mike Nichols.[10] The founder, Paul Sills, convinced a group of fellow actors to try experimenting with a set of improvisational children's games that his mother had been using in preschool classrooms. This unlikely group of nerdy undergraduates is the source of all modern improvisational theater. Second City is still going strong in Chicago, performing every weekend on North Wells Street to sell-out crowds of tourists and suburbanites. But in an ironic twist, Second City, the originator of improv, no longer performs any improvisation on stage.

In fact, Second City has a strict policy that they will *not* perform improvisations during their shows. Nonetheless, Second City continues to use improvisation during rehearsal, as a technique for developing skit ideas. If a good idea emerges during one of these improvisations, the cast collaborates to develop and refine the idea into a scripted five-minute comedy sketch. The TV skits on *Saturday Night Live* often seem rooted in an improvised rehearsal, because some of these ideas have the oddball unpredictability that you see in an improv show.

Although Second City has abandoned live improv, there are many other theaters in Chicago that have continued the original tradition of improvising on stage, and these groups sometimes criticize

Second City for selling out. Bernie Sahlins, one of the founders and owners of Second City, knows that his view of improv is controversial in the
theater community, but he is not apologetic. He says "Improvisation is a
tool for arriving at Second City material. It hasn't proven viable for anything else."[11] Sahlins believes that improvisation is an incredibly valuable technique for developing scripts, and their actors are trained in the
same improv techniques as any other improv group. But these improvisations stay behind the scenes and are not for public consumption.

Because Second City is a profitable business, and a good sketch
may end up being performed hundreds of times for paying audiences,
the issue of ownership of these scripts has come up repeatedly. The law
says that playwrights receive a royalty fee every time their plays are performed. But Second City scripts emerge from an ensemble of actors
improvising in rehearsal, so who owns the script? In fact, the owners of
the theater avoid these debates by requiring the actors to sign a contract
agreeing that all scripts will be the sole property of the theater. Needless
to say, this doesn't always sit well with the actors. They argue, with
some justification, that they should retain rights to the scripts they participate in developing, and that they should be able to perform the material in other settings. Sahlins responds that these scripts are the only
intellectual property that Second City owns, and that the theater would
not be profitable if they didn't retain ownership of the scripts.

As more and more businesses start to use brainstorming sessions to inspire innovation, the same issues come up. In a group brainstorming session, should the facilitator of the group receive special credit, even though someone in the group may come up with the brilliant
idea? How should an organization reward the creativity that emerges
from a group? In business, if you want to have an effective brainstorming session, the group must be told that they will share any credit that
goes to a creative outcome. How can you reward the one individual who
happened to voice the idea that led to the multi-million dollar product,
when that inspiration only occurred because of the collaborative interactions of the group? Of course, just like Second City, the corporation
retains ownership of these ideas. The employees are rewarded through
positive performance reviews, raises, and potential bonuses. In the same
way, Second City actors are rewarded with more shows and increased
exposure.

Just like Second City actors, many of us don't like the thought
that we might have an idea without getting all of the credit for it; and it's
human nature to think your contribution was larger than it might actually have been. In fact, some people will withhold good ideas during a
brainstorming session, so that they can later claim full credit for the idea.
But what they don't realize is that holding back will make *them* less cre-

ative, too. If everyone is holding back, no one will have the true insights that could only emerge from the group working together—the kinds of collaborative creativity that we examined at the end of Chapter 2.

Imagine a jazz musician deciding not to play his best solo, and instead planning to score it later as a composition! When jazz is recorded, the personnel on the album are all acknowledged to have played an essential creative role in generating this creative product, no matter who the big-name band leader is. Jazz DJs always list the personnel after playing a song; jazz fans know that if even one musician is different, you'll get a different musical conversation.[12]

This is one way that jazz is supposed to be different from classical music. When an orchestra performs a score, the conductor pretty much wants the musicians to be interchangeable—after all, they are supposed to perform exactly what's in the score, and exactly the way the conductor tells them to. Thus it seems that classical groups wouldn't benefit from this kind of rehearsal learning—they certainly don't improvise and develop new material themselves. Instead, they work from a common score, and they depend on the leadership of a conductor. In most major orchestras, the conductor is all-powerful; the musicians must obey his commands.

Maybe this is why jazz was considered deviant and dangerous when it first hit the scene, and why it still retains an aura of outsider music. The autocratic, hierarchical symphony orchestra is the complete opposite of jazz. In jazz, a group of performers creates without a conductor, and without a score. In a symphony, the performance is impossible without both a score and a conductor. Or is it? Is there something in the nature of European classical music that makes the jazz model fail? Does European music require a conductor?

A critically acclaimed orchestra in New York City is exploring this question. Since 1972, the Orpheus Chamber Orchestra has been rehearsing and performing without a conductor. Born out of the 1960s dissatisfaction with authority figures and hierarchy, a group of Columbia University students formed a sort of musical commune. All decisions—about what pieces to perform, about which musicians to use—were made collectively. No one controlled the rehearsal; any musician could say anything, at any time. This new approach appealed to some of the best young musicians in New York. By 1978, after only six years, the group performed in Carnegie Hall, and in 1984, it was signed by the prestigious recording label Deutsche Grammophon.

In the traditional orchestra, the rehearsal is controlled by a single conductor, who already has a vision of what the orchestra should sound like. He conducts the rehearsals with this vision in mind. In the absence of a single vision, how does a group rehearse a composition?

How do they arrive at a shared interpretation for the piece? With no conductor, the musicians have to make all of the creative decisions collaboratively. There is a lot more discussion and negotiation at an Orpheus rehearsal. The musician Eric Bartlett says "We're always fighting with each other, but we're always fighting it out."

Musicians talk about Orpheus using phrases that I've heard many improvisational actors use. They talk about the importance of *listening*, with "listening" given a special, almost reverent emphasis, in the same way that jazz musicians use the term. Each musician has to listen to all of the others, with a degree of concentration and intensity that becomes almost like a Zen state of consciousless-ness—they have to listen closely to each other, to coordinate their voices, and to non-verbally negotiate a common musical vision. Like improv actors, Orpheus musicians talk about *trust* in each other: trusting each of the other musicians to be listening to everyone, and to take responsibility for the entire piece, not only for their own part. Soloists who have played with Orpheus can hear the difference in the way the orchestra follows them, even when they slow down or speed up. This immediacy of response is different from a conventional orchestra, where the conductor hears the soloist slowing down, and then slows down his baton, and only then can the orchestra begin to slow down to follow the soloist.

Commercial success forced Orpheus to face some of the weaknesses of their democratic system. William Purvis, a horn player, says "It's a harder situation to play in than almost any other I can imagine." The main problem was with the rehearsals. Without a conductor to guide the rehearsals towards his vision, the musicians spent hours discussing details that a conductor would have dealt with in 30 seconds. Although the founding musicians were committed to their collaborative vision, they couldn't afford to pay musicians the going hourly rate for such long rehearsals. They eventually worked out a compromise: They elected a concertmaster from among the musicians to lead each piece. Still, the concertmaster did not stand in front of the orchestra waving a baton; he was one of the musicians and sat in his usual chair during rehearsals of the piece. Even with this compromise, it still takes Orpheus three times as long to prepare for a concert as a conventional orchestra.

But this inefficiency is what makes an Orpheus performance unique—it's what makes them sound different from any other orchestra. Their distinctive sound results from this collaborative, interactive process among the musicians—the slow, inefficient development of a shared vision.

Orpheus shows us both the benefits and the drawbacks of group learning through improvisation. The drawbacks are the inefficiency and the cost; these problems make it unlikely that the Orpheus model will be replicated. But the benefits, arising from the inefficiencies of the process itself, give rise to a special quality in the music that no conductor could ever duplicate. The critic James Traub says that at an Orpheus performance, you get "the feeling that the musicians were playing as much for one another as for the audience." The classical music audience is used to seeing a performance that is the realization of a conductor's vision. With Orpheus, they see a performance that is a product of a musical community—a group vision. When we hear an Orpheus concert, we hear the result of long hours of collective creativity and negotiation. And each performance is different, because the musicians are listening and interacting with each other *during* the performance, in a different way than if they could simply look up at the conductor.[13]

Children at play—like Orpheus, and like all improv groups—are learning without a conductor. They have to work together to improvise their drama—as we saw in Chapter 2, using implicit metatalk and other creative techniques. And like any performing ensemble, a preschool classroom is learning as a group—in a sense, learning to be an ensemble, learning shared play themes and inside jokes that even their parents might not hear about. Some innovative educators are trying to take advantage of children's natural ability to learn through group improvisation. Instead of the traditional, rather sudden transition from the play of kindergarten to the desks and structure of first grade, these educators are focusing on a more active, participatory kind of learning. In doing this, they are trying to replicate the natural creativity and groupwork of children's fantasy play.

At an innovative school in Salt Lake City, for example, teachers asked a group of second and third graders to develop a play to perform for their parents. But the children were not given a script, and the adults stayed in the background and did not direct the rehearsals. This *playcrafting* assignment was designed to teach children how to collaborate on tasks and how to develop plans and solve problems in groups.[14] Although these group skills are critical in most careers, the traditional school curriculum doesn't provide children with the opportunity to rehearse these abilities.

A group of psychologists at the University of Utah worked with the teachers to study these playcrafting rehearsals. They wanted to see how well the children collaborated during rehearsals, and how their abilities improved as they worked on this assignment. The psychologists didn't know what would happen. Would it be complete chaos, or could the children rise to the occasion? Happily, the children did remarkably well, generally had a lot of fun, and successfully performed the plays at the end of the one-month rehearsal period. This task is well within the abilities of 7-, 8-, and 9-year-olds. Children can work together to create a play, without being directed by an adult.

How did they do it? It turns out that the children frequently improvised during the rehearsals, as a kind of shorthand way of proposing new script ideas. That is, rather than explicitly propose their new idea to the other children, they start enacting a character, and speak their proposed lines *in character*. The children were not taught to do this—these improvisational techniques emerged spontaneously among the child actors. What's more, over the course of the month of rehearsals, the percentage of time they spent improvising in character increased. As the basic form of the play fell into shape, as they became comfortable with each other and had worked out ground rules for collaboration, they could spend more time improvising—negotiating in character—rather than having to step out of character and speak as a director.

For comparison, the teachers also asked adults to help some of the groups. In these groups, the children never improvised together. To see why, think of what you would do if you were assigned the responsibility for the children's play. The adult directors made all of the decisions, and told the children what to do. In fact, the children were expecting the adults to do that, and consequently they sat waiting for direction. But with no adult to direct, the playcrafting task allowed the children to practice important skills that no teacher can teach—skills that can only be learned by doing. By improvising and rehearsing together, the children were learning essential conversational and social skills: how to solve problems and develop plans in group settings, how to share decision-making, how to collaborate on a creative task—how to improvise.

THE SECRET HISTORY OF CONVERSATION

The circumstances of the creation of a myth are collective. Myths are anonymous; when a myth is repeated, the listeners receive a message that, properly speaking, comes from nowhere.
—Claude Levi-Strauss, *The Raw and the Cooked*[15]

Sometimes, the same conversation is performed repeatedly, changing and yet staying the same. A married couple tells of an event that happened on their vacation, and each time the conversation flows in a similar way, even though the audience is different each time. The first eight lines of a telephone conversation are almost always the same sequence of catchphrases. We explored these *scripts* in Chapter 1, and now we'll explore where they come from—their secret history.

Think about the last time that you repeated a joke. You almost certainly didn't repeat it word for word, but even so, it's still the same joke; no one expects a joke to be told each time using exactly the same words. In fact, it's the improvised personal touches—the pacing and delivery, tailoring the telling to the audience—that make one person a better joke-teller than another. Jokes aren't completely improvised, but they are embellished and creatively performed. There's no official version, and everyone tells a joke a little differently.

Another example of a verbal performance that changes and yet stays the same is the *urban legend*. One classic urban legend tells the "true story" of how Neiman-Marcus charged a shopper $250 for its cookie recipe, not the $2.50 the woman had been expecting to pay. As revenge on the store for refusing to reverse this charge, she now provides the recipe for free and exhorts others to pass it along. In fact, Neiman-Marcus didn't even make a special cookie until after this legend had spread so widely that customers kept asking for "the cookie." Variants of this legend have been around for at least 50 years. The earliest documented version appears in a 1948 cookbook, describing a $25 fudge cake recipe sold by a railroad. In the 1960s, the story was told about the Waldorf-Astoria hotel's "Red Velvet Cake." In the 1970s, a similar story was told about Mrs. Fields' cookies.[16]

Jokes and urban legends are examples of what folklore researchers call *oral culture*. A joke or an urban legend starts when some anonymous group of people comes up with the first draft; no one knows who created the story or where it was first told. If it's a successful joke or legend, it becomes gradually more refined and embellished, until it begins to take on a stable form. At this point, it has its own internal logic—a kind of script—that is sometimes hard to change. For most urban legends, this history will never be known—it will always be a secret history.

The example of the Neiman-Marcus cookie legend is an example of how oral culture is always both changing and staying the same. The story is recognizably similar across the decades, even though the details change. These sorts of issues—repetition, replication, development, and change—are important topics in contemporary folklore studies, but also in fields as diverse as the transmission of culture, the history of science, and literary theory.[17] These issues are also at the heart of the contemporary field of *memetics*, the study of how ideas, stories, and catchphrases reproduce and change over time, using insights and metaphors from biological evolution.[18]

A lot of children's games and rhymes are like this, because children never learn their playground games from books. Games like hopscotch and four-square are passed on for generations, in many cases without the participation of adults. And like jokes, children's games rarely have an official version—every town and every playground seems to have its own unique variation to the hopscotch game.

Where do children's games and rhymes come from? Like urban legends, their origins are largely lost to history. But the researcher Susan

Iwamura has documented an interesting case of children improvisation-ally developing new verbal games.[19] In 1980, Iwamura published a study of the verbal games created by two preschool girls, as they rode to preschool every morning. Iwamura taped and transcribed their verbal games at both the beginning and the end of the school year, and she doc-umented an amazing development—from improvisation at the begin-ning of the year, to an almost fully scripted, rule-driven game by the end of the year. The children developed these games collaboratively, and improvisationally, and they took an entire year to emerge. Iwamura called this long, slow process *ritualization*.

After a few months of improvisational game playing, the broad outlines of the game first emerged. These proto-games had a lot of flexibil-ity and room for embellishment—the rules were not developed overnight. Iwamura documented a regular pattern to the process of ritualization. First, the girls improvised to develop two-turn sequences of verbal catch-phrases; short, catchy exchanges that they embellished frequently. After they had developed a set of two-turn sequences, they started to combine them into longer sequences, or *routines*. These two developments were accompanied by a great deal of explicit metatalk—the children would stop the game, and talk about what they should say, what they were sup-posed to say, and what they might do differently. With repetition and refinement, a routine eventually developed into a *ritualized routine;* this final development tended to happen without much explicit discussion.

Towards the end of the school year, once a particular game became ritualized, it had its own power to control the children—the ritu-al structure of the game made it more difficult for either child to change. By this point, trying to improvise too freely had implications beyond the game itself; if one child broke out of the routine, the other child per-ceived it as a rejection of their friendship. As with all of the rituals of oral culture, once the game develops to a certain point, the children begin to lose control over their own creation; the game takes on a life of its own, and it constrains their creativity. This paradoxical dialectic rela-tionship is a major theme of Chapter 6.

This ritualized routine is a script that emerges within a single relationship. To become a part of oral culture, these scripts take on a life of their own and live on across many lifetimes; for example, many games and playground rhymes stay the same generation after genera-tion. In the 1950s, the folklorists Peter and Iona Opie conducted a major survey of children's games in Britain.[20] As part of their study, they explored the history of a single playground rhyme, which they first heard children use in 1939 and which was still being used in the mid 1950s. By researching written records of children's rhymes, they were able to trace this same rhyme as far back as 1725.

This playground rhyme seems to have a life of its own—it passes on from city to city, from generation to generation, with remarkably little change. In Figure 4.1, we are seeing the history of a rhyme. But the children who play this game today have no idea where it came from—just like we have no idea who created the cookie recipe urban legend. That's why I call this a *secret history*—the conversational performance has a history that no one is aware of; secret, because it is never written down; secret, because its origins are unknown to those who speak it. This playground rhyme has a life of its own, lasting longer than 200 years—longer than the lifespan of any single speaker. In this case, there is an additional irony—that an innocent children's rhyme has its origins in a barroom drinking song.

In America, we tend not to place much value on oral culture; all of our "high culture" is written down—novels, poetry, and plays. But in societies where most of the people don't know how to read—or where there is no writing—all of the culture is oral, and is passed on through repeated tellings, like we pass around jokes at the office. Oral cultures must be passed on verbally, from one generation to another. When a tradition is oral, verbal performance is central in a way that isn't the case with written literature.

Some of the classics of the Western canon, Homer's epic poems, are now thought to have emerged from an oral storytelling tradition. This discovery was revolutionary, because classicists had always assumed that Homer was a poet who sat in a room and composed the *Iliad* and the *Odyssey*. This "oral culture" hypothesis was first proposed by the folklorist Milman Parry in the 1920s, and he demonstrated that Homer's poems had poetic patterns that reflected their oral origins. In the 1950s, Albert Lord followed up on this research, by visiting a part of Yugoslavia where an epic storytelling tradition still survived. Lord found many storytellers who were capable of performing "Homerian" epic tales, with their performances going on for hours. Lord showed that these stories had the same poetic structures as Homer's epic poems.[21]

But still, some critics couldn't accept that Homer's epic poems were simple transcriptions of an oral tradition, because they were so darned long. How could anyone remember such a long story? It turns out that, just as with your jokes, the story is never told exactly the same way twice. Poetic structures like parallelism, rhythm, and rhyme are great memory devices for the overall flow of a story, but not so good for remembering the exact wording. Albert Lord discovered that these Serbo-Croation epics were performed in a more flexible and variable manner than had previously been suspected. The same song, sung by the same singer on multiple occasions, could vary in length by as much as several thousand lines. Even when the storytellers swore they were

1725
Now he acts the *Grenadier*,
Calling for a *Pot of Beer*:
Where's his Money? He's forgot:
Get him gone, a Drunken Sot.

1774
Whoes there
  A Granidier
What dye want
  A Pint of Beer

Whoes there
  A Granidier
What dye want
  A Pint of Beer

1780
Who comes here?
  A Grenadier.
What do you want?
  A Pot of Beer.
Where is your Money?
  I've forgot.
Get you gone
  You drunken Sot.

1907
Eenty, teenty, tuppenny bun,
Pitching tatties doon the lum;
Who's ther? John Blair.
What does he want? A bottle of beer.
Where's your money? I forgot.
Go downstairs, you drunken sot.

1910
Far are ye gaein'?
Across the gutter.
Fat for?
A pund o' butter.
Far's yer money?
In my pocket.
Far's yer pocket?
Clean forgot it!

1916
Rat a Tat tat, who is that?
Only grandma's pussy-cat.
What do you want?
A pint of milk.
Where's your money?
In my pocket
Where is your pocket?
I forgot it.
O you silly pussy-cat.

1939
A frog walked into a public house.
And asked for a pint of beer.
Where's your money?
In my pocket.
Where's your pocket?
I forgot it.
Well, please walk out.

1943
Rat tat tat, who is that?
Only Mrs. Pussy Cat.
What do you want?
A pint of milk.
Where's your penny?
In my pocket.
Where's your pocket?
I forgot it.
Please walk out.

1950
Mickey Mouse
In a public house
Drinking pints of beer.
Where's your money?
In my pocket.
Where's your pocket?
I forgot it.
Please walk out.

Figure 4.1. History of a playground rhyme

repeating verbatim the same story they had told a week ago, a close analysis of the audiotape showed that the words used were actually very different, although the structure of the story—the meter and the rhyme—remained the same. Here was additional evidence that Homer's epic poems were not inspirations from the mind of one man, but were transcriptions of a long-standing oral tradition.

Folklorists who study verbal art in cultures around the world have found that in all oral cultures, performances are always partially improvised. For example, they're often modified to fit the occasion—one version in the dark of a long winter's night, a different version at a spring celebration. They're also performed differently depending on who is in the audience; for example, a skillful storyteller can weave in subtle references to visitors from another village. In many oral traditions, the performer is *expected* to creatively add to the traditional text. The Yoruba singers of Nigeria, for example, are free to rearrange and manipulate the subject matter, to adapt the formulas presented by their tradition. In fact, their reputation as performers depends on the ability to skillfully improvise.[22]

Although all oral cultures allow variation across performances, and some even require improvisation, no oral culture allows their performers to speak or sing just any old string of words. In an oral culture, the performer uses something like a verbal erector set—lines and couplets handed down from tradition—and constructs the performance out of this set of formulaic phrases, themes, incidents, and plots. These are a little like the catchphrases and licks we use in everyday conversation—but imagine if *everything* that you said had to be a cliché or a catchphrase. For example, in the small islands of Eastern Indonesia, ritual performances are composed from rhyming couplets, and the performers are expected to creatively combine the traditional couplets to improvise an appropriate performance for the specific occasion. To be a talented performer, you have to memorize at least 1,000 of the traditional couplets, because performers are actually *forbidden* to invent new couplets; the performer's creativity is restricted to improvising the selection and ordering of the couplets.[23] But folklorists with tape recorders have found—just as Lord did in Yugoslavia—that even when the performers swear they are using the traditional couplets, across actual performances there is a great deal of variation and innovation within the couplets.

These performers aren't lying or misinformed. Instead, this is an example of a more general pattern: Performers in oral cultures have a different notion of what counts as "the same." The written word changes the way we think about verbal performance. What does a culture recognize as a creative innovation? In our literate culture, we think that any paraphrase is different, no matter how minor. Once a story is written down, we have the idea that it has to be repeated word-for-word, *verba-tim*, to be the same. But oral performances are never the same; watching a performance is not like reading a book. An audience perceives a creative, improvised process, whereas a reader reads a final, created product. The variability of performance means that there can never be a "correct" or "authentic" version of the performance text.[24]

So it wouldn't be accurate to say that these Slavic performers simply don't realize what they're doing—instead, these differences point out that our own ideas about performance are not universal: The concept of "verbatim" may not exist in an oral culture.

In oral cultures, every performance is a rehearsal for the next—subtly affecting what will be said on the next occasion. Although each change is minor, the changes can add up over time, just like in a game of Telephone. And because our creating conversations are improvised, they are much more like the performances found in oral cultures than they are like conventional Western stage performances; these performances are based on a written text—a script, a lecture, or a scripture passage. Perhaps that's why we have trouble seeing the connections between conversation and theater performance—because we are no longer an oral culture.

Like the performances of an oral culture, each conversation is connected to all of our past conversations, in complicated and invisible ways. Think of how the Neiman-Marcus cookie recipe started out decades ago as a railroad's cake recipe; or how a preschool hopscotch rhyme is sung differently by your children than you sang it decades ago. There is variation over time, but there is still a long series of connections, a secret history of conversation.

Jazz performances also have this secret history—"secret" because the audience never sees it. To understand this secret history, you have to be a serious fan and spend a lot of time listening to a group's recordings. That's why classic jazz CDs, re-issues of studio recordings from the 1950s, often have multiple takes of the same song. When a jazz group was recording, the engineer would typically have the group perform two or three takes of each song. Because much of the performance was improvised, each take was slightly different, and in the old days of vinyl recordings, the best take would be selected for the record. But with the expanded capacity of the CD, many re-issues contain all of the studio takes; that's because aficionados can then compare the multiple takes to hear exactly what was repeated, and what was improvised anew, in each take.

Some jazz fans can tell you exactly which month that a group developed a certain way of building to the end of a solo, because they have listened to tapes of all of the performances during that year.

Almost all jazz groups develop certain patterns to help organize the improvisations in the rest of the piece. Although some of these patterns are developed in rehearsal, most of them emerge in actual improvisation during a live performance, and the musicians retain what works for the next night. Sometimes the band members talk about it afterwards, but just as often, they all know what worked and they don't need to discuss it.

The improvisational music of the Grateful Dead exposed a rock audience to these collaboratively created patterns, because so many of the Dead's fans attended multiple concerts on a single tour, or listened to bootleg tapes of concerts only days apart. More than any other rock band, the Grateful Dead spawned a thriving subculture of bootleg tape trading, extending almost three decades. Most rock bands forbid concert taping, viewing it as a copyright violation—they'd rather make you buy their album. But the Grateful Dead realized they had a unique fan culture, and they decided to support it. In the 1980s they were the first band to announce that taping of their concerts would be officially allowed and even encouraged. In the 1990s, tape trading expanded to the Internet, allowing Deadheads in different cities to trade tapes. I started my own tape collection in college in 1979. With about 100 tapes, it's only a tiny fraction of all of the group's concerts, but many of my tapes are concentrated on concerts during the same few tours in 1970 and 1971. Listening to so many concerts from a short period of time helped me to realize how a group's improvisations subtly change and evolve during a concert tour. When you first listen to the Dead improvise a transition from one song to another—a unique aspect of their music—it may seem completely improvised. But when you listen to a tape of the same transition in another performance a week earlier, and then yet another version of the transition a month before that, you realize that all of these improvisations build on each other. Night after night, the group refines and elaborates on these group improvisations—they don't create from scratch each time.

A few years after college, I joined a Boston-area band called Slipknot, one of four or five Grateful Dead cover bands in the area. Such bands are surprisingly common, and are found even in small cities. Since the band's lead guitarist, Jerry Garcia, died in 1995, the number of these bands has increased nationwide.

Slipknot's greatest musical challenge was to reproduce the semi-improvised transitions between songs. That's because these don't appear in any songbook, and they're not on the albums. To do this, we all had to be familiar with a large number of the band's live performances, and we had to imitate a group improvisation. It's a paradoxical idea: How can you imitate something that is not fixed to start with? We were improvising with a certain model in mind: The Dead's own past performances. How could we all be improvising, if we were trying to sound like a taped performance? Was it *really* improvisation? And if it really was our own new improvisation, then why did it still sound like the Grateful Dead?

We could ask the same question of the original band: If the Grateful Dead's own improvised performances were often quite similar to prior performances, were they *really* improvised? Well, of course they were. As we learned in Chapter 1, improvisation doesn't mean there is a complete absence of structure, or that every note or phrase is something that no musician has ever played before. When Slipknot performed, even though we sounded like the Dead, we were still improvising. These improvisations reveal the complexity of change and rehearsal in improvisational performance: In all performances, much is the same, and much is improvised.

Such is the secret history of conversation. Over the years, we have repeat performances of family meals, morning greetings at the office, and dinner parties with our friends. These are like individual, private versions of the cultural scripts of Chapter 1. Each social occasion is similar to the last, yet each conversation is created a little differently; we improvise something that is partly new, and partly historical.[25] Our conversations are linked over the years, in the same way that each generation of children sings a playground rhyme that is both the same and yet different. In these ways, our everyday performances are always rehearsals for the rest of life.

One of my favorite movies—the offbeat 1993 comedy *Groundhog Day*—makes this point in a powerful, funny way.[26] Bill Murray plays Phil Connors, a news reporter from a Pittsburgh TV station. Every February, Connors is assigned to go to the small mountain town of Punxsatawny to do a local color story on their Groundhog-Day tradition of waiting to see if the groundhog, "Punxsatawny Phil," will see his shadow when he comes out of his hole. Connors is a type-A urban personality who complains about the provinciality of the town, and he can't wait to get back to urban life.

After a night in a quaint B&B, he wakes up to the clock radio—Sonny and Cher are singing "I Got You Babe." He grimly gets to work. He interviews the mayor of Punxsatawny, and the local guy wearing the groundhog suit. Right after the interview Connors and his crew start driving back to Pittsburgh. But a huge snowstorm has come in, and the Interstate is closed—a state trooper sends them back to Punxsatawny, and they spend a second night in town. The next day, Connors wakes up in his bed-and-breakfast, ready and anxious to return to Pittsburgh. But soon he thinks he's still dreaming, because "I Got You Babe" is playing on his clock radio when he awakens; the same weather report follows the song. Recognizing the weatherman's exact phrasing from the day before, he thinks the station has simply gotten their tapes mixed up. When he walks outside, everyone is again flocking to the town square to hear the mayor's speech. But Groundhog Day was yesterday! At first, Connors thinks this is a practical joke, a grand conspiracy on the part of the town to make him think he's crazy. He gets through the entire day, going to bed at the B&B and hoping that the next day will be the *next* day. But it happens again the next day: Everything happens exactly as it did on the first, and second, day. And it keeps happening. Connors is, it seems, condemned to live the rest of his life repeating Groundhog Day, in a town he can't stand.

After the initial shock, he decides to take advantage of the fact that he can foresee the future. He makes large sums of money gambling—but each day he starts again with nothing. He meets and seduces women, by creating "coincidences" that happen to bring them together and by making promises he knows he won't have to keep. He spends what seems like months working on the one woman he really wants, his producer, Rita. He never does successfully seduce her, because she always sees through his games.

The movie does a wonderful job of suspending us in time, just like Phil Connors. We never know how many days he's been there; it seems like a lot, but the movie never shows us a calendar or a countdown. After a while he goes crazy. He realizes there is no escape, and he decides to commit suicide. He successfully kills himself, but still wakes up to "I Got You Babe" the next morning. He kills himself over and over, but it doesn't work; he keeps waking up the next day, alive.

Then the movie goes through a subtle shift as Connors moves to a more aware, almost spiritual level. He decides to learn how to play the piano, since he can take lessons essentially forever. Each day, the piano teacher thinks it's his first lesson, and is progressively more amazed at how good he is "for a beginner." Connors also learns where traffic accidents happen each day in the town, and he works up a schedule so that he can appear there in advance of every one, to avert the accident. We never know how long Connors has been in Punxsatawny, but it seems like many years when he sits down at the piano and plays a virtuoso showpiece. After he attains a sort of Zen enlightenment—enjoying each day for the work of art it is—he finally receives the love of Rita, the producer that he had been pursuing throughout the whole movie. The morning after they sleep together, he wakes up and she is *still there* in bed, next to him. The radio finally plays a different song. He has found a kind of redemption, and his life advances to the day *after* Groundhog Day.

Groundhog Day is a series of rehearsals. Each day is improvised, but each one builds to an increasingly refined performance. Phil Connors's Groundhog Day is like a Grateful Dead classic—a song they improvise at every concert for years. Each performance is both the same and yet different. Although everyone else in town repeats the same script day after day, Connors is allowed to improvise different responses. He is a soloist, performing over a backup orchestra that keeps playing the same riffs.

Yet there is a difference between Connor's daily improvisations and the Grateful Dead's concerts. Successive Dead concerts don't build to an endpoint—each one stands alone. But Connor's repeated improvisations connect to each other to form a narrative; otherwise, the movie wouldn't have a dramatic structure. The movie gives him a series of goals: to get rich, to get Rita into bed, to learn piano, to make the town a better place. Each day is its own performance, but it's also a rehearsal for the next day, as Connors learns what works and what doesn't work. By the end of the movie, Connors has used his surreal situation to become his own work of performance art. His creation is a performance of "Phil Connors's Groundhog Day."

Connors's day is a metaphor for our own lives. Although each of our days has some structure, perhaps more and more as we grow older, there's always a chance to rehearse and refine our daily performance. What is repeated in each conversation, and what is new? And how do we change and grow from the rehearsals of everyday life?

* * * * * * * *

In this chapter, we've seen that conversations are rehearsals, and that these conversational rehearsals result in three kinds of change. In the first section of the chapter, we saw how *individuals* learn from rehearsal, and in the second section, we saw how *groups* learn—as an ensemble— through group rehearsals. In this final section, we have seen the secret history of conversation, when conversational performances—such as jokes, children's rhymes, or urban legends—take on lives of their own, apart from any one speaker or any single conversation. Each repeated telling is both the same and yet slightly different. Like an oral tradition, the performance takes on a life of its own, and changes and evolves under its own logic. Through creating conversations, the performance *emerges* as an independent object, a social creation.

In Chapter 1, we first encountered the phenomenon of emergence—when groups display complex, creative behavior, even without a central controller. Our centralized mindset often misleads us into looking for a script or a director, when, in fact, the group is doing it all through improvisational interaction. This is why the first folklore researchers tried to trace traditional stories or songs back to a single author. But when a songbook attributes a song to "trad." (traditional) or "anon." (anonymous), it means that this song probably emerged from a collaborative historical process. In this chapter, we've seen how the scripts of everyday life emerge across repeated rehearsals, like a Grateful Dead concert tour. These are all collective, emergent processes, emerging from the group's creativity.

The two types of learning that result from rehearsals are individual learning and group learning. Both kinds of learning always occur, because creating conversations are group improvisations, and they are collaborations with our conversational partners. We can't learn to improvise sitting at home alone—we can only learn in a group. Children learn conversation only in groups. Scripts and plays are often better rehearsed by the group. That's why it's often hard to draw a firm line between how *you* converse, and how *the group* converses—you're likely to talk slightly differently in each different group of people.

In the performance of everyday life, we experience a never-ending series of rehearsals, with each creating conversation serving as a rehearsal for the next. Although we are always improvising, our conversational performances are connected to all of our past conversations, in complicated and usually invisible ways. But whereas theater rehearsals work towards a final public performance, in the performance of everyday life, there is only a continuing series of rehearsals, and a never-ending process of development and change. There is no final goal—there won't be an opening night in front of an audience. Creating conversation is its own goal.

Chapter 5

Characters

All the world's a stage, and all the men and women merely players.
   —Shakespeare, in *As You Like It*

Shakespeare's famous line is a comment on those everyday situations when we feel like we're performing a role. We're especially aware of this when we're in more formal situations—we feel like we're performing, and consequently we don't feel like we can "be ourselves." In Shakespeare's time, belief in predestination was common—and his famous line implies that God is an omnipotent playwright. Perhaps the choices available in life were more limited in Elizabethan England—perhaps life provided fewer opportunities to improvise. But in modern life, we all have the opportunity to create our own characters, as we improvise the performances of everyday life.

Shakespeare created his scripts by starting with a plot idea—multiple plot threads, deceptions revealed, climaxes and denouements. But in modern theater, the plot is less important than the characters—today's playwrights form mental images of their characters even before they've selected a location or conceived of a plot. And as an additional aid to the writing process, some playwrights create a mental image of a conversation between these characters. A few playwrights even sound a little schizophrenic when they say that in writing the dialogue, they are just transcribing what these characters say—the script emerges from the conversations of these inner characters.

As we watch a play, we learn about the characters by listening to their conversation; what they say, and how they react to others, reveals their personalities and motivations. Although the playwright writes the dialogue, characters must be brought to life by actors. So who is the creator of a character? Is it the playwright or the actor? Actors and playwrights have been arguing about this since Stanislavsky founded the Moscow Art Theater in 1898. Before Stanislavsky, actors weren't expected to be creative interpreters. Playwrights were never comfortable with Stanislavsky's radical new method, because it shifted the creative emphasis away from the script to the actor. In Chapter 2, we saw how the Italian playwright Luigi Pirandello explored these tensions on stage in his influential 1921 play *Six Characters in Search of an Author*. Pirandello's play emphasized that this perennial conflict is built into the structure of theater; both the script and the actors are necessary, and both contribute to the creation of the character that we see on stage.

In the improvised performances of conversation, we are the actors, and because we don't follow a script, we are also our own playwrights. In this chapter, we'll explore how we use conversation to tell people about who we are. By focusing on improvised conversations, this chapter explores what some social scientists sometimes refer to as *the social construction of the self*, the process whereby individuals progressively modify and re-invent their public persona. Although many people remain essentially the same throughout their lives, others seem capable of frequently re-inventing themselves. As American society becomes more fluid and mobile, and we're constantly placed in new and unfamiliar situations, we are more likely to feel a need to consciously construct our public self. Theories of self-construction are largely associated with American researchers; it's not surprising that a mobile society like America would have embraced a theory of the self as being creatively constructed. In countries with a more stable social structure, or with a culture influenced by Marxist theory, the self is also thought to be socially constructed, but in a more deterministic way—determined by the structure and relations of the society and the economy.[1]

In conversation, we perform many different kinds of characters each day, presenting different facets of ourselves to family, friends, and coworkers. With the rapid spread of television and film, several theorists have proposed that elements of fictional drama have become built into the rhythms of our everyday lives; for example, children's play episodes almost always incorporate elements from popular culture, as we saw in Chapter 1. In a 1998 book, *Life the Movie: How Entertainment Conquered Reality*, the cultural historian Neal Gabler argued that the social construction of the self has become unavoidably dramatic; with movies and television permeating our experience, we create selves that are influenced by these media, and life has become "the biggest, most entertaining, most realistic movie of all, one that played 24 hours a day, 365 days a year."[2] Gabler argued that these modern developments change the way we think about our own social lives: as drama theorist David Hornbrook wrote, "when we try to make sense of our actions we do so with a consciousness which is *itself* dramatized."[3]

We create different characters to respond to new situations, and to participate in different kinds of conversations. In conversation, we're always responding to the characters of our friends and families; we could even say that they help us to create our characters. In this chapter, we'll explore some of the more creative ways that we enact characters in conversation—the ways that we talk to our children, how we behave when we're playing a part in a religious ritual, and how some people perform "virtual selves" in chatrooms and over electronic mail.

THE CHARACTERS OF EVERYDAY LIFE

Is you real or jest pretendin'?
    —Pogo to P. T. Bridgeport

Most of us can remember engaging in fantasy role play as a child. By enacting the characters of their parents, or of occupations like doctors or firemen, children seem to be rehearsing stock characters from the adult social world. Children often use these stereotyped roles to help structure their improvisational play. For example, in my preschool research I noticed that many children created their own distinctive play characters, and performed them repeatedly. John performed a robot character every day for two weeks, inserting this character into a wide range of play scenarios and locations. One day his robot had dinner in the doll corner; the next day it joined a group of boys on a spaceship travel to space. Jennifer used a plastic duck to perform the dinosaur "Cera" almost every day for two months, introducing this character in the sand table and the block area, in play with both boys and girls.[4]

Children instinctively realize the importance of character to improvisational conversation. Even though everything else about a play drama may be changing—including the location and the pretend activity—the children's play characters remain relatively stable. Enacting a play character provides a stable center for their play, and allows them to focus on other properties of the improvisation.

In improv training classes, actors are taught to establish their characters in the first lines of dialogue, and then to define a relationship between the characters. These are the same first steps taken by those playwrights and novelists who use internal mental characters to help them write. Once characters and relationships are created, the plot emerges from their dialogue. Drama theorist David Hornbrook has observed that stock characters are at the center of most world drama—from the Noh theater of Japan to Indian folk theater—and that improvising drama students often use stock characters as an "instantly recognizable shorthand," often without even realizing they're doing it.[5]

Second City improv theater classes teach students a heavily character-based acting technique called *character work*. Actors are encouraged to create two or three distinctive characters that they can use repeatedly in different improvisations. Because *Saturday Night Live* has its roots in Chicago improv, this is also the way their skits are written—the actors on the show are known primarily for the set of characters they are capable of performing. In the 1970s, John Belushi's Samurai character entered a wide variety of skits; more recently, Dana Carvey's characters included Church Lady and Garth, of Wayne's World.

In its emphasis on characters, *Saturday Night Live* is not so different from the 17th-century *commedia dell'arte*. This improvised Italian theater used a stock set of exaggerated characters, and every play contained roles from the same set of characters. Each character was always played by the same actor, allowing that actor to refine the role, and to develop extended bits of speech or one-liners that could be inserted into an appropriate point in the improvised dialogue.[6]

Although Second City has been successful with its character work, some improv teachers hate this style of improvisation. They claim that strong characters reduce the ensemble dimension of the improvisation, because the actors are enacting their characters rather than listening and responding to the unique features of the scene they enter. Belushi's Samurai character would enter any scene, and start chopping everything in sight with his sword. A comic genius like Belushi can pull this off; but when a mediocre actor does this, the rest of the group gets tired of it pretty quickly. Character-driven sketches are usually less of an emergent, group creation. That's because the actors often try to get quick laughs by enacting stupid or crazy characters, instead of putting their energy into the collectively created dialogue, the clever connections that actors can make between plot threads and events. When an ensemble doesn't use pre-rehearsed characters, the roles in each scene are more likely to be collaboratively created.

Like students at Second City, children at play are learning character acting and improvisation. They're learning how to integrate a character into an improvised dialogue with others. And they're practicing the process of forming a social persona, and experimenting with taking on different characters. In today's world, we have almost unlimited freedom to create our personal characters—especially in America, where it doesn't matter who your parents are or what city you grew up in, you still get to create your own self.

But by the time we reach adulthood, we have pretty much established the characters that define our social persona; we're so comfortable with our selves that we can smoothly shift characters without even noticing. Actors also become comfortable at enacting a specific type of character, and they sometimes find themselves repeatedly being *typecast* in that role as a result. This can become a trap in an actor's career, because each time they play this character type they become better at it, and directors won't hire them for anything else. We too can find ourselves "typecast" by our conversational partners: drawn into playing the same characters over and over. We don't notice that we're being typecast unless we somehow change, so that the old role no longer matches our new self. Then, we find out how stable these typecast roles are—and how difficult it is to act in a way that's different from what everyone expects of us. Even if we try, our actions may be interpreted through the lens of the typecast role that our friends have of us. This is why adults often can't help but behave differently when they visit their parents. We're not always in full control, because our daily characters are created collaboratively, during the performances of creating conversations—and because conversations are collaborative and emergent, conversation has its own dynamic that no one person is ever fully in control of.

Even though we like to think that we create our own characters, many of our daily characters are created to satisfy the demands of a situation that's not in our control. We have to behave in the right way towards our boss, or we won't move ahead in the company. When we get involved with a church service, we are expected to perform the ritual role in the traditional way. When we're engaged in these kinds of collective, organizational behaviors, our everyday characters are more rigidly defined, and they don't allow us as much creativity in how we interpret the character.

PROFESSIONAL CHARACTERS

Executives often project an air of competency and general grasp of the situation, blinding themselves and others to the fact that they hold their jobs partly because they look like executives, not because they can work like executives. They may even attempt to give the impression that their present poise and proficiency are something they have always had and that they have never had to fumble their way through a learning period.
—Erving Goffman, *Interaction Ritual*[7]

There are many professional situations where it's more obvious that performance is involved. These range from business meetings, to political negotiations, to diplomatic encounters. You're more likely to become aware of this when you first start your career—because in spite of your book learning from college, you still need to go through a process of *professional socialization,* a form of apprenticeship in which you learn "how to perform" the right character for the job.

Soon after college, I bought my first business suit, for a consulting job that required meeting with senior executives in New York. It was tough to get through these first few meetings. Around these experienced, hard-nosed businessmen, I felt very much like I was pretending to be a consultant, playing a role in an executive-suite drama. I'd rarely worn a suit before, and never spent any time with business people. I felt certain that all of these executives were pretending too, because they weren't acting like anyone I'd ever met. But they all seemed to be so good at it!

The sociologist Erving Goffman pointed out that we share an unspoken agreement—everyone has to take your performance at face value, and act as if you are who you pretend to be. He called this a "ritual courtesy" that we extend to one another in everyday life.[8] In these first consulting meetings, these senior executives treated me as I presented myself: as a knowledgeable consultant. If I faked it well enough to get through the meeting, they were obliged to go along with me. Eventually, after I did it enough times, the role became natural and I no longer felt like I was pretending. I became the character I was enacting.

To do this effectively, I had to learn the conversational style—the rules of turn-taking, the proper buzzwords and catchphrases, the degree of studied informality that demonstrates confidence and control. This learning process happens in all careers that require people skills—successful executives are talented performers. In large organizations they have to be able to shift among several characters throughout the day—playing one role with a superior, another role with a subordinate who needs to be motivated, yet a third role while negotiating with an outside contractor. Some of the most effective negotiators are aware of the fact that they are role-playing, and are able to use that awareness to strategic advantage, becoming angry or frustrated at will—in a performance that the best actor would envy.

You can be sure that I was extra careful about my language in these meetings. Think back to the last time you were in a formal situation, perhaps at a cocktail party where you were dressed more formally than usual, or in a business meeting with representatives from some other divisions of the company whom you hadn't met before. You probably didn't talk in your everyday casual style; instead, you were more careful than usual, using more formal speech.

In these more formal settings, we often become aware that we're playing a role. Because the roles are so different from everyday life, Goffman observed that formal settings have a ceremonial or ritual quality. He didn't mean that they were religious; but in both religious ritual and in formal settings, there are more rules and constraints on your actions than in casual conversation. People have more expectations of how you will act, and you're usually performing a character that is different from your everyday self.

In this sense, my young executive self was a kind of ritual role, and the business meeting had all of the qualities of a ritual, with its own rules, procedures, and characters. And at first it seemed like a secret society, where everyone there knew what to do. But through repeated practice, by participating in the ritual over and over again, I learned the rules and became more expert at performing the character.

Business performance is a good example of one of the central tensions in conversation—the tension between inner self and social self, the tension between your creative contribution and what the situation demands of you. Like business, many careers require you to manage this complex balance. Courtroom lawyers are expected to speak on behalf of their clients, and they have a professional responsibility to enact a character that believes in their client's case. Businessmen are expected to negotiate for the best terms for their company, even if they come to believe the other guy is getting a raw deal.

That's why several popular high school activities are designed to teach these skills, by using role-playing exercises and games. Role-playing in the classroom can make dry subjects come alive. I remember joining my high-school class for a Model UN field trip to Washington in 1977.

I'm starting to feel old, as I read about the 1990s version of the Model UN, which is, of course, on-line.[9] In one 1996 on-line session, two groups of students are role-playing Russia and the United States. Before they log on, the "Russians" decide on two main goals for the day's negotiations: tell the world that they support disarmament, and sweet-talk the United States into an alliance. Their goals: enhance both their stability and their global profile. Once the on-line performance begins, things quickly diverge from this plan. The "Americans" propose to tie each country's arms expenses to a percentage of GNP. They argue that this helps nations conserve money for basic social needs. The group of Russian students explodes, complaining among themselves how this proposal favors America. But on-line, they maintain a diplomatic speech style, dispassionately replying that this blatantly biased proposal does not further open cooperation between the countries.

Just like my high school in the 1970s, these kids are learning about world politics and about the nature of diplomacy. In our old-fashioned face-to-face version, I think that we learned more about how to improvise a negotiation on the spot, because we had to respond in character, without the luxury of being able to compose an email response. The trade-off is that these kids are also learning a lot about computers: how to log on, how to engage in email dialogue, how to send text files.

Over these 20 years, one important feature of the Model UN has stayed the same—students are learning that diplomats have to submerge their "real selves" to do their job. It doesn't matter what their *personal* reactions are; they have to put those aside, and act rationally and strategically to serve the interests of their government. The effective diplomat is an individual who is a spokesperson for his government. His own, inner self is irrelevant, and, in fact, his personal reactions can potentially interfere with his ability to do the job. Diplomats are most effective when they can create a character that is a personification of their government's policies. If they can't do this, they are expected to resign, rather than allow their own opinions to interfere with their ability to speak for their government.

The ability to bluff is a part of this kind of character performance. The same skills that we value in the diplomat or the negotiator are the skills that help a person win at poker, or make a conman an effective swindler. And perhaps most of all, these skills are required of politicians in today's media age—politicians have to be talented performers. Still, it's hard to trust a politician who seems to be a smooth performer. But like an actor, the politician has to satisfy his audience— the voters—to get re-elected. The merging of politics and performance became personified when the actor Ronald Reagan was elected President in 1980. But it's been going on since TV first presented Kennedy and Nixon as debate performers in 1960.

For better or for worse, most of what we hear politicians say these days is written for them by professionals. Politicians have entire staffs of handlers who become jittery whenever the candidate starts to improvise even slightly on the prepared text. Politicians perform because it works—it gets them the votes. But if they're too scripted—if they say only what their professional consultants and handlers tell them to—it seems like they're not authentic.

This has made us cynical, because we all know that candidates are just saying what they've been told to say. And because the performance is scripted, we assume it's not sincere; we're unhappy if our politicians are no more than actors. Instead, we place a lot more trust in appearances that are unscripted, where the candidate is forced to improvise: the press conference, the debate, the talk show, the town meeting. These improvised, off-the-cuff performances are thought to be more indicative of what the speaker *really* thinks.

On TV, we see the politician as a stage character, scripted by his professional handlers. But we also want to see the *real* self of the politician. In reality, we want both: Even though we want to know the real candidate, we are more comfortable with politicians who are effective performers. Some commentators have suggested that Bill Clinton creatively resolved this tension by being an effective political improviser, by merging his real self with his performed character. This both made him attractive to voters, and at the same time made us vaguely uneasy. Some asked, is it all performance, or is there a real person underneath?[10]

When we watch a favorite actor in a movie, we don't care that the actor's personality isn't the same as his character. We know that movies are collaborative efforts, where the words are written by a playwright and the scenes are controlled by a director. And of course, no one person can run the country alone—the presidency is a collaborative office. So shouldn't we have *more* trust in the carefully scripted statement? After all, it was prepared with days of effort and thought. Wouldn't that be more revealing than some casual, off-the-cuff statement? If not, why not? It's because we tend to regard spontaneity as an index of sincerity, as we first saw in Chapter 1 (pp. 27-28).

The confusion between performed self and real self is often unavoidable, because it's built into many of the performances of everyday life—we often have to balance our inner goals and desires with the performative demands of the conversational situation. As a result, it's often difficult to know where the performed self ends and the "real" self begins. This tension is exaggerated when we have to judge a person based solely on performance situations, such as television appearances or political speeches, but it's the same tension that we find in all creating conversations.

MULTIPLE CHARACTERS

I've spent the first part of the chapter talking about different kinds of characters, and about the unavoidable tension between your public, performed character, and your true inner self. These examples show us how much of our everyday life is performed, and how often the images we develop of other people are based on their conversational performances. We've seen how some careers, such as politics and diplomacy, require a highly developed performance ability. But diplomats aren't doing anything that we all aren't forced to do at some point in our lives; they've just perfected these creative abilities.

The workplace is only one of the many situations of everyday life, and for most of us, one character isn't enough. Most performers can't get through an acting career without being able to perform multiple characters. For example, *Saturday Night Live* actors have to develop between three and five distinctive characters before they can join the cast. And because our social characters are created, performed, and matched to the unique demands of the situation, we often develop different characters for different situations.

Most of us have the feeling that we are slightly different with different groups of people—our children, our colleagues at work, our old college friends. Some of us are more like "social chameleons" than others, having different characters that we perform for each situation; it's almost as if we have multiple roles in our performance repertory. Depending on how complicated your life is, you may have any number of different characters that you perform throughout a day. They probably won't be as distinctively different as an improv actor's characters. But without even thinking about it, most of us switch among our characters all the time, choosing the voice of the character that's most appropriate for the people that we're talking to, or the situation that we're in. The idea that individuals enact roles that are appropriate to a given situation originated with the American psychologist William James, who in 1890 was the first to use the term "self" in the plural—"selves"—to refer to the different aspects of the self.[11] This idea was elaborated in a post-World War II branch of sociology called *role theory*. Role theory is a theatrical perspective on social interaction: The idea is that individuals perform "parts" that are, to some extent, stock characters in their society. Each situation comes with expectations about how individuals will act, and in conversations, people simply act out scripts that are "written by" the culture.[12]

A version of multiple character theory has even made it to prime-time TV. The sitcom *Herman's Head* was released in the Fall of 1991 and lasted 3 seasons. Herman Brooks, the show's main character, is a single young man working as a fact checker in the research department of a publishing company in New York. To all outward appearances, he seems completely normal, but whenever he is faced with making a decision, the camera cuts to the workings inside a room in his brain. As he goes through everyday life, his decisions are made through a dialogue between four conflicting personalities "living inside his head." These characters represent intellect, anxiety, lust, and sensitivity (the only one played by a woman). The four characters debated, argued, and sometimes fought over what course of action Herman should take. The humor of the show comes from the struggle between the different desires and thinking styles of these characters. They represent four different aspects of Herman's personality, and their debates about what to do next, or about how to resolve a moral dilemma, are an inner dialogue that we all recognize. As the opening credits roll, the voice-over states that "The same struggle goes on inside all of us."[13]

Herman's Head is a rare example of a cutting-edge social science theory filtering into the pop consciousness. This idea that we all have "multiple selves" has emerged in fields as diverse as cognitive science, psychoanalysis, and philosophy. The famous artificial intelligence researcher, Marvin Minsky of MIT, released a book in 1985 called *The Society of Mind*,[14] with 270 essays arguing that the best way to explain our behavior is to propose that we all have multiple selves underneath the surface of consciousness, and that our actions result from "conversations" between these "selves." Remember the last time you were watching TV and your stomach started to rumble? You wanted to get up and go to the kitchen, but you didn't want to miss the climax of the episode. If only you can wait for the commercial. . . . Minsky explained this inner tension by proposing that you have a "hunger" self, internally fighting it out with a "TV-watching" self. His book takes this argument pretty far—claiming that it's nothing more than a myth that we think we are each a single, unified self.

Is it only a figure of speech when we say "I don't know what got into him," or "She wasn't herself this morning," or "one part of me wants this, another wants that"? Or is it really pointing to a fundamental property of human nature? Minsky thinks it's not just a figure of speech, and he's got lots of company among social scientists. The anthropologist Katherine Ewing titled a 1990 journal article "The illusion of wholeness,"[15] the psychologist Kenneth Gergen wrote "To be or not to be . . . a single self"[16] in 1967, the French sociologist Pierre Bourdieu titled one article "The Biographical Illusion,"[17] and the computer scientist Mitch Resnick has written of the "decentralized mind," comparing the mind to other emergent phenomena like a flock of birds, an ant colony, or market economies.[18] Plausible or not, *Herman's Head* represents the state-of-the-art in psychological theory.

Several therapists have begun to use this concept, applying their experience with multiple personality disorder (MPD) to healthy, non-MPD patients. This method has been called *internal family systems therapy*, or *cast of characters therapy*. The basic idea is that the therapist helps the patient to personify competing, internal desires and wishes, and to encourage the patient to "voice" as each of these characters in turn, having a conversation with themselves, as it were.[19]

Most of us find these theories a little hard to accept. We might be willing to accept that we behave differently in different situations, but it's a big jump from that to accept that we have different "selves" inside our head. We think, *of course* there is only one person in my head! But these theories are interesting because, if there is some truth to them, then we can begin to think of thought itself as a kind of improvisational performance, an interaction of improvising characters inside one person's head—as with the conversations inside Herman's head. In the same way that a creating conversation emerges from the actions of all of the participants, these theories suggest that our own actions and decisions emerge from the interaction of inner selves, and that the self is an emergent phenomenon. Although the multiple self theory may be counter-intuitive, it's one of the basic assumptions guiding modern research in Artificial Intelligence—Minsky and Resnick represent a large army of researchers studying concepts such as distributed intelligence, large interconnected networks of intelligent agents, and parallel distributed processing.

Because we all develop our personalities in deeply social environments, surrounded by family, engaging in pretend play with other children, all the while practicing for everyday life by improvising conversations all day long, it's not so surprising that our inner selves might mirror the improvisations of everyday social life. If our everyday encounters are improvised, emergent events, then why not thought itself? Indeed, why not our very selves?

Role-Playing Games

"This is the Temple of Malphagoras," says Lee, a professional by day who is now wearing a flannel shirt and an old pair of blue jeans. He is refereeing a friendly session of Dungeons and Dragons in his living room. Around him are eight game players, including his wife Katy. They are sitting around a large table covered with D&D books such as *Monster's Compendium* and *Dungeonmaster's Guide*, scraps of notebook paper, and about 20 white, gray, and black figurines, two inches tall, that look like little monster soldiers. Another group of figures is perched upon the Temple of Malphagoras, which has been built from a few videocassette boxes.

Lee, who is in charge of running the game, is the "Dungeon Master." His role is to act as a director for the rest of the characters in the drama. Each of the eight players is represented by one of the toy figures. D&D is the original and most popular of a class of games that are called role-playing games, because each player is supposed to enact his toy figure as if he were really living and fighting in the fantasy world created by Lee. Lee points to the different toy figures and fills us in on the current state of the drama. "These are the player characters trying to overtake the Temple. These are zombies. These are ghouls. The Temple is ruled by an evil unholy undead monster." The undead monster is too horrible to be represented by a mere plastic toy; Lee shows a picture of the evil ruler that he has drawn.

"We're in combat now." He asks the players what actions they want to take in this battle. "Am I still invisible?" one player asks. The others say he is. Another player asks, "If I'm giant-sized now, can I ascend the Temple in one move?" The Dungeonmaster says "No, you have to fight the ghoul first." During the fight, one player's figure is standing in the way of one of the evil clerics that guards the temple. He's in danger, and Katy shouts "You're radically good and you're standing on his alter!" In fact, all of the players enact good characters. Because Lee is the Dungeonmaster, he controls the evil characters. He announces "The evil cleric shoots a black beam from his hand straight at you. You scream out the name of your deity!" The player rolls a dice, and luckily, rolls a number that saves him from the evil beam.

Role-playing games such as Dungeons and Dragons have grown in popularity since their origin in the 1970s, despite their unshakable nerdy image. After 250,000 copies were sold in 1979, Forbes magazine declared D&D "the hottest game in the nation." By 1991, the company had developed a fantasy fiction division that outsold all competing publishers. These games provide the players with a stage—the fantasy world—where they have a chance to create a fantasy character.

D&D is not like a traditional game, with a board, some pieces, and rules. Instead, the "rule book" is a set of guidelines for loosely structured improvisations, and this improvisationality is what gives D&D its unique appeal. Many aficionados say that the best players are good actors. One DM says "Like a good character actor, they do what their character would do, even if it gets their character killed. They're admired for this—role-playing to the bitter end." He continues, "Role-players have serious insight into their characters and have the ability to project themselves into their characters. They have to be actors."[20]

Because the game requires a group of players, a D&D session is always a collaborative, improvisational performance. The dungeonmaster plays a role similar to the director of an improv theater company, and the best DMs are the ones that help their players achieve more creative and interesting improvisations. The DM creates the setting—the "dungeon"—and the evil characters that provide the conflicts for the players. Most groups of players embellish on the published guidelines, improvising their own unique version of the game. Many groups continue playing together for years, with each person playing the same character in one dungeon after another.

The dungeonmaster is responsible for providing an overall plot for the players. He starts out by giving the players a *campaign goal*—for example, to overthrow an evil ruler. The DM also creates a rough narrative structure for the team, by specifying sub-goals that have to be accomplished along the way towards the campaign goal. The DM is like the writer of a *commedia dell'arte* scene-play—he provides the basic plot outline, but the details emerge from the improvisations of the players.

The best game sessions seem like improvised performances. For example, the players have conversations while they are enacting their characters. They take on the voice of their imaginary character, and perform as their figure, almost like children do at the sand table. Players prefer to play with a talented dungeonmaster, because he is able to create a world where the challenges are perfectly matched to their role-playing skills. These players experience flow; that's why they can go on for hours or even days at a time.

When I was at MIT in the late 1970s, it was the nerdiest of the nerdy who played D&D; since then, role-playing games have spread to a much broader audience. But it remains the case that role-playing games are more popular among people who tend not to be so comfortable with everyday social interactions. I'm not surprised at the popularity of role-playing games, because they provide players with a chance to improvise in a group—without the pressures of performing on stage, or the social anxiety that goes along with performing "as yourself." When you're performing as a character, you get all of the enjoyment of creating conversation, without the stress of having to perform as yourself. For some people, the challenges of everyday conversation are too great for them to be effectively creative—their skills aren't up to it, and instead they experience only anxiety. The fantasy world of D&D reduces the challenges just enough to match their improvisational skill level, and gives the players the opportunity to reach a flow state through improvisation with others.

The popularity of role-playing games like D&D shows us just how important improvisation is for everyone. Even people who are uncomfortable with the improvisations of everyday conversation still need to express the creativity that goes along with group performance— we all have a creative urge to improvise in collaboration with others.

Virtual Characters

With the explosion of the Internet, many on-line role-playing games have spread like wildfire, because you can play a game with people you've never even met without having to leave your computer. These games allow people to create virtual characters in cyberspace. In the Internet worlds that Sherry Turkle describes in her 1995 book *Life on the Screen: Identity in the Age of the Internet,* people are given a chance to create and enact characters on-line, without even the structure that a dungeonmaster provides.[21]

Turkle is an anthropologist and a professor at MIT, known for her studies of computer subcultures. She uses her training in anthropol-

ogy—a field devoted to the study of foreign cultures—to help us understand the uniquely modern subcultures that have emerged around computers. In *Life on the Screen*, Turkle turned her attention to the Internet
and the fascinating "virtual communities" that were beginning to form
without concern for geographic location, age, race, or gender. Because
no one can see you—they only know your online persona—you can
assume a character of your own creation, with no limits. In *Life on the
Screen*, Turkle argued that this new form of self performance is leading
to "a fundamental shift in the way we create and experience human
identity." For example, she described how people reacted to a popular
role-playing game, TrekMUSE, which allowed thousands of players to
participate. The players were allowed to create their own characters and
to interact with any of the other characters, all by typing descriptions
and commands at their keyboards. "This is more real than my real life,"
said one character that Turkle interviewed, who turned out to be a man
playing a woman who was pretending to be a man. In these kinds of
games, Turkle wrote, "the self is constructed and the rules of social
interaction are built, not received." These computer users are engaged in
a new form of improvisational theater, where they create the characters,
the stage sets, and the rules of dialogue, all at the same time.

The Internet technology that makes this interaction possible is
called a MUD, or Multi-User Dungeon. The name indicates the role-
playing connection with Dungeons and Dragons; the first MUDs were,
in fact, fantasy games. As MUDs have spread in popularity to non-game
applications, the acronym is sometimes reported as "Multi-User
Domain" or "Multi-User Dimension." A user who participates in a MUD
enters a virtual space where he can navigate through the space, build or
add on to spaces, and converse with other participants who have
entered the same MUD. As of 1995, there were over 500 MUDs with
hundreds of thousands of participants.

These MUDs are a new stage for creating conversations, and
Turkle compared the MUDs to collaboratively written literature, script
writing, performance art, and improvisational theater. However, there
is a difference: The players become much more closely attached to the
characters that they have created. In a sense, the MUD allows people to
become authors of a new self, constructing this character through on-
line creating conversations. One player said, "You are who you pretend to be." And because there is no limit on the number of different
user IDs a person can login with, many of the (mostly) men that participate in this culture have created multiple characters, each with its own
personality.

The MUD is a particularly dramatic example of how the Internet
provides new opportunities for people to construct and modify their iden-

tities, through different performances of created characters. But even the everyday technology of electronic mail allows you to perform a character. Because so many of my friends also have email addresses, and communication is free, the long-distance phone call and the post office are starting to seem like strangers. With an email message, I have the opportunity to create my on-line performance: I can edit my message as much as I like before I send it out. If I decide I don't want to come across with a certain tone, I can move the cursor up to line 3 and rephrase the sentence. In person, or over the phone, once you've said it, you can't unsay it; but on-line, you can spend as much time as you want "editing your self."

These on-line personas are another example of Goffman's "presentation of self" in everyday life: how we create a role for ourselves and enact this role in our everyday encounters. He used the term *face* for a person's performed image, using the word in the sense it has in the phrase "to save face." Goffman was particularly concerned with the performances that people engage in to keep up this image, to "maintain face" in an interaction, and he studied the characters that individual enact in a social encounter, the impressions they make, and the style of dialogue that they choose to enact this character.[22]

The Internet provides a whole new set of opportunities for us to create characters. Because the performance is all based on words—there is no body language, no facial expression—creating conversations do it all. We have much more control over our performance on-line. First of all, if you don't feel up to participating, you don't have to type anything; in contrast, if you're conversing in person you're still visible even if you're not talking. Your friends can still monitor your reactions, checking your posture, your facial expression, to see what you think about what they say. If you want to stop performing, you have to excuse yourself and leave the group. But on-line, if you don't type anything, you become a peripheral participant (see pages 80-83); in fact, no one has to even know whether you are logged on or not. This peripheral participation is called *lurking*.

On one level, I'm excited about these new styles of creating conversations. Interaction over the Net is a lot like conversation, and it requires almost the same creativity. But there are many critics of the Internet, people who argue that it's destroying our public social life, allowing us to stay at home alone and stare at the screen instead of going out to a bar with "real" people. Likewise, I'm a little nervous that we might lose our ability to improvise in face-to-face interaction if we spend too much time interacting through the keyboard; there's an immediacy to conversation that gets lost in computer interaction. Creating a conversation is a complex skill that we have to practice to stay good at. Although the computer allows us to connect with people in a new way—forming new groups and subcultures—it's no substitute for the performance of everyday life.

On the Internet, we can perform multiple characters, and as multiple-self theory proposes, we might even *be* multiple characters. Now I'll turn to another kind of performance where just the opposite happens—where it takes more than one person to perform a *single* virtual character. This super-character is collaboratively created, with everyone's talk joining in a *group voice.*

Many of us have spent a lot of time watching sports. All of us—men and women both—are familiar with the kind of "spectator talk" that goes on when a group watches a sports event together. Say you're watching a Chicago Cubs game, televised from Wrigley field; after an impressive catch by an infielder, the fans all shout at the TV:

Whoa!
What a catch!
The Cubs kick ass!
Look out, Boston!

It doesn't really matter who says what. Each person is speaking for everyone in the room—in fact, for all fans in TV land. This kind of talk is associated with men; as humorist Dave Barry observed, "The women watched the game; the men actively controlled the outcome by shouting at the screen."[23] The researcher Donald Carbaugh says that sporting events give us a chance to participate in a "collective social identity." After all, this is why you go to the game, instead of staying home where you can see it better on television. When you shout out in a crowd of fans, you are engaging in a very public performance of a distinct, almost ritualized, kind of person; you are participating in the creation of a group voice.[24]

This kind of conversation pattern is also common among a team of players, after a skillful play or a score, and in the locker room, after a game:

Way to go!
Alright!
Get tough!
Good job!

Once again, it doesn't really matter who says what. These are not individualized, personal statements, but rather, exclamations for the entire team.

When we do this, we're all speaking in a group voice. No fan, or player, is enacting a solo dramatic character—instead, they all participate in creating a single group character. The group voice is common in team sports and among team fans, because it serves the function of building solidarity and strengthening group identity. Many sociologists think that this collective group identity is exactly what makes sporting events so important to our national culture.

So many of these examples are found in stereotypically male groups. Why do men do this more than women? In my preschool research, I've found that boys are socialized into this group-voice style of talk as early as the age of three. Among preschool boys, group talk often has a competitive feel to it. In the following group talk that I observed in a preschool classroom, Artie, Eddy, and Muhammed are in the block area. Each of them builds his own rocket using wooden blocks. They are about five feet from each other, and each boy's eyes are focused on his own construction as he speaks. They don't look at each other, except for occasional glances.[25]

(1)	Eddy	I am making a rocket like . . .
(2)	Artie	That's not even a rocket, that's a small rocket
(3)		Mine is bigger than yours
(4)	Eddy	Mine is even bigger, mine smaller than yours
(5)	Artie	You can't even sit on it
(6)	Eddy	I am this...
(7)		make a rocket...
(8)		looks like a rocket, but it's not a real rocket
(9)	Artie	That not a real rocket at all
(10)		(laughs)
(11)	Muhammed	Mine shoots poison in their eyes
(12)	Eddy	Mine shoots poison all the poison in their eyes
(13)	Muhammed	Mine shoots billions and billions of poison in their eyes
(14)		. . . kind of poison
(15)	Artie	Doesn't this look like a dumb rocket?
(16)	Eddy	(laughs as his rocket falls down)
(17)	Artie	I eat lots of food
(18)	Muhammed	I don't need lots of food
(19)	Artie	Yes we do, I have been in space for nine years

I spent a year in this classroom, and in all that time I never saw a girl involved in group voice. If a girl joined a group of boys, the boys would stop talking in group voice, and switch to a different style of conversation.

Could there be a connection between boy's preschool play talk and the ways that men talk while watching sports? Eddy, Artie, and

Muhammed are collaborating to create a group identity. Girls' play is different—their dramas have more complex characters, with more elaborate relationships. That's why we often think that girls' play is more sophisticated. But speaking in a group voice may require its own sort of conversational skill, a social awareness that develops into the classic kind of sports team voice that we see on TV, at the stadium, and in our living rooms.

VENTRILOQUISM

I remember seeing a ventriloquist on TV as a young child. The ventriloquist sat in a chair with a big-headed puppet on his lap. He held the puppet in his right hand, and the puppet's head was by his shoulder. For his performance, the ventriloquist had a "conversation" with the puppet. Like most children, I was amazed at the illusion, because when the puppet spoke, I couldn't see the man's own mouth moving.

A skilled ventriloquist can give a puppet a real personality. Not only does he open and close the puppet's mouth; he also manipulates its eyebrows and turns its head from side to side. In the classic act, the puppet has all of the personality. The ventriloquist plays the straight man and the puppet makes all of the jokes, often by insulting the ventriloquist. This dramatic contrast in personality exaggerates the illusion. We wonder: How could this plain-talking, boring man be the person responsible for creating this wisecracking, irreverent puppet's voice?

One of the classic examples of ventriloquism is from *The Wizard of Oz*. Dorothy and her companions are cowering in front of the huge, frightening Wizard, who is hovering in the air over an imposing altar. Suddenly, the dog Toto runs to a nondescript curtain hanging at the side of the room, barks at it, and pulls it aside with his mouth. The group turns and sees a white-haired man behind the curtain, who quickly glances back at them as he talks into a microphone, while furiously manipulating levers and switches at a console. As they watch, looking back and forth at the terrifying Wizard and then at this harmless man, they hear the Wizard command,

"Pay no attention to the man behind the curtain!"

But they also see that the man is speaking these words into the microphone at the same time. Then the truth dawns on them: They realize that the Wizard is a fraud, only a puppet controlled by this unthreatening old man.

This is a fascinating example of performance, because for a split-second, there are two wizards in the room: The Wizard-Man is a ventriloquist, throwing his voice into the Wizard-Image. What gives this scene its tension and resolution is that the participants start out with different understandings of what is going on. At first, the Man is the only one who knows what is going on. Dorothy's group sees only the frightening performance of the Image. When Toto pulls the curtain there is a brief moment of transformation, when the Image speaks of "the man behind the curtain" but as *if* he is a third role, an irrelevant bystander. There's a brief moment of confusion for Dorothy, when it seems as if both the Man and the Image are speaking. Then it dawns on her that they are speaking exactly the same words. What makes it conversationally complex is that the Image is referring to the Man in the utterance. By speaking in this way, speaking of "himself" in the third person, the Wizard is trying to convince Dorothy that the man behind the curtain really is a different character.

The Wizard is trying to recover from Toto's frame-breaking act, and to incorporate his deception itself into the deceiving frame. We can see that it's a plausible attempt—the Image continues to talk in his powerful, authoritarian tone of voice. Yet somehow it's touchingly inadequate, and sad. Does the man really think Dorothy won't notice that the two speakers are the same? That the "man behind the curtain" is not the animator of the Wizard? In this moment, the movie audience feels sympathy for the old man, preparing us for the next scene of reunion and return.

This scene from the *Wizard of Oz* demonstrates one of Erving Goffman's most important observations: that it's too simplistic to think of a conversation as involving only two roles—as Goffman archly calls them, "the primitive notions of speaker and hearer." In Chapter 3, we explored how complex the "hearer" often is. And in many cases, you also have to examine how the "speaker" is split out into multiple distinct roles. Ventriloquism is a special case that makes this particularly obvious: In Goffman's terms, the puppet is the *animator*, but the words are created by the puppeteer, the *author*.[26]

Ventriloquism isn't only found in the theater. Some of the most creative conversations happen when people "throw their voice" through another object to engage in conversation. For example, we see a kind of ventriloquism everywhere on the Internet, with new technologies allowing us to voice through computer characters. But although the computer gives us many new opportunities to ventriloquize, it's not a new ability—in fact, like so many conversational skills, it begins in children's play. When children play with plastic toy figures, they often throw their voice into the figurines, and speak for them, a type of play talk that I call *indirect performance style.*[27] Sometimes children do this when they're playing alone, because they can manipulate a whole set of characters, creating conversation all by themselves—enacting a play performance by speaking all of the parts.

And groups of children often create an entire play performance by speaking through their favorite toy figures. For an impromptu stage, they use the sand table or a block structure that they've built. Each child manipulates one or two figures. In contrast to role play, where each child performs a role like an actor on a stage, each child is more like a puppeteer, speaking through their toy to enact the play character.

As with all children's play, each child often has a different idea about how the play drama should unfold. If they want to play together, they have to listen and respond to each other, just like improvising actors work together to build a scene. Improvising actors create their performance by staying in character, never breaking the fourth wall. But children can't always communicate a new twist to the play by speaking as their toy figure. For example, if a child wants to spice up the drama by pretending that an earthquake has occurred, the child may step out of character, speaking as a director, and say to the other children, "Let's pretend there was an earthquake." If the other children agree, they can then return to in-character dialogue, working through the drama of an earthquake.

Although stepping out of character interrupts the flow of the play drama, it's often an effective play negotiation technique. And it's exactly this difference with improv theater that makes play so valuable for children. That's because during toy figure conversation, children have to both enact the performance, and at the same time, manage and modify the play drama as it emerges. They have to speak in two voices at once: the voice of their toy figure, and the voice of a director. Once children develop this ability to "double voice," their play conversation quickly gets more complex, because they start blending the two voices together in the same utterance.[28] Here's an example from a sand table play session, where Eddy explicitly suggests a new direction for the play (the director's role), but while speaking in his play character's voice:

(1)   Eddy   And sometimes they would   Speaking as his toy man.
              put us in jail.
(2)   John   No they wouldn't.   Speaking as his toy man.

Eddy is speaking as his toy figure, wiggling the toy up and down as he speaks. And he says "they" would put "us" in jail; by "us," he is referring to the play characters, in the play world, not referring to the boy's real selves. But because he is proposing a new event for the evolving play drama, it's a director-type suggestion. Because the proposal is tentative and explicit, John has the option of accepting or rejecting it. He rejects it by also speaking in character.

Performing at these two levels allows children to experiment with improvisation, helping them learn how to create conversations in an unstructured, unscripted setting. In our everyday lives, we don't have the option of stepping out of character and directing our conversation. Because our everyday conversations are unscripted and undirected, we have to collaborate using the kind of implicit, in-character directing that improv actors do on stage. Children of preschool age can't quite handle this complex, improvisational social skill—toy figure play allows them to practice these skills.

Anthropologists have discovered that children in all cultures engage in improvisational play—it's a universal need. But although improvisational play is universal, there are cross-cultural differences in *how* children engage in creating conversations. These differences in play conversation can give us some unique insights into cultural differences.

The anthropologist Bambi Schieffelin has spent years studying the Kaluli tribe, an isolated cultural group in the mountains of Papua New Guinea.[29] When she went to the rain forest in the 1970s, she decided to try something new. Most anthropologists had been studying "men's issues" such as politics, warfare, and religious rituals; Schieffelin instead studied child-rearing, spending most of her time with mothers and children. She found that Kaluli mothers involve their children in conversations in a very different way from American mothers; Kaluli mothers teach their children how to participate in conversations by using a unique form of ventriloquism. Within a week after birth, Kaluli mothers start to involve their infants in interactions with others. Rather than face their babies, speaking to them in baby-talk like we do, Kaluli mothers face their babies outward so that they are facing the other people in the group. For example, when an older child speaks to the infant, the mother moves the baby, and speaks for it in a special, high-pitched, nasal tone of voice. Just like the ventriloquist's puppet, the child looks as if he is talking to someone while his mother speaks for him.

When children first begin to speak, mothers continue to speak for them, but now they teach the child to repeat what they say. For example, when another adult meets the mother and child, that adult will look at the child and say something to it, even though the young child doesn't yet know how to participate in conversation. The mother will respond to her friend, speaking *as the child,* and then use a special instruction to the child, *elema,* which means "Say it like that." The child then repeats what the mother has said, to the other woman, word for word. The mother is teaching conversation for the child, by providing a model to imitate. Imagine a director trying to get an actor to express a line with a certain tone of voice and emotion, repeating the line with the inflection he wants the actor to use. By supplying infants with a voice—and with a sequence of appropriate lines, before they are capable of appropriately creating conversation—mothers help the children learn how to participate in the improvisations of everyday talk.

In contrast, American mothers almost always face their children and talk directly to them. Our children can't participate in conversation until they've developed the ability to construct their own improvisational responses; they certainly don't participate before they learn to talk. But this Kaluli method of ventriloquizing gets children involved in creating conversations even before they can say a single word.

These contrasts in child-rearing are a reflection of the differences in our two cultures. The Kaluli are much more group-oriented than Americans—they live in small villages where they are rarely alone, and there are always many adults nearby. It makes sense that they would raise their children to be able to engage in group conversation, and that mothers would start to orient their children out towards the rest of the tribe, almost from birth. The tribal village plays a larger role in life than in our individualistic society. Our families are smaller, and each family lives in its own house. American children aren't raised with people constantly walking in and out of the house; they spend most of their time talking to parents or siblings. And adult life is much more compartmentalized and individualistic than the tight-knit villages in Papua New Guinea.

This is an example of a general pattern in social life, as you look around at the world's cultures—conversational differences are often related to cultural differences. And it's not surprising that children would be raised differently, raised in the way that will teach them to participate in the conversational styles of their own culture.

THE REAL SELF AND THE SOCIAL SELF

We often find ourselves in situations where we know we're performing a character. And each of us has multiple characters in our repertoire. We know how to create conversations differently with different types of people—our families or our colleagues—and we may perform different characters in different settings—in a courtroom or in a sports bar. When you realize how many different characters we all enact every day, you realize how incredibly creative we have to be in conversation. While talking, we are managing all of these different roles, and creatively combining and modifying them as the situation requires. We constantly switch character as we go through our day, enacting one character with our boss, another when we call the hardware store, and yet another at home with our family. And at times—in the group voice—we even join together with others to create a single character. Most of us manage all of these transitions smoothly and without having to think that hard about it; it's amazing how quickly we can perceive what's going on around us, and immediately start enacting just the right character.

Our characters are created through conversational performance—this is what Goffman meant by "the presentation of self."[30] But many readers find that Goffman is a little too cynical—implying that all social life is a con game, that no one is ever genuine, that your personality is nothing but a performance. Many social theorists react the same way. The prominent anthropologist Clifford Geertz described Goffman's social world as "an unbroken string of gambits, ploys, artifices, bluffs, disguises, conspiracies, and outright impostures";[31] the moral philosopher Alisdair Macintyre argued that Goffman's theory had no place for morality, writing "for Goffman the central error is to suppose that there is a substantial self over and beyond the complex presentations of roleplaying."[32] Goffman's world view is radically unromantic, and strikes many people as depressing.

Is your socially performed self "really" you? Most of us feel that the *real* you is inside, even while you are performing a character for everyone else. In the yuppie era of the mid-1980s, a spate of self-help books appeared to help us deal with this feeling—the buzzword was the *impostor phenomenon*.[33] But yuppies didn't invent the impostor syndrome. Scott Fitzgerald's 1920s character, Jay Gatsby, performed the character of the old-money playboy, but at his core he was still an insecure Midwesterner from a modest family. Like Gatsby, today's impostors may achieve business success, but they feel that they're only fooling everyone into thinking that they are talented and competent. Inside, they are extremely insecure and feel like it's only a matter of time before the rest of the world discovers their secret: They are only pretending to be talented and successful. These 1980s self-help books all provided the same good advice. If you are capable of pretending to be talented, of acting exactly as a talented person would, then that acting ability itself requires just as much talent!

In many conversations—such as these professional encounters— the character that you perform is more important than how you feel inside. Although this particular self-help fad came and went with the age of the yuppie, the phenomenon reflects an eternal truth, because at some level social life is always a performance. Everyone has been in situations where they felt like they were performing a character. Maybe you were at a formal dinner party with important executives from your company, and you were on your best behavior. Maybe you were meeting your future in-laws for the first time and trying to behave like a suitable son-in-law, hiding the part of your self that wanted to race motorcycles or to live like a pauper in India for a year.

In 1892, William James wrote about the multiple "mes" that social life requires; but he also proposed that there was an inner self, which he called the "I." James argued that the "I" was different from all of the "mes" that an individual performs, but he found it difficult to clarify exactly how it was different. James concluded that the "I" doesn't have an independent existence—it's not a homunculus inside the head—rather, it's nothing more than a stream of consciousness, a series of passing thoughts. His discussion ends with a famous comment: "The thoughts themselves are the thinkers."[34]

Most of us believe that we have a real self inside—not just a series of passing thoughts—and that these different characters are no more than faces that we present to the world. If so, how can we best understand the relationships between our inner self and our socially performed selves? Are we always the same self, deep inside, and just pretending to be a different character in each different situation? It seems that there are two *levels* to our personality: the real, inner level, and the social, performed level. By focusing on conversation, this chapter is about the social level—the characters we perform.

We have a lot of control over our socially performed characters, but we've seen that we're not always in complete control—as when we're typecast by old friends or family, or when we're on the job. Over time, if you keep performing these socially created characters, the performance can start to have an influence on your real self, too. For example, I didn't realize how much my own personality was influenced by everyday performance until I first traveled overseas after college. Before visiting Europe, I didn't think I was a very typical American. In college in the 1970s, I had long hair, wore old clothes, read alternative magazines, and listened to the Grateful Dead. In a rebellious young way, I liked thinking that I was far outside the mainstream of our society. But when I visited France for the first time, I came face-to-face with my own American-ness. I realized that I was hopelessly, deeply American—even my way of rebelling was distinctively American. For example, the Grateful Dead, and the Deadhead scene, could never happen in France.

I had discovered an important and humbling lesson—the culture that you grow up in results in certain kinds of characters and selves. There's no way that I could have simply decided one day to "be French"; the choice was not mine to make. There are many different forces at work in the creation and formation of socially performed characters, and not all of them are under our control. I hadn't only been pretending to be an American character my entire life; I really was an American. The characters that we perform have an effect on the selves that we truly are inside.

To truly understand our selves, we can't look only inside our own heads. We have to look at all of the factors that influence the performance of everyday life—our nation, our subculture, our region, the unique dynamics of our family. My experience in France emphasizes the powerful social forces that influence the construction of the self—the roles that culture, environment, and social context play in the formation of your personality.

Conversation is the medium in which we construct these social selves. The anthropologist and psychologist Michèle Koven recently studied the construction of self in French-Portuguese bilinguals;[35] she reasoned that if your language really does play an important role in the formation of your personality, then a bilingual person might be expected to have two different "selves," a different self depending on the language being spoken. Koven asked her subjects to tell a story about an event that happened to them, first in French, and then to tell the same story again in Portuguese. Afterwards, she interviewed them about how they felt while telling the stories; and she played audiotapes of these stories to other French-Portuguese bilinguals, to find out what sort of messages were being sent implicitly by the storyteller's speech style. In the interviews, her subjects reported the experience of having multiple selves—feeling as if they were different people, depending on which language they were speaking. When Koven played the two versions for other bilinguals, she found that they formed a completely different image of the storyteller, depending on which version they listened to. Koven then linguistically analyzed the story audiotapes, and discovered that the speakers were indeed using "speech styles" that indicated different character types.

These examples show us the importance of the social and cultural context in the performance of self in everyday life. In fact, Koven notes that the experiences of these bilinguals is not fundamentally different from monolinguals—because everyone has to perform multiple selves, in the many different contexts and situations of everyday life. Speech styles and conversational contexts are the topic of the following chapter; we'll examine the social settings of creating conversations, and explore how conversations change depending on the situation.

Chapter 6

Settings

Improv theater groups don't use any props or sets; they create objects by miming them, and they create physical spaces—furniture, walls, doorways—by moving "around" them. The transcript below is taken from the very beginning of a one-hour fully improvised show by the Chicago theater group, Jazz Freddy.

Lights up. MAN carries a chair to front stage right and sits facing audience. He mimes working at a desk—takes a cap off of a pen, opens a book, starts to make underlining motions as he studies the page. He stops to rub his eyes. He then turns the page, and underlines some more. The other 9 actors watch intently from the left and right sides of the stage; the audience is completely quiet. After about 20 seconds, WOMAN stands up from her position at stage left, and walks across the stage to MAN, miming the act of carrying something in both hands, held in front of her:

1	WOMAN:	Here are those papers.	Puts down the "papers."
2		(2 second pause)	She remains standing.
3	MAN:	Thanks	Looks up to face WOMAN
		(2 second pause)	
4		I really appreciate your doing those copies for me.	

5	*A second man, MAN 2, approaches from stage left, also carrying "papers," and stops next to WOMAN.*		
6	MAN 2:	Here are those papers.	Puts down the papers.
7	MAN	Thanks a lot,	Still facing the two
8		You guys have really been great. (2 second pause)	
9		I'm gonna stop booking for now	Closes book on desk.
10	WOMAN:	//OK//	
11	MAN 2:	//Sure// (1 second pause)	
12		I'm gonna go get some more papers.	
13	MAN:	Alright (1 second pause)	He stands up
14		Thanks a lot, I appreciate it.	
15	MAN 2:	You're welcome. (1 second pause)	
16		We mean it.	
17	*(As he says "We," MAN 2 touches WOMAN's arm; woman reaches up her other hand to grasp his hand; they stand holding hands.)*		
18	MAN:	Thanks for being in my corner.	
19	MAN 2:	We always will be.	

In this brief two minutes of dialogue, the actors have created a setting. We know that MAN is working at a desk—using a highlighter as he reads books. We know that he is in a room, in a place where others are available to help him—perhaps an office, or perhaps the study of a house; "more papers" are stored nearby.

But this physical setting is only the tip of an iceberg; we've also learned about the *social setting*—what's going on between the characters. At this early stage, much is still ambiguous, but we can guess that it's late at night, that MAN has two friends—or perhaps colleagues—who are working hard to help him, and that they are working as a team. We also have some idea that MAN 2 and WOMAN may be romantically involved.

Unlike improvisational theater, when you arrive at a conventional theater, the stage is set and ready for the action to begin. Many modern theaters don't use a stage curtain; after you take your seat, you have a few minutes to look over the stage—is it a bedroom or an office? What time period does the furniture represent? This setting gives us a lot of information about what kind of play it is. But as with improv, we don't learn anything about the social setting until the action starts. Is this a formal or an informal situation? Are the characters good friends, or strangers? What meaning does the physical setting have for the actors? Again, we learn about the social setting from the actors' dialogue; their conversation tells us if this a formal or an informal situation, if the characters are good friends or strangers, and who has more power or status.

Creating conversations also take place in physical settings that affect how the conversation flows—in an office or a cafeteria at work, in the kitchen over dinner at home, or in front of a TV in the den. You talk differently waiting at a bus stop, having dinner with your family, and drinking in a bar with your college friends. And as with the theater, the social setting of a conversation is always more important than the physical setting. The social setting includes who is in your group, how much time you've spent together, whether you are joking with each other or are more serious, whether you are waiting for someone else to arrive, what you were doing just before this conversation, or what plans you have made for where you are going to go next. Some settings are more formal, and our conversation is more restrained—think of the annual performance review with your boss. In these formal situations, we probably will speak more carefully and less creatively. But most of our conversations occur in casual, informal situations, where there are no rules about what to talk about, or what to say. In these conversations, we have more opportunities to creatively determine the social setting, and our improvised talk helps to create this invisible setting.

In an improvised performance like the one above, actors work together to create characters, relationships, emotions, events, and a plot for the scene. After only two minutes, they have created the outline of a social setting, and as the dialogue moves forward, they have to stay consistent with that setting. The next few minutes of dialogue, although continually improvised, must now be consistent with the "studying" theme. As the setting becomes progressively more elaborate and detailed, the actors have an increasingly challenging task: to improvise within the emerging structure.

In everyday discourse, this emergent setting also influences how we create our conversations. As the conversation emerges, we are faced with the tension between creatively contributing something new, while remaining consistent with the setting. And we often have to negotiate what the setting is, because different participants may develop different understandings of what is going on. You can't always assume that just because the setting seems obvious to you, everyone else has the same idea of what's going on. Actors describe this by referring to the *POV*, or *point of view*, of a character; in an improv game called "POV" (or sometimes called "Rashomon") the actors re-enact the same scene several times, once from the perspective of each character. The humor of this game comes from the inevitably different perspectives on the social setting.

In this chapter, we'll explore two complementary aspects of the conversational setting, which researchers usually call the *context* or the *frame*. First, how do settings influence our creativity in conversation? We'll see that we create our conversations differently in different settings. Second, how do we create or modify the setting through the conversation itself? By creatively using language, we can often establish what the social setting is—what kind of conversation we're all having, and what sorts of things are appropriate to say. We'll see that there's a constant dialectic between these two complementary influences—we create our conversational contexts, even while being constrained by them. It's been difficult for researchers to get a handle on these simultaneous, twin directions of influence. Most researchers have dealt with this difficulty by focusing only on one half of the dialectic—they focus on either the influence of context on conversation, or they focus on how conversation is used to create context.

The first half—the influence of context on conversation—is the subject of a branch of linguistics known as *pragmatics*. Pragmatics researchers tend to start with the assumption that the context is already fixed, and that all of the participants share an understanding of what it is. This assumption underlies the most prominent schools of pragmatics research, including speech act theory and Grice's theory of conversational implicature.[1] Of course, this assumption holds true in many everyday situations—if you're sitting in a business meeting at the office, it may be perfectly clear to everyone what the setting is.

But there are many everyday conversations where the context is not fixed in advance, where it has to be created and negotiated by the participants. Conversation researchers have more recently started to examine the second half of the dialectic—the ways that context emerges from an ongoing conversation. Dick Bauman and Chuck Briggs describe this new line of research as a shift "from context to contextualization," with the term "contextualization" emphasizing that context is created through a continuing, collaborative process.[2]

In this chapter, I'll try to put these two perspectives together, showing the complex, dynamic processes whereby conversation creates the setting, at the same time that the setting is influencing the conversation. It's a complicated dialectic, and understanding this two-way relationship is perhaps the biggest problem facing conversation researchers.

FORMAL AND INFORMAL CONVERSATION

One thing that stands out about the Pogo comic strip is Walt Kelly's clever use of distinct lettering for each characters' words. We all know that the fancy lettering goes with a fancy way of talking. In one strip from 1950, Deacon Mushrat—whose dialogue is always printed in old-English script—comes upon Albert the Alligator chasing a puppy, who has stolen his hat:[3]

Albert: Aaargh! You li'l varmint—you is chewed up my hat!
Deacon: 𝕯𝖊𝖘𝖎𝖘𝖙! 𝕻𝖚𝖗𝖘𝖚𝖊 𝖓𝖔𝖙 𝖙𝖍𝖎𝖘 𝖕𝖔𝖔𝖗 𝖚𝖓𝖋𝖔𝖗𝖙𝖚𝖓𝖆𝖙𝖊 𝖞𝖔𝖚𝖙𝖍–𝕺𝖍, 𝖘𝖕𝖆𝖗𝖊 𝖙𝖍𝖊 𝖗𝖔𝖉!
Albert: But look at my hat—Deacon Mushrat!
            (*Deacon picks up and pats the puppy*)
Deacon: 𝕳𝖆𝖛𝖊 𝕮𝖍𝖆𝖗𝖎𝖙𝖞, 𝖒𝖞 𝖋𝖗𝖎𝖊𝖓𝖉–𝕿𝖊𝖒𝖕𝖊𝖗 𝖞𝖔𝖚𝖗 𝖜𝖗𝖆𝖙𝖍 𝖜𝖎𝖙𝖍 𝖐𝖎𝖓𝖉𝖓𝖊𝖘𝖘–𝕺𝖍, 𝕴 𝖘𝖆𝖞, 𝖞𝖔𝖚𝖗 𝖍𝖆𝖙 𝖎𝖘 𝖆𝖘 𝖓𝖆𝖚𝖌𝖍𝖙 𝖈𝖔𝖒𝖕𝖆𝖗𝖊𝖉 𝖙𝖔
            (*At this point, the puppy grabs his tie, jumps down, and runs*)
Deacon: 𝕲𝖔𝖔𝖉 𝕲𝖗𝖆𝖈𝖎𝖔𝖚𝖘! 𝕸𝖞 𝕮𝖗𝖆𝖛𝖆𝖙!
            (*Deacon begins chasing after the puppy.*)

The rural South is known both for its dialects and its deep awareness of social class distinctions, and Kelly captures these with the eye of a sociolinguist. When I read a Pogo comic strip, I can almost hear the voices of the characters—speaking formally, casually, or sweetly. Kelly's different lettering lets us know that the residents of Okefenokee are talking in different speech styles.

Most of the time we never think about the speech styles that we're using. When we do notice different speech styles, it's often when we're speaking with an unusual level of *formality*, like with Deacon Mushrat's Old English script. A formal speech style usually goes with a more formal social setting. For example, when I meet someone, I can say either "What's up" (informal) or "How are you tonight" (formal). The words mean the same thing; choosing to speak more formally is a choice about speech style, not about the meaning of the message itself. Because speech style is communicated by the overall structure of your words, rather than their literal meaning, it's an example of what I called in Chapter 2 *speaking poetically*.[4] Speaking formally is a poetic use of language, because you're communicating more than what's on the surface of the words. Because speaking formally indicates something about the setting, it's also an *indexical* use of language.[5] By choosing to speak formally, I send the indexical message that "This is a formal conversation" or "This is a formal situation."

Informal conversation seems more natural to most people, and we're more likely to feel like we are being ourselves. In contrast, in a formal setting, we feel like we have to act polite and watch our language—if you want to say "damn," instead you might do a formality check and translate to "darn" in such a setting. All this monitoring of our language takes effort—that's why you feel like you can't be yourself. When I was in my first job just out of college, I remember taking my girlfriend to the company holiday party. It was a small company, and I introduced her to just about everyone, including the president, a rather formal man who was from Europe. I still remember how odd it was when the three of us were talking. With the president standing there, even when I said something to my girlfriend, it was more formal than I would have normally been; it seemed stilted and unnatural. I became very conscious that, in a way, we were performing for the president.

Such situations pose additional linguistic challenges for speakers whose native language is not English, or who speak a non-dominant version of English. The sociolinguist John Gumperz analyzed discourse strategies in speakers who are fluent in more than one language *code*: a dialectic, speech style, or even a different language. For example, Gumperz pointed out that among English-Spanish bilinguals, Spanish is typically associated with in-group and informal activities, and English is associated with more formal, stiffer, and less personal out-group interactions. If I normally spoke Spanish with my girlfriend, and was forced to speak English with her in front of the company president, my feelings of "performance" would have been even more extreme.

Gumperz analyzed many example of speakers creatively using multiple speech styles. Often, speakers use each speech style to speak to a different audience. The following example was observed by Gumperz in the mid-1970s:

> Following an informal graduate seminar at a major university, a black student approached the instructor, who was about to leave the room accompanied by several other black and white students, and said:
> a.   Could I talk to you for a minute? I'm gonna apply for a fellow ship and I was wondering if I could get a recommendation?
> The instructor replied:
> b.   O.K. Come along to the office and tell me what you want to do.
> As the instructor and the rest of the group left the room, the black student said, turning his head ever so slightly to the other students:
> c.   Ahma git me a gig! (Rough gloss: "I'm going to get myself some support.")

Gumperz then played an audiotape of this encounter to black and white students, and asked them what accounted for this code switch. Most whites felt that this final comment implied a rejection of the white instructor and of the academic enterprise. But blacks had a more subtle and complex interpretation of the encounter. They argued

"He was trying to justify himself; he was appealing to others in the group, as if to explain his earlier remarks by suggesting 'I'm still in control,' 'I'm just playing the game'." They pointed out that, in fact, graduate students of this speaker's background do not talk that way; in (c) the speaker used an exaggerated form of black English that he usually didn't use, thus distancing himself from his own words even further, and again conveying the impression that he is in control and knows what he's doing.[6]

People often use different codes and speech styles in groups of three or more people. For example, whenever you and a close friend are in a group of more casual acquaintances, you can't use the informality and the shorthand you would normally use with each other, because the others in the group would be left out. I'm particularly aware of this when we have a foreign visitor, someone whose English isn't very good. Even though I might be talking to my American friend, I'll slow down and avoid slang so that our foreign guest can follow along; we end up speaking in a very different style than we usually do together.

Like Molière's Monsieur Jourdain, who was surprised to find out that he had been speaking in prose, we are usually unaware that we are speaking in a speech style. Many of us talk using the same style as all of our friends and family, so that we go through most of our lives speaking only one style. And if your home language is standard English, you'll probably use the same speech style at work and at home. But nondominant groups—like Gumperz's examples—have to be more attuned to these speech styles. And many other cultures are more attuned to speech styles than Americans, because they are expected to use different speech styles in different social settings.

For example, of all the advanced industrial economies, Japan has perhaps the most elaborate system of speech styles.[7] Most Japanese statements can be expressed in any one of six or more different speech styles—each with a unique combination of grammatical features and word choices—that indicate degrees of politeness, the degree of humility of the speaker, and the degree to which the subject of the sentence is being honored. No Japanese sentence is completely neutral; a speaker is forced to make decisions about the speech style, for even the simplest of statements.

The choice of one style or another depends on a whole range of features of the situation. Japanese speakers talk differently with people who share some social connection with them—for example, colleagues at the same company, or graduates of the same college. Sharing membership in a peer group has a pervasive influence on speech styles. For example, if you're talking to someone *outside* your social group, you will speak more formally if the topic of conversation is another member of your group than you will if you're talking about a stranger. But there's no universal rule for how this works—the rules vary from one group to another. For example, when University faculty talk to non-faculty about their colleagues, they tend to be more formal than business executives talking about other executives in their company. And there are many other subtle rules that all Japanese know intuitively. They speak more politely to a stranger than to an acquaintance, and more politely over the phone than in person, all other things being equal. These conventions are followed differently by young and old, because Japan has become progressively more egalitarian since World War II.

How does anyone ever figure out how to talk, with so many choices? Indeed, it turns out that the system is so complex that not all Japanese can master all of the proper speech styles and their rules of usage; some people are better at it than others. The Japanese feel that it's a mark of good education and good upbringing if you know how to use the more elaborate, more deferential expressions. In fact, many educated Japanese use the polite forms simply to indicate that they know how, to demonstrate how cultured and educated they are—even if a less polite form would be technically more appropriate. Speaking in a certain style can end up saying more about the speaker than about the setting, and English speakers do this too—that's why we laugh at Pogo's Deacon Mushrat, who speaks formally even though he's in a backwater swamp.

With Japan's increasing economic and political importance, more and more Europeans and Americans are learning their language. However, non-native speakers are taught a more-or-less neutral speech style, and we're allowed to use the same speech style in all situations without anyone getting offended. But native speakers of Japanese cannot do this without being considered low-class, poorly educated, or just plain rude.

Japanese is one of the most formal languages of any industrialized country. But many European languages have a similar type of formality built into the grammar—they have at least two different words that both mean "you." In your first year of high-school language study, you learn about these "formal" and "informal" pronouns. For example, French has two pronouns that both translate to "you": *tu*, the informal, and *vous*, the formal. French is like other European languages, in that the formal pronoun is also used as the plural. You have to use *vous* if you're talking to a group of people, even if it's an informal setting. My high-school French teachers taught me a simple rule, that you should always use "vous" when you first meet someone. So when I made some French friends just after college, I started using *vous* with them. This made them uncomfortable; they teased me about being so formal and assured me that they used *tu* with all their friends. So why did my high-school teacher get it wrong? It's because these rules change from generation to generation. My French friends told me about 80-year-old Parisian women, who had known each other all of their lives, who still exclusively used *vous* with each other. People of this older generation still considered it vulgar and rude to use *tu* with someone that they respect. But my French friends told me this story to emphasize that only old people spoke this way. Of course, just because these young French people used *tu* with each other doesn't mean they've stopped using *vous* altogether—although the rules have changed, they are just as complicated as they ever were.

A lot of interesting social dynamics is played out through the use of these pronouns. The French language even has two special metatalk verbs to refer to these different ways of talking: *tutoyer* means "to use *tu* with someone," and *vouvoyer* means "to use *vous* with someone." Imagine if we had a verb in English, "to formal" someone, meaning "to speak formally to" someone.[8] Although English doesn't have a formal speech style that is encoded in the grammar, we've already seen that many English speakers have different speech styles in their repertoire. These speech styles tend to fall along a single dimension, from polite or formal at one end, to casual or informal at the other.

The setting doesn't always make it obvious which speech style should be used. In these more ambiguous situations, the selection of a speech style creatively communicates a specific idea of what kind of interaction is going on. Gumperz documented several situations where speakers creatively negotiate the setting through the selection of a speech style.

> A graduate student has been sent to interview a black housewife in a low income, inner city neighborhood. The contact has been made over the phone by someone in the office. The student, who is also black, arrives and rings the bell, and is met by the husband, who opens the door, smiles, and steps towards him:
>
> Husband: So y're gonna check out ma ol lady, hah?
> Student: Ah, no. I only came to get some information. They called from the office.
>
> (Husband, dropping his smile, disappears without a word and calls his wife.)[9]

The student later reported that the interview that followed was stiff and quite unsatisfactory. Being black, he knew he had blown it by failing to recognize the husband's speech style and to respond in kind. Instead, he was intent on following his methodological training and doing well in what he saw as a formal interview. Using an "in group" speech style, the husband was attempting to creatively define the encounter in one way; the student's response—in formal, standard

English—creatively selected another definition of the encounter, in effect rejecting the husband's opening move.

The code switches documented by Gumperz have some of the flavor of the subtle messages that can be sent by creative selection of a formal or informal pronoun. Gumperz referred to these messages as *contextualization cues*—by choosing a speech style, a speaker sends a message about what kind of speech context this is. Some of my favorite examples of the social dynamics of formal and informal pronouns are taken from the Russian language, which has the two pronouns *ty* or *vy*, used in almost the same way as the French *tu* and *vous*. The linguist Paul Friedrich has identified some wonderful examples of dialogue in the Russian novels of Tolstoy, Dostoyevsky, and Gorki. In these conversations, status relations are negotiated implicitly through the creative selection of *ty* or *vy*.[10] Russian novelists are masters at communicating drama through well-timed shifts in pronoun usage, and it's very hard to communicate these subtleties in English translation.

Russian speakers can step out-of-frame and explicitly metatalk about these pronouns. For example, in Dostoyevsky's novel *Village of Stepanchikovo*, there's a telling bit of dialogue between a man and an upper-class woman, Foma Fomich. The man asks, "Aren't *ty* joking, Foma?" She is offended by the informal pronoun and the use of the first name both. She haughtily replies, "In the first place, I am not *ty* . . . but *vy*, and don't forget it. And I am not Foma, but Foma Fomich."

These two simple pronouns can be used to mean so many things more than social status. There's a famous scene between Dunja and Svidrigailov at the end of *Crime and Punishment*. Svidrigailov is extremely intelligent but also psychopathic, and has fallen hopelessly in love with a young woman. They had been neighbors in the country, and when they meet again in Moscow, they use *vy* with each other, as was normal for two members of the gentry during the early stages of courtship. Eventually, he lures her into his apartment, but continues to use *vy* even when declaring his love for her. She tries to escape, but finds the door locked. He says "*Vy* are agitating yourself in vain." At this point, because she is excited, Dunja switches to *ty*: "*Ty* open the door immediately, base man . . . so this means rape!"

But Svidrigailov continues with *vy* while he explains that, since they are alone, she would never be blamed for surrendering to his advances, and that in any case, no one would believe her story about rape. At this point, Dunja pulls out a small revolver. Svidrigailov shouts, still using *vy*. Dunja starts to yell, switching to *ty* a second time as she accuses him of being responsible for his wife's death by poison: "*Ty*! Ty hinted it to me yourself." After being called *ty* many times in this accusation, Svidrigailov also switches to the informal, saying, "Even if it were true, *ty* were the reason." They continue to use the informal while she shoots him, but when she misses Svidrigailov switches back to *vy* to scoff at her. When the pistol misfires the second time, she tosses it away, and Svidrigailov approaches and puts his arm around her waist. Trembling, she says "*Ty* let me go."

Dostoyevsky, the narrator, himself makes a metatalk comment at this point: "The *ty* was not being pronounced as it had been a moment before," meaning that this time, Dunja's use signals hatred and disgust rather than excitement. Switching to *ty*, he quietly asks, "So *ty* don't love me?" His *ty* is not one of disgust, but of intimacy. Never, she says. At this, Svidrigailov releases her, stands still for a moment, and then hands her the keys to the door, saying "*Vy* take them, go away fast!" Shortly after, he commits suicide.

This brief but tragic scene covers only four pages, with the pronouns shifting four times. These shifts show how these two pronouns can be used to create and negotiate the setting, to propose and reject differing ideas of what is going on in the situation. Dunja's three switches to *ty* mean three different things: terror the first time, contempt the second time, and hatred the third time. In contrast, Svidrigailov's two switches to *ty* signify intimacy, and are attempts at seduction. This is a wonderful example of how speakers can use language creatively to define the setting as a particular social situation, or to negotiate their social relationship. Svidrigailov uses *ty* to propose that they are lovers, although Dunja has never agreed to this and continues to use *vy* to keep her distance. When she does switch to *ty*, it is not as a lover, but to insult him as a base and evil man.

In this scene the speakers are not using some simple formula to decide whether *ty* or *vy* is more appropriate for their setting—every shift has its own unique meaning. This is an example of a general fact about speech styles in conversation: The speech style that we use is rarely an obvious choice. Instead, every situation provides us with a range of speech styles that could be appropriate. Creative speakers know how to choose from among the many available styles, to match their goals and to match who they're with. And the choice helps to create the social setting. In the same way that the dialogue at the beginning of a play tells us a lot about the setting, the initial lines of our creating conversations are often used to create or subtly modify what kind of social setting we're in. Through your choice of a speech style, you creatively negotiate whether you are lovers or co-workers, cultured members of the upper class or regular guys, arguing or simply having a polite discussion.

Of course, English doesn't have formal and informal pronouns; but, as Gumperz documented, we nonetheless can negotiate the social setting through the creative use of speech styles. Gumperz's examples tend to be of speakers using radically different speech codes, as different as two different languages, but speakers are incredibly sensitive to even subtle shifts in speech style. Michael Silverstein, an anthropology professor at the University of Chicago, tells a story about English speech styles in his legendary course on language and culture. He and his wife were taking a taxi home from an evening downtown, and they lived on the opposite side of town from the campus. The professor and the cab driver were engaging in the usual small talk you might have in that setting—in a very informal style, the driver speaking in a working-class voice, with a liberal amount of slang. I doubt that women talk to taxi drivers as frequently; the usual effect of such conversations is to reflect an egalitarian masculine solidarity, because many Americans are uncomfortable with such obvious status asymmetry.[11] Often such conversations are about the universal conversational topic that crosses class lines: sports.[12] Halfway through their ride home, Silverstein said he was a professor at the university.

Instantly the cab driver completely changed his speech style. He explained—dropping his working-class slang and using extremely polite language—that he was a graduate student at the same university, working his way through school. He was quite educated in fact, and to compensate for his earlier performance as an "ordinary taxi driver" he began to speak in very correct, deferential language, addressing Silverstein as "Professor" for the remainder of the ride. Of course, he was right to speak casually at first—no one wants a cab driver to put on airs. But after finding out that they played such asymmetrical roles within the hierarchical structure of the university, the taxi driver decided that it was inappropriate to use a speech style that assumed solidarity or equal status.

If this scene had been played out in Paris, the taxi driver would have shifted from *tu* to *vous*. But even though we don't have a *tu*/*vous* contrast, we use different speech styles to communicate the same social information in our conversations. The taxi driver felt he had been rude to use such a casual speech style with one of his own university's professors, and indicated the asymmetrical status of their relationship—and his inferior position—by switching to a formal speech style. The professor, occupying the higher-status role, was not required to use the formal speech style, and Silverstein didn't change his speech style during the cab ride; the informal style that he used with the "cab driver" is the same one he would use with the "student." This asymmetry in usage is found all over Europe; in French, a higher-status person can use *tu* even while being addressed as *vous*.

At one level, the cab driver's style shift was an attempt to show the proper respect and politeness. But on a deeper level, his shift showed that he was an educated individual, one who was capable of speaking in the more formal speech style. Recall that educated Japanese often use a more formal speech style than is necessary. Because it takes education and sophistication to use it properly, the fact that you *can* use it sends a message about you—when the cab driver switched to a formal speech style, he was demonstrating that he was more than just a cab driver.

Because English doesn't have two different second-person pronouns, it's perhaps less obvious when we're speaking formally or informally. But Professor Silverstein's cab ride shows us that we can't avoid doing the same types of things with our everyday conversation. One of the ways that we indicate formality is the way that we address a person—for example, the cab driver addressing Silverstein as "Professor." Titles like "Doctor" and "Professor" are called *honorifics*. Compared to many other languages, English speakers' use of honorifics is quite sensitive to setting. American graduate students who address their professors as "Dr. So-and-So" in the office will switch to first name at a party or a picnic; but Japanese and Korean speakers, in contrast, never change their speech style to their professors, no matter how informal the situation is.[13] By American standards, the cab driver has selected a relatively exaggerated use of the honorific "Professor," a choice creatively made to emphasize his embarrassment and his apology.

We have many other ways of naming the people in our lives: first names, last names, nicknames, *kin names* like "son" and "Dad." Choosing one of these names indexically communicates something about your relationship with the listener. The Harvard Medical School professor Dr. Alvin F. Poussaint, who is African American, tells a story about being stopped by a white policeman in 1967. The policeman walked up to his car window and asked:

"What's your name, boy?"
"Dr. Poussaint. I'm a physician."
"What's your first name, boy?"
"Alvin."[14]

This negotiation about what name should be used shows how important and strategic the choice can be. The policeman insults the professor by referring to him as "boy," and by refusing to use the prestigious honorific that his position warrants. Everyday conversation has many more innocent examples. For example, only your parents will address you using your first, middle, and last names all at once; if one of your friends does it, it always invokes the image of a parent's admonishment. In my university, the students refer to me as Dr. Sawyer, but I am expected to call them by their first names. This asymmetry of address corresponds to an asymmetry of status, and the norms vary among universities, primarily along East Coast-West Coast lines. It's known among professors across the country that in California, students call professors by their first names. In fact, the professors insist on this to avoid seeming like authority figures. Mutual use of first names—an informal style—indexes equality and solidarity.

Why is English the only European language that doesn't have formal and informal pronouns? In fact, English used to have the same two pronouns; many of us have had the experience of reading the Bible and encountering the old-fashioned pronouns *thee* and *thou*. No one uses these anymore except the Amish. But English speakers used to use *thee* all the time, along with *you*; we used them in the same way that the French still use *tu* and *vous*, as informal and formal pronouns. Note the first letter of the obsolete pronoun: *t*. Just like the French *tu* and the Russian *ty*, that's the clue that these no-longer-used pronouns were the informal pronouns. (Why do we hear these in church so much? I'll get to that in a minute.)

We've already seen some examples from French and Russian of how these different pronouns are used in different situations. The most simple rule is that you use the formal pronoun if you're talking to someone who has superior status to you. You can only use the informal if you're speaking to a subordinate, like an employee or a servant. Even without the pronouns, we still have this distinction in many parts of America; service employees, such as high-rise doormen or office secretaries, are often addressed by their first names, whereas the building residents or the executives are addressed by their last names, preceded by Mr. or Ms. In this case, the two speakers in a conversation are of asymmetric status, and are using different names to address each other.

If you are roughly the same status, how do you decide whether to use informal or formal? To explain this decision, the linguists Brown and Gilman identified a second principle, *solidarity*. You can use informal together if you are in the same social group: buddies, coworkers, immigrants from the same country. You may start out using formal with a new acquaintance if you have no common bond; but later, you might switch to informal, once you become sufficiently good friends. These pronoun shifts can carry many different meanings—in post-war France, for example, mountain climbers who used *vous* with each other would shift to *tu* once they reached a certain critical height on the mountain; it was almost as if this was the point where their lives began to depend on each other, perhaps the extreme example of solidarity.[15] These rules vary widely around the world and in different social groups—for example, in highly class-stratified societies, the formal style may always be used among upper-class friends, simply to signify their superior status.

The solidarity principle explains why we use the informal in prayers—to indicate the intimacy of the relationship with God. That's why there is so much use of the informal—thee and thou—in the Bible; it turns out that in all European languages with two pronouns, the informal is used to speak to God.

Why did the informal fade from use in England, while it remained in the languages of the European continent? And why did we keep the formal pronouns, and not the informal ones? The historical story shows how complicated language change can be. It all resulted from the Protestant reformation sweeping Europe in the 17th century. In England, one of the most successful of the new Protestant churches was The Religious Society of Friends, sometimes known as the Quakers. They believed in a radically egalitarian view of society, inspired by their belief that all men were equal before the Lord. This was revolutionary at a time before the Declaration of Independence and the American Revolution. The founder of this church, George Fox, insisted that all Quakers use a type of speech that he called *Plain Speech*, and this required saying "thee" to everyone. Thus, as a matter of religious principle, Quakers refused to use the formal "you" with anyone in a superior position, as was expected at the time. For the new convert to the Society of Friends, the universal *thee* was especially difficult. For example, sons that had spoken the formal *you* with their fathers their entire lives now were required to start using *thee,* and needless to say, the fathers weren't happy about it. And imagine how much worse it must have been when a Quaker had to go to court or before a representative of the King, and insisted on using the informal pronouns.

Well, this all sounds downright American! Why aren't we all using thee and thou, just like the Quakers? During the French revolution, *tu* became the preferred standard form among *citoyens,* for the same egalitarian reasons the Quakers chose it. All of my young French friends insist on using *tu* with each other, because the formal seems stuffy and old-fashioned. So why did the English settle on the formal pronoun? It probably resulted from a popular backlash against the Quakers, who were ahead of history's democracy curve; they were perceived to be extreme radicals, and most of the English just thought they sounded rude. It got to the point where a non-Quaker couldn't use the informal pronoun without people thinking *he* might be a Quaker, too. Gradually, the informal pronouns died out in England, and remained in use only among Quakers.[16] The Amish continue to use thee and thou with each other, for the same reasons the Quakers started doing it over 300 years ago; however, even the Amish use these pronouns only with each other, and say "you" to outsiders. They've realized that the pronouns don't have the social class connotations that they once had, so it's no longer an important religious issue.

In an indirect way, the Society of Friends accomplished their goal—English no longer has a two-level pronoun system. But three centuries later, we still indexically communicate status asymmetries with our conversation—as we've seen in our examples. With or without special pronouns, speech styles are always used to send important social messages about the setting, and about who we think we are. As with most indexical poetic uses of language, using speech styles effectively requires amazing conversational creativity.

RITUAL AND IMPROVISATION

Various theories have been proposed to explain the origin of drama, but the most widely held theory is that drama evolved from ancient religious rituals. Even the most modern, avant-garde theater is connected to these prehistoric rites and religious practices. Rituals are performances; our churches are the theater. Like theater, churches have a stage in the front, and a cast of regular characters—the priest, minister, or rabbi and assistants—who enact the ritual. Like theater, rituals often have a script that specifies what everyone should say. For example, most American weddings are entirely scripted. We have an intuitive sense that the most important uses of language are found in such ritual situations.

Goffman argued that much of our everyday discourse is ritualized, as well, with a ceremonial aspect that reflects the individualistic culture of America: "Many gods have been done away with, but the individual himself stubbornly remains as a deity of considerable importance."[17] In the little rituals of everyday discourse, we show our respect for our partner's individuality. Of course, our everyday conversations are much more improvised than a religious ritual; but some everyday situations are more formal—job interviews, dinner with the boss—and our talk becomes more structured and more scripted. In these situations, when we aren't as improvisational, we could almost say that our conversations become *ritualized*—because our speech style takes on the characteristics of formal, ritual speech.

Anthropologists have discovered four universals in ritual speech that can help us understand the relationship between ritual and everyday discourse. First, the speech styles that are the most highly valued in a culture—those used in the most important rituals, such as weddings or funerals—are almost always the *least* improvised—they are formal and scripted. Improvisational genres are the least valued, and this explains why we often fail to take everyday conversations seriously. This bias against improvisation seems to be a cross-cultural universal.[18]

One example of this universal pattern is found in th‹ tory of Bedouin Arabs in Yemen. These nomadic tribes ha٢ ent genres of performed public oratory, and they are each very different. One is highly improvised and collaborative, one is completely scripted, and one falls in between these extremes. *Balah,* the most highly improvised of the three, is performed competitively by a group of men; it's a group improvisation. It's often performed at weddings for entertainment. The *balah* is like a modern-day poetry slam, or like the "dozens" of African Americans, because the poets compete by spontaneously composing lines of verse to see who can outsmart the other guy. The lines are never written down in advance. At the other extreme, *qasidah* is the most highly valued type of performance, and it's usually composed in advance by the speaker. *Qasidah* is the pinnacle of oratorical art and only the best poets can compose it, whereas many poets can perform *balah.*

When the tape recorder was introduced to Yemen, the Yemeni immediately began recording and circulating the best *qasidah,* but *balah* was not considered valuable enough to be recorded. Following the universal pattern, the scripted style is highly valued, and the more improvisational style is not thought to be very important.[19]

A second cross-cultural universal is that the language used in ritual situations is also extremely poetic. In ritual language, poetic devices—overlapping and interweaving—reinforce the meaning of the words. An interesting fact about these multi-layered poetic texts is that it's very difficult to change them without destroying the structure on at least one of the levels, thus reducing the overall effectiveness of the text. It's almost impossible to improvise on a very poetic text—you can't modify it without messing it up. The poetic structure of both ritual language and formal language contributes to its stability over time; this partly explains why rituals often use archaic speech, or why formal speakers sometimes sound old-fashioned.

A third cross-cultural pattern is that the most improvised form of performance is also the most collaborative: For example, in *balah* there is always more than one poet, and always in a competition. And *balah* reveals a fourth universal pattern: The most improvised form has the most audience participation. For example, *balah* poets are carefully monitored by the audience, and by each other to make certain they follow the rules of the game. These four patterns of preferences are found around the world, in all cultures that have both formal and informal verbal performance.

These four universals also apply to genres of musical performance. In ritual and formal settings, we find music that is more composed and structured, and in informal everyday settings, we find music that is more free-form and improvised. We can see this pattern right here in America, where our most improvised music, jazz, has received much less respect than classical music. And jazz is consistent with the other three universals as well: It's the most improvised, it's the most collaborative, and it's based on more audience participation than classical music.

Comparing performance across cultures leads us to an interesting question: Do some *cultures* encourage more creative improvisations in everyday life? That is, would a more uptight, formal cultural group be less improvisational throughout their lives, than a less formal cultural group? Would a group that has memorized a lot of cultural scripts, and uses them in everyday life, improvise less than another group that has no scripts?

Americans—and English speakers in general—are often said to be uninterested in verbal creativity. English speakers value clarity in speech over artistry—we say "just the facts," "get to the point," "what's the bottom line?" These preferences have found their way into many Anglo-American theories about conversation; Grice's theory of conversational implicature emphasizes clarity, brevity, and efficiency, and Austin's speech act theory focuses on explicit speech acts even though most everyday speech acts are indirect.[20] These theorists are just reflecting cultural assumptions that all English speakers share; we're suspicious of the rhetorical flourish, of those who speak with poetic license; we think it must mean they're trying to hide the fact that they have nothing to say.

In contrast to English-speaking cultures, anthropologists have found that many other cultures value verbal artistry. Some have even proposed that some cultural groups use a more improvisational style in their lives. Which types of people use more improvisation? Most researchers think that it's the people who have less money, fewer material advantages in life, and less access to power in a society. This research suggests that such people are required to improvise more just to get through life. If you have money and connections, the thinking goes, you can take advantage of these resources, rather than being forced to creatively improvise.

If everything that you need or want is available just for the asking, then you don't need to improvise. If you're a well-paid lawyer, and your car breaks down and needs $500 of work, you take it to the dealer and get the work done; you have the resources to take advantage of the rules and procedures of the society. But if you're unemployed and don't have $500, you have to improvise a cheap solution: a quick fix with a coat hanger, or a deal with a friend to find a used part for less.

Mary Catherine Bateson's book *Composing a Life* argues that women, more than men, are forced to improvise their lives. Throughout her book, she describes women's lives as "an improvisatory art."[21] Women improvise for the same reason as disadvantaged cultural groups: because life is not as easy for them as it is for men. But Bateson also thinks it has something to do with personality. She suggests that men focus on a life struggle towards a single goal, which has the effect of making their lives more scripted. In contrast, women are more receptive to the fluid, improvisatory, and discontinuous nature of life.

Ingrid Monson, an ethnomusicologist who studies jazz, has identified many parallels between the improvised nature of jazz and the highly improvised speech genres found in the black community: ritualized insults and boasting genres, called the *dozens, sounding,* or *joning.*[22] Improvisation in verbal art seems to be less valued among European Americans. In words that reminded me of Bateson's view of men, a Chicago jazz musician told me that this was why white people would never be able to play jazz: because they structured their lives in a logical, verbal, rational fashion that was antithetical to the fluid, improvisatory nature of jazz.

So it seems that some cultures and groups may be more improvisational. If we're from a privileged group, does this mean that we're doomed to be bad improvisers? That's probably too simplistic. In some cases of cultural contact, the dominant group is more improvisational. For example, the semiotician Tzvetan Todorov has argued that the Spanish were able to easily conquer the Indians of Central America, in part because "the Indians are inadequate in a situation requiring improvisation, and this is precisely the situation of the conquest. . . . The art of improvisation matters more than that of ritual."[23] Todorov argues that Spanish improvisational ability helps to explain a historical mystery: how Cortés and a few hundred Spanish were able to seize the kingdom of Montezuma, even though he commanded several hundred thousand men.

These are exaggerated contrasts. In most cases, it's more a matter of style and degree; as we saw in Chapter 1, both structure and improvisation are ever-present in our daily lives, and improvisation is required in all conversation, even those that contain scripts. Once you realize that it's not either-or—that both structure and improvisation are always present in conversation—it becomes harder to make broad generalizations about how cultures compare to one another.

Of course, improvisational creativity is a skill that can improve with practice, and it can atrophy if never used. The more we improvise—the more we respond creatively and contingently to everyday situations—the better we will get at creating conversations. And if we spend more of our lives in predictable situations, speaking scripts and lines we already know, we will lose our ability to improvise.

Thinking of everyday conversation as a creative improvisation should help us to be more respectful of cultures that place a high value on verbal art. We have a lot to learn by being exposed to the different styles and settings of improvisation.

NEGOTIATING THE SETTING

In most conversations, we know what's going on. And we're usually in sync with our friends. But some conversations are more ambiguous, with several potential meanings. Think back to the Jazz Freddy dialogue at the beginning of the chapter. During this dialogue, none of the actors know what the setting is, and none of them know where the conversation is going; all of these things emerge slowly, over the course of the performance. In minute 5 of this performance, we learn that the MAN who was studying, is studying to be a baseball umpire in the Olympics. In minute 8, we learn that MAN 2 and WOMAN have hired this umpire for $2,000 a day. In minute 16, the two have turned against the umpire, after he makes several bad calls in a practice game. But none of this could have been known—neither by the audience nor the actors—in this initial dialogue, because these elements of the drama had not been created yet.

Many conversations occur in ambiguous settings, where no one is sure exactly what kind of conversation is about to happen. Because we like to leave our metatalk implicit, sometimes these conversations continue even though everyone has a different idea of what is going on. You assume that you know what the topic is, or why your friend said something in a certain way, but you find out later that your friend saw it differently. When the conversation finally reaches a point when this confusion becomes obvious, we all have to step "off-stage" and do some explicit metatalk: "Oh, I thought you were talking about . . ."

In everyday life, confused conversations can continue indefinitely. Business meetings are structured to avoid this all-too-frequent possibility—a secretary takes minutes; at the end, the boss explicitly summarizes what happened; someone is assigned to write down who agreed to do what and by when; and later, the secretary prepares and circulates the minutes to everyone. But in other situations, such as diplomatic meetings, all of the participants in the conversation may actually prefer to have some ambiguity. That is, each participant may be fully aware of the ambiguity of the conversation—of the possibility that the others are leaving with a radically different understanding of what has happened—and this may be a desired outcome. For example, in the superpower summits of the Cold War that brought together the presidents of the United States and the Soviet Union, both presidents had to be able to return home and claim success—to claim that they had prevailed. During the negotiation, both of them realized that they each had this need. Skillful statesmen can conduct conversations in such a way that this ambiguity of interpretation is built in, allowing both of them to return home and claim success. Or they can communicate primarily through indexical messages—with the surface meaning directed primarily at the home audience, but with the implicit messages still being understood.

Settings are much more likely to require negotiation when a conversation has many participants. In groups where there are distinct audiences, each with a different setting in mind, a conversation is performed on many stages at once. Goffman referred to these stages using the metaphor of the *frame*—like a picture frame borders a photo, a conversational frame surrounds a conversation. In conversation in large groups, two or more frames can be simultaneously in play. The conversation researchers Charles and Marjorie Harness Goodwin have conducted several studies of multiple frames in group conversations.[24] For example, Figure 6.1 shows the positions of six speakers at a dinner table:

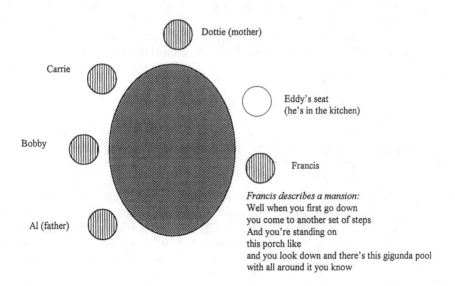

Figure 6.1. Dinner conversation

Eddy has gone to the kitchen to get more food. Francis is describing a visit to an elaborate mansion, and we'll examine closely the brief portion of her story in Figure 6.1, in which she describes the mansion's swimming pool. At the beginning of this pool description, Bobby—her sister's boyfriend—starts to make fun of Francis, at about the same time that Francis's mother is trying to pass her a bowl of potatoes.

Like most multi-party interaction, it's incredibly difficult to tease apart all of the non-verbal interaction that's going on. The researcher has to repeatedly replay videotapes of the encounter—watching for micro-second overlaps of timing—to reconstruct what was really going on in the encounter. Through this kind of close analysis, the Goodwins identified three simultaneous and overlapping frames in this brief encounter, with some members of the family playing simultaneous roles in multiple frames; the three frames are represented in Figure 6.2. If you look only at the text of Francis's story, it seems that there's only one thing going on: frame 1, the storytelling frame. To see how the participants handle the competing, overlapping frames, we have to break out the different utterances in her story.

1   Francis   Well when you first go down
                   you come to another set of steps

Francis gestures a lot while she talks, and as she says this she's holding her hands on both sides of her head and shaking them excitedly, perhaps depicting stepping motions of descending a staircase. Bobby, who's been heckling Francis all evening, imitates these hand motions, but exaggerates them to form rabbit ears, and then sings the lines from a children's camp song:

2   Bobby   Little Bunny fou fou

Bobby leans towards Carrie and looks at her as he sings this, trying to get her to join him in his heckling activity—this would start up a second frame, frame 2, which would take Carrie out of Francis's storytelling frame, frame 1. Francis ignores Bobby's heckling; instead, she stares straight at Carrie while she speaks, making it more difficult for Carrie to turn away and look at Bobby. How does Carrie handle the competing claims of frames 1 and 2? Rather than explicitly interrupting the story to metatalk about the situation, we'll see that everyone handles these competing frames nonverbally.

3   Dottie   (offers bowl of potatoes to Francis)

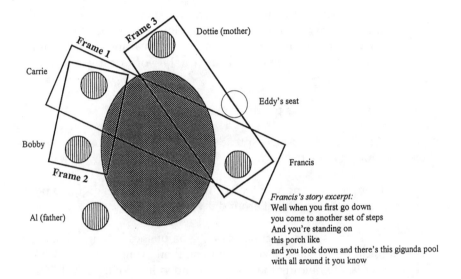

Carrie

Bobby

Al (father)

Frame 1

Frame 2

Frame 3

Dottie (mother)

Eddy's seat

Francis

Francis's story excerpt:
Well when you first go down
you come to another set of steps
And you're standing on
this porch like
and you look down and there's this gigunda pool
with all around it you know

**Figure 6.2. Dinner conversation, showing 3 overlapping frames. Carrie
and Francis are both handling competing frames**

Just as Francis is trying to make sure Carrie stays in her frame—
frame 1—her mother is trying to engage her in yet another frame, frame
3. In this frame, her mother is offering her the bowl of potatoes, which
has been going around the table. But if Francis looks away from Carrie
to acknowledge her mother, she runs the risk of losing Carrie to Bobby's
competing frame. Initially, Francis simply choose to ignore this proposed interaction with her mother, who is holding the potato bowl in
midair, waiting for Francis to take it.

4   Francis   And you're STANDING on

Francis raises her voice to compete with Bobby—whose teasing
song overlaps with her story—and the word "standing" overlaps with
Bobby's "fou fou" line. Carrie continues to look back at Francis, ignoring

Bobby, so he gives up on his "bunny ear" gesture; he sees that Carrie has chosen to stay in frame 1, and starts to put his hands in his lap. As his hands are about halfway down, Carrie reaches over and pushes his hands down further, and then quiets him with:

5   Carrie   Ssssh

She still doesn't turn her gaze from Francis, but she does smile a bit to indicate an appreciation for Bobby's joke. She's managed to non-verbally handle the competing claims of frames 1 and 2, managing to participate in both frames simultaneously—offending neither her boyfriend nor her sister.

6   Francis   this porch like

At this point, Francis spreads her arms out in an expansive gesture, to depict a large flat surface.

7   Francis   and you look down and there's this gigunda pool, with all around it you know

As Francis says "gigunda pool," she pushes her right hand outward to indicate the large size of the pool, then brings her arms back in. Her mother is still holding the bowl suspended in midair, and at "gigunda pool," she makes a push with the bowl to make sure Francis sees it. But Francis still doesn't want to yield the floor; she's worried that if she pauses in her story, Bobby will jump in with a snotty comment. To respond to her mother's offer without pausing in her story, as Francis says "you know," she repeats her expansive gesture, but this time directs her right hand gesture at the bowl. This repeated gesture reinforces the description of the "gigunda pool," but it also indicates that she doesn't want the potatoes; the mother gives up and hands the bowl across the table to Bobby. Francis has handled the competing claim of frame 3 non-verbally, while verbally continuing her lead role in storytelling frame 1.

In this perfectly normal dinner conversation, we see that a complex set of frames are in play, overlapping and simultaneous. Whenever there are many different potential frames in a conversation, we have to listen closely to what is going on, and fit our words to the unique, ever-changing, emerging setting. These situations require a great deal of collaborative, conversational creativity, because so much is negotiated implicitly and collectively.

Goffman pointed out that participants can't know how to interpret a comment until they know what conversational frame is active;

every conversation takes place within multiple overlapping layers of potential frames.[25] Some frames are always available, to be invoked in conversation. For example, every conversation takes place within the broad frame of a culture, and also within the frame of a geographic region—the country, the city, and the neighborhood are different frames that speakers can choose to invoke. And nested within these broad frames are the intimate frames that form our lives—family dinners, pick-up basketball games, or lunch at work.

All of these nested frames have an effect on how our conversations unfold. And when we're creating conversation, our words can subtly influence what we all think the setting is, and what features of the setting are seen to be the most important. Do we choose words that emphasize that we're all in a city? Or words that remind everyone of our shared family history? When so many potential settings are out there, overlapping and intersecting in our everyday conversations, we can use language creatively to tell everyone which settings we think are the most important for this conversation. Goffman's term for this creative selection of a frame was *keying*—speakers "key" a frame when they indicate that they think that frame is the relevant one.[26] This concept is similar to Gumperz's notion of a contextualization cue—a conversational move that sends an implicit metatalk message about what the context currently is. And because other participants don't always agree with a keying move, speakers often end up negotiating about what the frame of the conversation is.

* * * * * * * *

In this chapter, we've seen that there are two relations between conversations and settings; a true dialectic, a continuing spiral of creative influence. First, we create the setting with our words; then, once it's in place, it constrains our creativity; our words then further modify and negotiate the setting, in a never-ending spiral. As Goffman wrote, "conversation has a life of its own and makes demands on its own behalf."[27] These ephemeral, emergent frames constrain improvisation, in much the same way as the scripts of Chapter 1. As we saw in that chapter, just because there's a structure doesn't mean that conversation is no longer creative; it just reflects the truth that improvisation always occurs in the presence of structure.

This is the constant dialectic of creating conversation—creative improvisation is constrained by a setting that the group creatively improvised. This setting—as we've seen in this chapter—can be more or less specified in advance, more or less improvised or ritualized by the participants. But all conversation occurs within a setting, even as that setting is always created in conversation.

Chapter 7

Performances

In the last six chapters, we've explored the many ways that we create conversations. In "Scripts," we saw how our conversations are collaboratively improvised, and how bits and pieces of our dialogue are sometimes scripted. In "Dialogues," we explored the techniques that we use to create our conversations together with others. In "Audiences," we saw that conversations change depending on who we're talking to and who might be listening in. In "Rehearsals," we learned about the ways that our conversations change over time, and how they connect to each other over the years. In "Characters," we examined the different ways that we talk throughout the day, and saw how much of our image and reputation comes from our conversational performances. And in 'Settings," we learned how we create our conversations to match each situation, and how often we can use conversation creatively to influence everyone's perception of what's going on.

Now we'll bring all of these perspectives together, to gain insight into some of the situations of our everyday lives where conversational creativity is particularly important. We'll start by looking at some of the most ordinary performances of everyday life—telling stories, gossiping, making friends. Then we'll turn to an exploration of conversation in some more structured settings: how we use conversation to get things done at work; how children learn by working together or by talking to their parents; how teachers and leaders react creatively and improvisationally to novel situations.

THE PERFORMANCE OF EVERYDAY LIFE

John Guare's 1990 play *Six Degrees of Separation* has several interesting themes.[1] Most people think that the main theme is implied by the title: Everyone in the world is connected, through a chain of friends-of-friends no longer than six people: six "degrees of separation." But there is another important theme in this play: performance in everyday life. The play tells the story of Paul, a gay black teenager from the ghetto, who convinces his white prep-school lover to teach him how to "act preppy." Paul is a quick study; he goes through a remarkable transformation, changing his dialect, his clothing, and his choice of conversational topics. It's like *My Fair Lady*—another movie about the performance of everyday life. A poor cockney flower-girl is taken in by an upper-class linguist, who transforms her into a princess of the old European aristocracy.

Paul uses his new preppy persona to con his way into the fancy Park Avenue apartment of a wealthy art dealer and his wife, Ouisa. He convinces them that he is the son of Sidney Poitier, and a boarding-school classmate of their son. Of course, none of this is true—Paul's entire existence is a performance of a false self. He ends up staying for the night, and the couple gradually discovers his secret. Although the art dealer is angry at being conned, Ouisa becomes fascinated with Paul's convincing performance, and quizzes him about why he's done it. Towards the end of the play, Paul becomes implicated in a crime; he is arrested, and the story of "the prep school conman" makes the covers of all of the New York tabloids. He disappears into the prison system, and Ouisa never does learn anything about his "real" self.

The 1993 movie version of *Six Degrees* uses a narrative device that was not in the play—it begins with the couple at a friend's cocktail party, after it's all over and Paul is in jail. They're sitting on a couch, telling the story of what happened to them; surrounded by attentive listeners who have just heard about this conman through the newspapers. The movie constantly shifts perspective, first showing the couple telling a bit of their story, and then cutting back to show the action of the story itself as it unfolds. The entire play takes place in the art dealer's apartment, with only one set—one dramatic frame. But the movie depends on two nested frames—the original frame of the play is embedded with the storytelling frame.

In the movie we see the couple doing something that married couples often do—they tell us their story in a kind of *conversational duet*.[2] They finish each other's sentences: The husband describes one event, and the wife the next. Because they've had the same experience—and they know each other's style of talking so well—their storytelling is collaborative. Even though both of them are talking, in a sense there is only one storyteller, and only one story.

This "conversational duet" style of storytelling is common among friends and couples. The *Six Degrees* example is familiar—it's something we've all heard and participated in—and it's a good example of how stories are told around the world, even in exotic and faraway folklore traditions. Folklore experts study styles and traditions of storytelling around the world. They've discovered that cultures have different ways of telling stories, and that these differences tell us a lot about society and everyday social life. In some traditions, the storyteller is expected to hew to the literal truth; in others, creative embellishment is encouraged. Some traditions value humble speakers, others prefer boastful speakers. And some traditions allow the speaker to perform alone, whereas others encourage *co-narration* and audience participation.

In co-narration, two or more speakers join together to participate in the telling of a story, something like the conversational duet. Some societies even have performance traditions where three or more speakers work together to tell their culture's most traditional tales. And in many storytelling traditions, the audience participates in the creation of the story. In *Six Degrees of Separation,* everyone at the cocktail party listens politely; interrupting or joining in would be considered rude. But they still influence the flow of the story with non-verbal feedback—by raising their eyebrows in shock at a particular aspect of the story, or by looking confused when they can't understand a particular comment. And in most informal gossip and small talk, our friends don't sit there quietly, either; they make assenting or evaluative comments, the *back channeling* of Chapter 3.[3] Even if our friends are politely listening, we choose our words and our style to keep them engaged, to make sure they stay interested. If someone suddenly looks confused, we notice and then pause a second to clarify what we just said.

There are many cultures where audience participation is encouraged during gossip and storytelling; researchers have found that gossip is some of the most creative conversation. Most societies have a genre of conversation that we could recognize as gossip; it seems that gossip is universal. Several psychologists have recently hypothesized that gossip served an important evolutionary function. And in a 1996 book, the psychologist Robin Dunbar presented an intriguing and novel claim: That language evolved in humans *specifically* to make gossip possible. His argument: Cohesive social groups are more evolutionarily successful. Apes and monkeys groom each other constantly, not so much for hygiene, but to maintain and reinforce social bonds. But when a group gets to be too large (early human tribes were about 150 people, much larger than any ape group), it's impossible to find time to do all of the grooming that would be required to maintain social stability. Dunbar argued that gossip evolved as a more efficient way of "grooming" each other, of maintaining and reinforcing social cohesion.[4]

But although gossip is universal, the conversational techniques that are used during gossip are not universal. Like so much about conversational style, there's a lot of variation from one culture to another, and these variations often tell us about more than language alone—they can give us insights into the most basic cultural differences.

My colleague Don Brenneis studied a particularly creative style of gossip during his research in a rural community in Fiji, a small Pacific island. Brenneis spent most of his time in Fiji with a large group of Hindi-speaking Indian immigrants, who immigrated to Fiji generations ago. These Indians work hard, and they think that the native Fijians waste a lot of time sitting around and talking; that's why the word they use for "gossip" is a word they've borrowed from the Fijian language. As we learned in Chapter 2, personality stereotyping often results when two cultures have different ideas about how much talk is appropriate; the more silent culture thinks that the talkative one is superficial, or is wasting time. The more talkative culture thinks the silent one is uptight, unemotional, cold. In America, this pattern is sometimes found between European and African Americans, or between Jewish and WASP New Yorkers.

The Fijian word for gossip is *talanoa* and it translates roughly to "idle chatter," and in Fiji, only men talk talanoa. The English word "gossip" has exactly the opposite gendered connotation—when we use this word, we typically conjure up an image of two women talking. It somehow doesn't feel right to use the word to describe two men at a bar, talking about work.

Like Ouisa and her husband, describing their experiences at a party, *talanoa* stories are always told collaboratively: Two or more men join together in a conversational duet. What's more, listeners are expected to jump in and contribute to the story; sometimes a *talanoa* story is more like a conversational trio or quartet. Different speakers are always interrupting each other to continue the story; but no one complains about it, because it's an expected part of the collaboration.

Talanoa gossip is spoken in a rhythmic, almost poetic style of talk, with "lines" that have a metric structure like our own traditional poetry. Because of this rhythm, everyone knows when a line is going to end. And because there are clear pauses after each line, it's easy for someone to jump in and take over the story. When a man jumps in and takes over the storytelling role, he often begins by repeating the last line, and then continues the story in the same tempo and meter. Watching this, you get the impression of a connected verbal performance—a collaborative poetry.[5]

There's a reason that *talanoa* stories are always performed collectively. In the small country villages where these Indians live, it's important not to directly insult another person, because word of it is guaranteed to get back to the person you're talking about. So if two or more people are telling the story together, neither one of them can be blamed for talking behind your back. And if the audience keeps jumping in and participating, they're equally guilty. The *talanoa* style of group storytelling distributes the blame for whatever is said. At the same time, it provides an opportunity for a kind of male bonding—the smooth flow of this kind of creative conversation makes it clear to everyone how much they share. In America, this is the kind of bonding that women experience when they talk together; maybe American men need to gossip a little bit more.[6]

What do these Indian and Fijian men get out of this kind of collaborative poetry? They obviously enjoy it. Collaborative conversation is fun—you get the same high that improv actors get during a good performance. Think back to the last time you had a great conversation—you may not remember what you talked about, and you probably lost track of the time. You weren't thinking too hard about what to say next, because your words just flowed naturally. You didn't have to work to understand anyone; instead, you had a feeling that you clicked with them. Sometimes the sun will start to rise before you realize how many hours you've been talking.

Of course, you can't make this happen all by yourself; great conversations can only happen when a group of people are on the same wavelength, because it takes two or more to talk. Jazz musicians and improvisational actors both say that the reason they love improvising is because of this smooth-flowing interaction with the other performers. A good conversation, like a good improv performance, flows naturally.

The psychologist Mike Csikszentmihalyi is famous for his studies of these *flow* experiences.[7] Csikszentmihalyi refers to them as *peak experiences,* because they are some of the best moments of our lives. We experience flow whenever we're doing something where our skills closely match the challenges of a situation. You won't experience flow if the situation isn't challenging enough—you'll just get bored. For example, some conversations aren't that creative, and we don't experience flow. This is true of many ordinary conversations, when you're making small talk, or using a lot of catchphrases—there is no creative challenge. But if a conversation is over your head, or if everyone is speaking too quickly, or if you can't understand what's going on, you won't have flow either; instead, you'll just get frustrated. According to Csikszentmihalyi's theory, we experience flow in between these extremes—in conversations where the creative challenges are just right for our conversational abilities.

Improv actors often describe their best performances using the same flow-like descriptions as dancers, mountain climbers, and basketball players. That's because people experience flow in situations where they have to improvise. Mountain climbers have to respond to the mountain, moment by moment, deciding where to place each hand and foot. Basketball players have to respond to their opponents creatively with split-second timing. It's not surprising that we often reach a flow state in creating conversations: Almost nothing else is so improvisational.

It doesn't happen in all conversations, because everyone has to be at the same level. In an improv group, one inexperienced actor can keep everyone from reaching this peak state. In our everyday conversations, a poor conversationalist can ruin the flow with one ill-timed remark. It takes skill to improvise these conversations—to connect with what has already been said, while at the same time introducing new ideas. To reach the flow state, our abilities should be matched to those of our conversational partners—we're not likely to experience flow if we're conversing with someone who is not as skilled a conversationalist, because we get bored.

Children love to play in preschool because their group improvisations lead to flow.[8] Play leads to flow because it requires the same improvisational collaboration as conversation, jazz, and improv theater. A child's level of skill is constantly matched by the challenges of these play performances. Eventually, children master the ability to play; their level of skill moves beyond the challenges of the task, and they don't experience flow anymore during play. That's why children engage in less dramatic play by the first or second grade—by this age, children have mastered the improvisational skills needed for dramatic play, and they take these skills and move on. They use these same skills to begin engaging in creative conversations, improvising social encounters with friends in school.

We usually become friends with the people that we have conversational flow with, because those are the people that we seek out and see over and over. A friendship is something that we create together, emerging from a series of conversations over the years. A good friendship is a joint performance with a long run, a series of conversational performances that are embellished with variations and novelty each time. The more formal relationships that we have—with our boss, with our co-workers, or with a clerk at the Division of Motor Vehicles—are more scripted and less creative. We don't have to be very talented improvisers to get through these kinds of conversations. But with friends, we're more likely to improvise. In fact, one of the characteristics of a good friendship is that the conversations are so smoothly improvised, like the dialogues of a seasoned improv theater group. This is why it takes a while to warm up if you've been apart from an old friend for a long time—you have to get used to the improvisational rhythms that have fallen out of practice. Because you're attuned to each other's conversational patterns and styles of talking, you are free to be more creative, because you know that you will be creative in a way that works with your friend. In conversations with friends, we experience the balance between skills and challenges that leads to a flow experience. A 1997 study at Carnegie Mellon found that people with the most diverse networks of family, friends, and acquaintances were four times less likely to catch colds, as those with the sparsest ties.[9] The lack of a social connection was a greater risk factor than any other variable: low Vitamin C, stress, or even smoking. Perhaps it's the positive flow experiences of conversation that result in these health benefits; the new field of *positive psychology* is just beginning to examine the causes of a happy, healthy personality.

Think about the last time you started talking to a stranger at a party. At first, you don't know anything about each other. Little by little, you find out about each other's children, profession, and hobbies; this knowledge emerges in different ways, depending on the flow of the conversation. If the two of you click and have a lot in common, you probably spend a lot of the conversation identifying these areas of shared interests, jointly creating the basis for a new friendship.

You may selectively reveal certain facts about yourself based on how the conversation is emerging, and by doing this, the other person begins to react to this presented version of you; your presented image is thus partly collaborative and emergent. Just as in improv theater, the two of you have together improvised not only a dialogue, but also a pair of characters, and a social setting—a new friendship.

Of course, not all conversations are wonderful flow experiences. Some conversations take effort, and can even be unpleasant. For example, this is what happens when we're disagreeing about something. Heated arguments are extremely challenging—usually so challenging that we don't experience flow. Of course, some people are so good at arguing that they enjoy it and seek it out. If two people like this find each other, they can have a creative, flowing argument. Linguist Deborah Schiffrin discovered that different cultural groups attach differing meanings to argument; in her classic 1984 paper "Jewish argument as sociability" she claimed that among her subjects—primarily lower-middle-class Jews living in an urban area of Philadelphia—argument was not necessarily perceived as a conflict, or as a way to arrive at some shared truth, but was more of a way of demonstrating and building solidarity among the speakers.[10] This is, of course, a familiar stereotype of New Yorkers, demonstrated in the dialogue of any episode of *Seinfeld.*

But in many cases, arguments don't feel like creative conversation—they're emotional, we talk with raised voices, we respond quickly without thinking about what we're saying. We interrupt each other more than we do in most conversations. But it's exactly this quick, unthinking responsiveness that makes an argument so improvisational. For example, we almost never *plan* to have an argument. They come out of nowhere, when we are unprepared or when we least expect them.

In an argument, like all creating conversations, there is no director and no script. The outcome is unpredictable—it emerges from the dialogue itself. But the creating conversations that we've talked about so far are all situations where everyone is working together, agreeing with each other, supporting and accepting each other. In improv theater, for example, everyone is participating in a shared endeavor, working towards a common goal. But in an argument, there is no common goal; instead, there is conflict and disagreement.

Still it takes two to argue; there must be some level of coordination happening. All improvisations, even arguments, must be jointly created by the people doing the arguing.[11] But if we're so busy arguing, how can we manage to coordinate our talk at all? Coordinating conversation is hard enough even when everyone agrees to work towards a common goal. So imagine the additional difficulty, improvising with another person when we're disagreeing with them. People who are arguing with each other still need to respond to each other, just like improvisational actors. If you can't do this, you won't win any arguments.

Sometimes things do get out of control, and an argument falls apart. We can't even talk to each other anymore; we just have to leave the room. It's a fine line, but we usually know when this has happened. When things get to this extreme stage, we realize that up until that point, we actually were coordinating our words, and we shared some common ground. Now that things have degenerated to this point, we are no longer creating a verbal performance together. To continue an argument, we have to collaborate, in an odd way, to create an improvisational performance. This was Tannen's critique of the "argument culture" in her 1998 book of that name; her definition of an "argument" was a situation where there is no collaboration and no common ground, and her examples included the current-issues talk shows where "left" and "right" provide their distinct perspectives, never meeting in the center.[12] These encounters are more like people talking past each other, than they are like conversations.

In these sorts of talk shows, the speakers are more interested in coming up with a quotable sound bite than they are in genuine discussion; it's a different task than the arguments of everyday discourse, where we have to collaborate. If you can't manage the creative demands of this situation, you probably won't be able to win many arguments, nor will you be very convincing when you're trying to persuade someone that you're right. In fact, it's usually the less creative individuals who walk out of an argument, when they realize that they don't have the verbal skills to win fair and square.

CREATING CONVERSATION AT WORK

In the experience economy every business is a stage, and therefore work is theater.
—B. Joseph Pine II and James Gilmore, *The Experience Economy*[13]

Conversation is an important part of every job, especially in those businesses where the employees interact with the public on a regular basis. Pine and Gilmore's book is a study of service businesses that create "experiences" for their customers, such as Disneyworld and Starbucks. The most successful of these companies, they argue, are those that stage memorable performances for the customer. Even in an office job, those situations that have the biggest impact on your career are in groups: meeting with the boss, working with colleagues, negotiating with a client. Like all conversations, workplace conversations are creative and collaborative, and unexpected things often emerge from them. Conversations are never predictable and scripted; likewise, business settings are also unscripted. For example, many business meetings don't have a predetermined outcome. And although some meetings are run by the boss, other meetings—such as contract negotiations or brainstorming sessions—are not controlled by any one person. Informal conversations in the elevator or the cafeteria can strengthen a relationship or pave the way for a future meeting. All of these workplace settings provide us with opportunities to collaboratively improvise with our colleagues. In fact, top business schools—including Vanderbilt and the University of Chicago—teach their MBA students improvisational theater techniques, as a way of helping them learn these essentially improvisational communication skills.[14]

When we think about creativity, we often think of a solitary genius, alone late at night in his studio or at her typewriter. But in today's information society, some of the most important creative products result from this kind of collaborative group process. It's more and more rare to find a significant innovation resulting from a lone genius, sitting in the library for months, alone. The great innovations of our time are collaborative products, emerging from the creative actions of many people—movies and TV shows, technologies like the personal computer and the Internet.

Collaboration is a fact of life in business. The whole reason that business organizations exist is to accomplish tasks that are too big and complex for one person. Some scientific papers have over 100 authors listed on the title page, reflecting the collaborations that are common in modern science. And many creative fields require collaboration—think of the long list of credits that scrolls by after a movie. Still, it's hard for us to lose our romantic image of the entrepreneur, or the innovative employee trapped by an oppressive bureaucracy.

Our legal system of copyright and patent is based on the "lone genius" model of creativity. Whoever originates the idea owns it, and retains the right to sell it for a profit. But our legal system of intellectual property rights doesn't do a very good job with collaborative creativity. How do you assign credit and split up the profits? Our copyright law sometimes makes it hard to encourage truly collaborative creativity. For each participant to fully contribute, they must be convinced they will benefit more than by working alone—that the final product will be more successful than if they had struck out alone.[15]

In Chapter 4, we learned about theater groups that use rehearsal improvisation to develop script ideas. These rehearsals are collaborative creative processes, group interactions that result in a comedy skit script. This emergent script is a collective group product, and could never be associated with any single actor. Second City avoids the issue of ownership by not giving *any* of the actors any ownership rights; the resulting scripts are owned by the institution—the theater itself.

Brainstorming

It's not so hard to believe that a group of professional actors could collaborate to create an improvised performance. After all, these are both extremely creative fields. But it's perhaps harder to see the creativity in everyday business conversation.

Sometimes a project team is faced with a real obstacle. Everyone is stumped; no one has been able to come up with a good solution. Here's a situation where only a true insight will save the day; but it doesn't seem likely, because everyone is just going in circles. One way to get out of this rut is to get everyone together to brainstorm—to think out loud about the problem. Brainstorming is based on the theory that "two heads are better than one." You all start thinking out loud, free-associating on each other's ideas.

The Harvard business professor, John Kao, calls this collaborative creativity *jamming*, comparing it to a jazz improvisation.[16] Jazz performances are collaborative, with each musician constantly introducing new melodies, rhythms, and embellishments on the basic song form. The other musicians take this material and play off of it, developing it further into something different yet again. What emerges is a performance that depends on all of the player's improvisations together.

Brainstorming works because new ideas often emerge from creating conversations. When the creativity researcher Mike Csikszentmihalyi interviewed 100 creative people, they all said that they couldn't have done it without conversation—they got some of their most important insights during creating conversations.[17] Brainstorming has become big business these days, because new product innovation is so essential to the future of so many companies. Many companies hire creativity consultants to visit for a day, acting as facilitators who guide a brainstorming session. They use a few simple rules for these creating conversations. The most important rule is that no idea can be criticized, all ideas are accepted. Like improv theater, there is "no denial." The goal is to encourage the maximum number of ideas to emerge.

Like all improvisations, brainstorming is an unreliable technique. You can't predict whether a good idea will emerge or not. But real business innovations can't be planned or scheduled. Revolutionary ideas can only emerge from improvised, creating conversations. Even the best improv group has good nights and bad nights. Sometimes they perform at a peak; other times, they're tired from a week on the road. This is why fans of the Grateful Dead—a band that emphasized group improvisation—used to attend three or four concerts in a row; they knew that a real peak performance wouldn't happen every time, and they wanted to increase their chances of seeing a truly great performance. When a manager gives his workers the time to spend in a brainstorming session, he's taking the risk that it might end up being a waste of time.

Psychological research provides some explanations for why brainstorming works. Researchers have found that the creative process has two steps. The first step is to have lots of ideas, without worrying about how good they are; psychologists refer to this as *divergent thinking*, because your ideas are expanding outward—"diverging." This is the goal of brainstorming—to enhance this divergent thinking step, to get more raw ideas on the table. Of course, most of these ideas will not work. But you hope that at least one idea will be great. One great idea can justify all of the time spent in the brainstorming meeting.

Divergent thinking is hard because it's just the opposite of the kinds of skills that we're all tested on in school, where we're expected to come up with the one correct answer. To be effective at this first step of creativity, we have to unlearn everything that our schools have taught us. That's why IQ tests don't predict who will be creative. These tests all require us to come up with the one right answer to a question—exactly the opposite task from coming up with as many answers as we can think of.

But no business could survive if it pursued every crazy idea that came out of a brainstorming session. Once all of these ideas are on the table, how do you decide which ones are worth pursuing, and which ones are duds? This involves the second step in creativity: *convergent thinking*, because now you are homing in—"converging"—on a single solution. Business innovation requires two steps to be effective: First, a divergent period where the team generates lots of possible solutions, without worrying about how good they are; then, a convergent period, where they evaluate all of the ideas, throw out most of them, and hopefully end up with one or two good ones. The goal of a brainstorming session is to clearly separate these steps, and to get everyone working at the first step—divergent thinking.

Like all creating conversations, brainstorming is improvisational, with the results emerging from everyone's participation. We don't have to be taught how to brainstorm; we just have to be reminded how much it's like everyday conversation. That's why businesses can learn a lot about creativity from improv theater. Improv actors can be trained, and a group's rehearsals improve their public performances. Can we develop "rehearsals" for business innovation? Yes, and these training classes should focus on improvisation. A good brainstorming session requires all the same things that a good improv performance does: trust among the group; the ability to *listen* and to *respond* to each other; the ability to work without a script or a director. Cutting-edge businesses have to create new products to survive. If every meeting follows the agenda (the script)—if every group is guided by the iron hand of the boss (the director)—then nothing new or unexpected can emerge from the meeting. Like good improvisations, true innovation happens in the absence of a script and a director. Innovation can't simply be willed into existence; it has to emerge, unpredictably, from the unstructured interactions of a group of talented individuals.

One problem is that the cost of failure is high. In improv theater, if you have a bad night, no big deal; a different audience will be there tomorrow for the good night that invariably follows. In business, you can't always afford a "bad night," a dud product. And when time is money, you can't afford to have everyone engaged in divergent thinking all of the time. Businesses that use improvisational techniques must be prepared to handle failure gracefully and supportively. If improv actors had to worry about looking stupid, nothing creative would ever happen; that anxiety would be paralyzing. Improv training classes incorporate a wide range of exercises to overcome this fear of looking stupid. Actors are told over and over, "anything goes; say the first thing that comes into your head." If you really want a more creative organization, you have to convince your employees that improvising in this way will work for them.

Employees who experience this kind of improvisational creativity at work can easily get addicted to it. What they're addicted to is the flow state that comes only from good collaborative improvisations. These conditions are rarely found in large organizations, which tend to focus on structure, script, and process, and limit the opportunities for improvisation. Individuals sometimes seek out this flow experience by avoiding large corporations and joining small, entrepreneurial firms, or by working on their own. As the management researcher Eric Eisenberg points out, "Entrepreneurs are people looking to jam."[18]

Performance in Negotiation

In brainstorming, everyone is pretty much on the same page. But even adversarial meetings are improvisational. For example, contract negotiations are improvisational conversations. Like all improvisations, you can't predict the outcome; the result of a negotiation session is never the unilateral decision of one person—it emerges from the negotiation itself. Negotiations are collaborative conversations, and the resulting agreement emerges from the collective, improvised actions of two parties.

Like an argument, negotiations often begin with strong differences of opinion. You'll try to get the best deal for your side, even if you know it might not be a great deal for the other side. As with an argument, it's hard to see how you're collaborating—negotiators don't seem to be working together. But even in the face of bitter disagreement, the two sides share the desire to negotiate a mutually agreeable contract. As long as neither one of you stomps out of the room in disgust, you're both doing something to keep the negotiation on track.

Like all creating conversations, negotiations are rarely predictable, and never scripted. That's why it takes skill and strategy to negotiate well—negotiation is an improvisational skill, and it depends on many of the abilities that improv actors use: listening closely, making connections, integrating your position with what everyone else is saying.

Children start practicing negotiation soon after they've mastered the basics of conversation. Many of the playground games of children—especially in primary school—involve constant improvisation, even though these games have rules. Some of the most popular playground games have rule negotiation built into them; for example, in Four square, the player in the A square gets to make up her own rules; but even then, some rules are not acceptable and are rejected by the other players. What counts as an "acceptable rule" is a constantly shifting, constantly negotiated group norm. In hopscotch, each group of girls creates its own local rules. For example, Candy Goodwin documented a group of girls whose version of the game allowed a player to take three "small steps" within a square, before throwing the beanbag to the next square—but only in squares six and above. Goodwin observed that the exact meanings of these local rules are constantly probed and negotiated during the play of the game. In which numbered squares are "small steps" allowed? Exactly how big can a "small step" be?[19]

These playground games contribute to the development of planning skills, negotiation skills, and the ability to engage in effective arguments. David Bearison, of the Graduate Center at the City University of New York, studied negotiation and collaboration among elementary-school-aged children by creating a novel task for them: They were asked to invent a new game, using a set of abstract game pieces and game boards. There were no rules, and there were no words or defining marks on either the pieces or the boards. Bearison videotaped groups of two children while they created a new game together.

What would you think these children would do in this situation? We might guess that the children would first agree on a set of rules, and then start playing the game. Adults almost always start out a project by first developing a plan. But the children's sessions were much more complicated than that. It turns out that they started playing "the game" almost right away, with only the barest of outlines, with only one or two rules specified. Almost all of their game-designing negotiation occurred *while they were playing*; they conducted their entire negotiation, their entire collaborative game creation, during and through the playing of the game!

Even after the kids had developed a few rules, they didn't faithfully follow the rules. Children are doing much more than simply following rules when they play games. They are continuing to use the same improvisational techniques that they used during preschool fantasy play. Even once a few rules have been agreed upon, there is always room for creative negotiation—they continued to negotiate the rules throughout the session, improvising and embellishing along the way. For these children, planning, negotiation, and collaboration all merged together in play.[20]

Creative Leadership

So what are the implications of all of this for managers and project leaders? It's your job to lead, after all—you can't just drink a beer while your team improvises. But if you want to make maximum use of your staff's creative potential, you can't plan and script everything either.

These are big issues for contemporary businesses, because everyone realizes that innovative organizations have to be flexible. In 1995, the *Harvard Business Review* published the article "Changing the role of top management: Beyond structure to process" (January-February 1995). The article encourages managers to focus on improvisation and collaboration, instead of structures and scripts like business plans and organizational charts.[21] The article starts by observing that large organizations have traditionally had complex structures, graphically represented by the infamous "organizational chart." This corporate structure was hierarchical, with a straightforward chain of command leading up the hierarchy. The rigid, hierarchical management structure worked fairly well for several decades. But in the early 1980s, the business environment started to change much more rapidly, due to three primary forces: the rapid introduction of new information technologies, the increasing globalization of the marketplace, and government deregulation of key industries such as telecommunications and banking. I was a management consultant in the 1980s, when "structure" first began to be seen as the problem; executives began to realize that rigid organizational structures were blocking innovation, keeping the organization from responding quickly enough to these changes, and stifling entrepreneurial talents of employees, forcing them to leave and found their own companies. Major companies spent millions in consulting fees in the attempt to design more responsive, innovative organizations. During a three-year consulting assignment with one large telephone company, I watched this massive company reorganize, on average, every six to nine months!

In 1988, while I was in the middle of this project, the prolific management theorist Peter Drucker wrote an influential *Harvard Business Review* article suggesting that the "new organization" of the future would be structured like a symphony orchestra.[22] Drucker used the symphony metaphor to emphasize that the new organization must be improvisational and collaborative. He noted that in both the symphony and the new organization, each professional—the musician or the knowledge-worker—"directs his own performance." He emphasized the lack of hierarchy within the orchestra; all of the musicians are highly trained professionals, responsible for their own creativity and without answering to a hierarchy of managers (there are no "group vice-president conductors" or "division VP conductors"); and he suggested that in the new organization, innovation will emerge from the interaction of specialist professionals, just like a musical performance emerges from the actions of all of the musicians together. Drucker pointed out the essentially emergent nature of organizational creativity when he noted "A business has no 'score' to play by except the score it writes as it plays."

Much of this is now the conventional wisdom in management circles. Structure is bad, process and innovation is good. But still, there are certain individuals in charge, executives and board members who are responsible for the organization's products and profitability. If the new organization is going to be an improvisational, collaborative effort, then what is the proper role for the leaders of the organization? What will leadership look like in the improvisational corporation?

In the 1990s, two prominent creativity researchers turned to the study of leadership, having realized that many of the innovations that have changed the world have required not only a spark of insight, but also the ability to communicate these new ideas, and to mobilize groups of people to carry through on these ideas. Howard Gardner, at Harvard University, published *Leading Minds: An Anatomy of Leadership*, after many books about creativity in the arts and sciences. Dean Simonton, at the University of California at Davis, after a decade of research on scientific creativity, published *Greatness: Who Makes History and Why*.[23]

Thus two fields—the business-school study of innovation and the psychological study of creativity—are converging on some common themes. The common themes are all related to the observation that creativity doesn't occur in a vacuum—that it's not a matter of a brilliant individual having the key insight that magically leads to new products and increased market share. After several decades of research into the individual's internal mental processes, psychologists have realized that the most important aspects of successful creativity are often interpersonal and extremely dependent on a person's interaction with the rest of the organization, the whole industry, and the customer base: the ability to bounce ideas off of other people and benefit from constructive feedback, the ability to absorb the work of other people into one's own evolving creative framework, the ability to recognize which of all the new ideas floating around are worth pursuing, the ability to communicate new insights to groups of people who can use them, and the ability to mobilize organizations to successfully implement new ideas.

Psychologists have turned from the attempt to identify the creative *individual*, to the attempt to identify creative *social groups*. At the same time, management research has turned from the attempt to find the best organizational structure, to the attempt to identify those interactional, social processes out of which innovations are most likely to emerge. In both areas, researchers are focusing on the improvisational, emergent nature of group creativity.

Leaders of the future will not be successful if they just create the structure and then manage that structure. Leaders who are structure-focused will not be effective at managing the group process of organizational creativity. Instead, the leader must become a participant in an ongoing, improvisational process; a facilitator of collaborative, group creativity. Rather than imposing a predetermined structure on the organization, the leader will be the director of the improvisational performance.

LEARNING BY CREATING CONVERSATION

When we think of learning, we usually think of schools and classrooms. But a child learns the most important things about life from informal conversations: social skills such as how to converse, how to make friends, how to express emotions, and how to deal with insults. As we grow and mature, we continue to learn simply by participating and performing in everyday life. Just like aspiring actors, we learn to become better improvisers by continually improvising.

This is one of the unavoidable facts about improvisational creativity—it's not a body of knowledge that you can write down in a book, and learn by studying; the only way to learn it is by doing it. Nowhere is this more obvious than with conversational skills. The only way to become a more creative conversationalist is by engaging in more and more conversations.

You learn best when you're right in the zone of flow—when your current level of ability is equally matched to the demands of the situation. And in fact, you'll probably learn the most when you're pushed to the edge of the flow zone—where the challenges *almost* go beyond your skills. This is the essence of Vygotsky's concept of the *zone of proximal development*, an influential idea in education and development psychology.[24] No matter what kind of conversationalist you are now, you can always find a group of people who are matched to your style and level of creativity. We all naturally seek out that match in our friends, because we all want our conversations to be right in the flow zone, not too difficult and not too boring.

Many of the skills required in the workplace are improvisational skills. Brainstorming, collaboration, planning, and negotiation are types of creating conversation. You can't learn these skills by studying late in the library—you have to find another way. Paradoxically, you have to start participating in these types of performances, even before you have the skills to participate fully. It's like a form of apprenticeship—in an apprenticeship, the apprentice has to begin working in the shop even before he has been taught anything, and he gradually acquires expertise by working under the guidance of the master. In fact, all of us have gone through these kinds of learning experiences, in a workshop in college, or in our first job. Creating conversations are essential to on-the-job learning, like apprenticeship and mentoring.

And children learn almost everything about the social world by participating in creating conversations. As we saw in Chapter 4, learning doesn't only happen when adults explicitly tell children things; much of it is *implicit*, indirect, with children picking up knowledge in the course of everyday life. We're all familiar with the idea that children learn things better by doing, rather than just by book learning. Our usual image of this kind of active learning is a child repeating or imitating what their teacher or parent does first. But creative conversational skills can't be learned through imitation. Creative conversations are collaborative, with both parent and child participating together, responding improvisationally to each other. Children learn by doing it *together* with their parents. By participating in improvised conversations, children learn about the norms and practices of their culture, they acquire the social skills necessary to enter the first grade, and later, to participate in social groups with friends.

How do children learn by participating in conversations? In recent years, developmental psychologists have started to go into the home and the classroom to observe how children actually learn. This new research has confirmed something that parents intuitively know: Children are creative performers in their everyday settings, and they are not passive recipients of knowledge that parents wisely impart to them—they actively participate in creating conversations. A child's early social performances can, of course, be helped or hindered by the guidance of parents and the challenges of peers, conversational partners that vary in both social skill and social status.

Anthropologists have recently begun to look at child-rearing practices in non-Western cultures, to learn how different societies teach their children about social life. These researchers have found that in all cultures, children are extremely active participants in social life. And this research also shows that children learn to improvise in the conversational style that predominates in their culture. It turns out that children in non-industrial, rural cultures encounter a broader range of social situations than children do in America. For example, in the typical American home, there are only one or two children, and only one parent home most of the day. Contrast this situation with a mountain village in Guatemala, where there are always children from multiple families around, several mothers, and extended family members such as aunts and grandmothers. Dr. Barbara Rogoff, a psychologist who studies child development in different cultures, spent years observing families in a remote Guatemalan village. She heard multiple conversations everywhere she went; daily life has the conversational complexity that we Americans find only at a cocktail party. Another difference is that in American families, the workplace—the daily activity of adults—is outside the home. But in Guatemala, children are surrounded by the everyday work of adults—piecework weaving, or small-scale subsistence farming. Thus they can learn not only by participating in the social world, but also by participating in the economic world, alongside their parents, as apprentices.

Rogoff found that parents interact with their children very differently in Guatemala and America. American mothers tend to "teach" their children—guiding activities step by step, or passing on specific facts. And because there are fewer adults and children in the home, the mother spends a lot more time talking one-on-one with her children. In Guatemala, children learn about work by observing and participating—through *apprenticeship*, rather than through explicit verbal instruction. Children are constantly observing adult activities, and increasingly allowed to participate in those activities as their skill level improves.[25]

When a novice participates in an ongoing activity with an expert, the novice has a special interactional status—he or she is a *peripheral participant*. The novice is participating in the activity, but his activity is much less central than the expert's—especially at the very beginning of the apprenticeship, the novice is "peripheral" to the main activity. Apprenticeship is an effective learning technique because it allows novices to initially participate in a more peripheral way, and to become gradually more involved in the work as their expertise increases. Developmental psychologists have had great success in using this concept as a way of understanding how a child learns conversational and social skills. Unlike Goffman's "bystanders" or the non-participant overhearers of Chapter 3, novices are *legitimate* peripheral participants, because even though they are not central or actively talking, they are acknowledged to be part of the activity. Through apprenticeship and legitimate peripheral participation, Guatemalan parents allow children to develop skills through their own initiative, rather than through explicit guidance and teaching.

Apprenticeship is the model of learning that we find in most improvisational performance genres, including jazz and improv theater. If you want to be a great improviser, you go to Chicago to study with a master. This model of learning is quite different from the contemporary classroom, where students learn by being taught from a book, outside of the context of any real-world activity. Our child-rearing practices in America—explicit instruction, one-on-one conversation—are quite similar to what goes on in a classroom, and this smooths the child's transition to formal schooling. But for students who come from an apprenticeship-style culture of child rearing, the transition to formal schooling can be more difficult.

Apprenticeship is an improvisational interaction, a private performance between an experienced performer and a younger learner. This is how children learn conversational and social skills—there is no schoolbook that tells you the rules of social life. By skillfully adjusting his or her responses during the performance, the master (or parent) can lead along the novice (or child) in the art of creating conversations.

What kind of knowledge do children acquire in these everyday situations? It's not a set of facts that you could write down in a book. Instead, they learn how to improvise in everyday life. Children need to learn how to participate in these performances—to respond contingently and appropriately to each situation, each new group of people that they encounter. This learning is a lot like how aspiring young musicians learn how to improvise jazz—they learn by jamming with other more experienced musicians. By improvising with senior improvisers, both jazz musicians and young children become socialized into a community.

Often, when we think of how our children learn from us, we think about all of the knowledge that we have, and how we can best teach it to them. Most American parents try to help their preschool children by providing them with explicit instruction throughout the day. We tend to do this especially to teach them vocabulary—if we encounter a new object, we make a point of defining it for our child. But this situation is not as participatory as it could be—it's more like classroom instruction. How can we make our parenting more like an apprenticeship?

All parents know that you can't be an effective parent simply by following the rules that you read in all of those books you bought when you found out you were going to have a child. Parents have to improvise—to respond appropriately and immediately to unexpected and unpredictable situations. Parents who are poor improvisers—who require a great deal of structure in their lives—will probably not raise children who are talented improvisers, because children need to practice improvising with others to learn this essential social skill. Social skills are learned and practiced in groups, and to learn effectively, children have to learn by participating with others. Musicians can't learn to play jazz by practicing at home alone, no matter how many hours and years they practice; they have to go out and jam with other musicians, to learn how to converse with other musicians and to integrate their musical ideas and their musical voice with the voices of other musicians. For the same reasons, children can't learn to participate effectively in social life if they stay at home alone.

Children love to play with children their own age; social play seems to be a strong instinct. By some estimates, over 50% of all American children create imaginary companions. Developmental psychologists now believe that children create these pretend friends simply to extend the fun of social play—rejecting the common belief that imaginary companions are a sign of psychological disturbance. For example, children who create pretend friends are usually extremely social, and enjoy interacting with others. For these children, even with frequent opportunities for peer play, it's still not enough—the imaginary companion provides a "social" setting even when they're alone.[26]

Most adults are notoriously bad at improvisational play. Children get most of their pretend play experience with peers, in settings like the preschool, the local playground, or with their siblings. Parents almost never engage in this kind of improvisational play with their children; instead, parents tend to observe, rather than enter the game as full partners.

Studies of American families typically find that if another child is available, over three-fourths of a child's social play is with that child, rather than with a parent.[27] Similar studies in other cultures usually document an even larger percentage of peer play, probably because many cultures have more open households and more other families close by, providing more peer play opportunities. Children's pretend play may be one of those rare finds in anthropology: a cross-cultural universal.[28]

What are the implications for parents, once we see that conversations, and much of social life, are improvised performances? How can parents raise their children to be more effective performers and more creative improvisers as they grow to adulthood?

If you want to help your child learn to improvise, you can't just *tell* your child what to do. Improvisational knowledge is not a list of facts. Most of all, it's important for parents to *interact* with children frequently, to engage in as much conversation as possible. And in these conversations, children should be encouraged to be creative, active participants in the talk. It's not improvisational if the adult determines everything that will happen next. It's not improvisational if the adult allows the child to determine everything that happens next. Parents tend to either plan everything for the child or to respond positively to every-thing the child proposes. Neither of these extremes results in a collabora-tive improvisation. The improvised conversations of adult life are char-acterized by the active, creative actions of all participants, and the key to effective conversation is the ability to integrate your creative contribu-tions with everything that has been said by others before you, and to creatively contribute something that has the potential to further the interaction's improvisational flow, something that your partners can work with and build on.

In addition, parents should create opportunities for their children to engage in unstructured, improvisational play with other children their age. It's too difficult for most of us to pick up on the creative rhythms of children's play improvisations, but it comes naturally to children.

Children seem to be born with this ability to learn by participat-ing. And this ability stays with us throughout life—in fact, it's the kind of learning that adults go through every time they start a new job. It's especially important when you're starting your very first job after col-lege—when you are learning the kinds of knowledge that can't be found in textbooks. And it's particularly important in professional fields like law and medicine.

Law and medicine are highly technical fields that require years of graduate education. Legal education is focused on the written word—the court transcript, the volumes filled with records of prior decisions. Law schools rarely teach students how to *talk* like a lawyer—the unwrit-ten assumption is that good legal language should sound just like it's being read.[29] But of course, no one's speech sounds just like the printed word—this is just a legal version of our script-think bias. Whether they realize it or not, every profession has its own distinctive ways of talk-ing—its own speech patterns, catchphrases, shorthand symbols—that tell others "in the know" that you are one of them.

That's why becoming a lawyer involves more than simply learn-ing what's in the textbooks. First-year law students are told by their pro-fessors that the purpose of law school is not to teach you any particular facts, but is rather to teach you how to *think* like a lawyer. Law schools do this by using a conversational method of teaching: the Socratic method, a structured dialogue. First-year students don't learn only by sitting in lectures and reading books; they interact intensively with pro-fessors, with the rest of the class looking on. Sociologists refer to such education as *professional socialization*; professors teach students "how to think like a lawyer" by coaching and mentoring them to converse like a lawyer.[30] This method teaches them how to read a legal text—because a precedent-setting decision can rarely be applied to a new situation with-out interpretation. Law is more than what's in the books—it's being *con-*

versant with these legal texts, knowing how to use them creatively in the courtroom performance.

There's another benefit to professional socialization—to be taken seriously as a lawyer, you have to perform and speak like a lawyer. Even if you got straight As in law school and you are a brilliant lawyer, if you don't play the part properly—by speaking as everyone expects a lawyer to speak—then everyone will be suspicious of your credentials. For example, in the courtroom, the judge expects a certain style of speech, and expects the lawyer to know the basic interaction patterns of the trial format. This kind of knowledge is difficult to teach explicitly. In fact, law schools don't even try to teach lawyers about speech—the major textbook dealing with language and the law focuses exclusively on the written word. And trial practice, in general, receives low priority in law schools. Performing in a courtroom, or advising a client, requires a type of conversational creativity that is perhaps best acquired by working closely with a knowledgeable mentor, someone who already knows how to talk and act like a lawyer, scientist, or doctor.

Why can't lawyers speak in plain language? Most of us are suspicious of this Latin-laden jargon, pejoratively referring to it as "legalese." We cynically think that the only function of this jargon is to preserve a professional monopoly—you can't be a lawyer if you don't know how to talk like one. But there are some good reasons why legalese exists—just as there are good reasons why doctors and physicists use a specialized language to communicate with each other. In fact, most courtroom dialogue is spoken "to the record," couched with the potential of an appeals court in mind. Everyone trained in the law has learned these conventional ways of speaking, and there are hundreds of stock phrases that work like a conversational shorthand, communicating a very specific legal meaning to everyone else that knows the language. As frustrating as it is for the rest of us, legalese helps lawyers communicate with each other.

That's why most professional fields don't consider your education to be complete after you get the degree. You then have to go through an apprenticeship out in the field, where you work closely with a senior figure, who serves this function of socializing you into the discipline. Lawyers work as associates for at least seven years before they become partners. Professors work as assistant professors for seven years before they can be promoted to tenure. And doctors go through as many as eight years of residency after medical school before they become licensed to practice on their own. Mentorship—learning by working with a senior experienced professional—is built into the structure of these fields. Through mentoring, an advanced form of apprenticeship, you learn to think and talk in an appropriate manner for your professional role.

We often make a distinction between the on-the-job learning that we get from apprenticeship and mentoring, on the one hand, and the more formal instruction of the classroom, on the other. But if participatory learning is so effective for learning on the job, then why shouldn't it work in the classroom? We all know that the worst teachers are the ones who read their lectures, never interacting with the students. When we think of the great teachers that we remember, what made this person such a great teacher? Good teaching requires a special kind of creativity; unlike artistic creativity, creative teaching doesn't leave behind a brilliant painting or scientific theory when it's over. Instead, it leaves something invisible in the mind of the student. Good teaching, like good improv, is found in the *process* of teaching, not in any product that we can point to. A teacher's classroom performances are created for the unique demands of that classroom, at that moment, and the only thing left when the class leaves the room is the impression that remains in the head of the student.

Creative teaching is an improvisational performance, and the best teachers are good improvisational performers. But it usually takes years of practice to be an effective classroom improviser. For the first few years, young teachers tend to stick with the rigid curriculum and lesson plans that they were taught to use; they get nervous if a child does something unexpected that takes them off schedule. But as teachers gain more and more experience, their teaching becomes increasingly improvisational.

In a 1989 study of improvisational teaching, Hilda Borko and Carol Livingston of the University of Maryland compared experienced mathematics teachers and student teachers.[31] They found that the experienced teachers improvised in every class. They made decisions on the spot to respond to the unique demands of that class. Rather than preparing a detailed lesson plan, they prepared a flexible outline that allowed them to be responsive to the students. One expert teacher said, "I play off the kids," comparing his teaching method to a tennis match.

In contrast, inexperienced teachers developed specific and detailed lesson plans. They planned ahead every few pages of the textbook, and they rehearsed a script for each class, which the experienced teachers almost never did. One new teacher said, "I can't ad-lib it too well." When the students did something that veered the class in a different direction, the inexperienced teachers had trouble, because their ability to improvise a response was not fully developed. Some new teachers dealt with this by not allowing students to ask questions!

If we want to improve teaching, we need to teach improvisational skills. How can we teach improvisation? We can start by looking at how jazz musicians learn their craft. Aspiring jazz musicians rehearse the same song over and over before they attempt to improvise it on stage. The current way that we train teachers is through student teaching—they teach many different lessons during a semester. Although the school calendar might not permit it, what if we had them teach the same lesson plan several times in a row, but to different classes? This would be like the jazz musician who practices the same Miles Davis tune for weeks at home alone, before improvising it in a club. And working so closely with one lesson through repeated performances would let the student teacher feel what it's like to develop this improvisational ability; with every other improvisational art, skillful performance can only emerge after several times through the material.

Good teaching is an improvisational performance, and that's why so many educational fads and curriculum reforms fail—they don't examine how to make a teacher's improvisation more creative. Unfortunately, most reform efforts are biased by one of the two misconceptions that I introduced in Chapter 1, either *script-think,* a focus on the scripts of teaching—the curricula, the lesson plans, the standardized tests, or the *centralized mindset;* a focus on the directors and producers of the classroom performance—the principals, the administration, the organization of the school board. By focusing on scripts and directors, reformers often seem to be trying to "teacher proof" the curriculum, to remove all creativity from the classroom.[32]

But a better script, or a more effective director, does not necessarily result in a more creative improvisational performance, and this is the dilemma facing everyone who cares about education. A teacher who follows the script—no matter how well-conceived that script is—will be unable to respond effectively to the unique needs of each situation. And we can't develop a centrally administered plan to make teachers better improvisers. Improvisation, by its nature, requires collaboration, flexibility, responsiveness, and emergence. Different things work in different situations. Improvisational performances, by definition, will look different in every school, and in every classroom.

For too long, educational reformers have focused on the scripts and the directors of the classroom performance; that's why school administrators and curriculum experts have traditionally held a higher status than the teachers doing the work. It's the same way in theater— the playwright and the director have a higher status than the actors. The original motivation of the first improv group, The Compass, was to free the actor's creativity from the domination of the director and the script. In education, we need to free the teacher's creativity from the rigid constraints of the script (lesson plan) and the director (curriculum experts and administrators). We need to realize that good teaching is improvisational. Like all creating conversations, there is always some structure—

there are goals to education, and certain content must be taught—but thinking of the classroom as an improvisational performance can help us to harness teacher creativity in accomplishing these goals.

Epilogue

As I finish writing this book, I'm more excited than ever about the current state of conversation research. There are still many interesting and important questions to be studied, and the topics we've explored—performance, improvisation, interaction, collaboration, communication—come up repeatedly in many disciplines, including psychology, sociology, and anthropology. No single scientific discipline can give us a complete picture—that's because understanding conversation requires us to integrate many different perspectives on social and human behavior. It's hard to get a handle on all of these different perspectives at once. That's why universities are separated into different departments, such as psychology and sociology—each department focuses on a different *level of analysis* (see Figure 1). Psychology studies the individual; sociology studies the societies that people live in. Each perspective has its own strengths and weaknesses; psychology is pretty good at helping us to understand individual creativity, but doesn't do such a good job of explaining why all Americans are one way, whereas all French are another. Anthropology, in contrast, focuses on differences between cultures, and consequently doesn't spend as much time thinking about individual differences and individual creativity.

Level of Analysis	Discipline	Study of Conversation
Society	Sociology	Roles, statuses, participation frameworks, speech styles, socialization processes
Culture	Anthropology	Scripts, myths, rituals, catchphrases, audience-performer relations, metatalk variations, parent-child relations
Conversation	???	Improvisation, turn-taking, context influences, metatalk processes and strategies, influence of audience, collaboration
Individual	Psychology	Personality, goals, individual style, individual development and learning, improvisational ability

Figure 1. Levels of analysis in the study of conversation

There's an empty spot in Figure 1—that's because there's no single discipline dedicated to the study of the conversational level of analysis. Understanding conversation is an interdisciplinary project, cutting across many levels of analysis, and that's why I've drawn on so many different scientific fields in this book.

Levels of analysis are related to the phenomenon of *emergence,* a theme throughout this book. As we learned in Chapter 1, emergence occurs when interactions at one level of analysis lead to novelty at the next higher level of analysis. For example, the "V" shape of a bird flock is not centrally planned, but instead it emerges from local decisions made by each bird in the flock. The "V" is a *higher-level* phenomenon, emerging from the "lower level" actions of individual birds. The dramatic structure of an improvised play is a higher-level structure that emerges from the lower-level, moment-to-moment conversational decisions of each actor. Emergence comes into play whenever scientists are trying to understand phenomena that require simultaneous analysis at multiple levels. How can scientists best understand these phenomena?

Reductionism is the belief that the best way to understand any phenomenon is to break it down into its component lower-level parts, and then to analyze lower-level interactions. Reductionism has been immensely successful in the physical sciences: cells are analyzed in terms of their constituent proteins, protein structure is explored by analyzing the molecules in the protein, molecular structure is understood by reference to the physics of constituent atoms. Reductionism even works pretty well for many emergent phenomena. For example, it's fairly easy

to "reduce" the overall shape of a bird flock to the individual, local decisions of each bird. In fact, in 1987, Craig Reynolds wrote a computer
graphics program that generated a "virtual bird flock" on screen; the
program contains only local decision procedures for each bird, but no
central controller.[1] By generating such models—often called *distributed*
or *connectionist*—scientists are able to better understand emergent phenomena, by reducing the higher-level patterns to their lower-level com-
ponents.

   But strange things start to happen when you use reductionist
methods to study the collaborative emergence of an improvised performance. By analogy with the bird flock, a reductionist explanation of any
single performance would require you to model each actor's moment-to-
moment improvisational decision making and the communication
processes that we've studied in this book. If it worked, your model would
generate the same improvised play, just as Reynolds' computer program
generates a flock shape. But with collaborative improvisation, there are
two problems with reductionism. The first is practical: Current science has
no way to model the millions of neurons interacting in the human brain;
we are years away from understanding an individual's improvisational
behaviors; and we're just beginning to understand conversational interaction. Even if we knew everything there was to know about the mental
make-up of each performer, we would still have difficulties predicting the
flow of a group's improvisation, because there are so many possibilities
for change and transformation at each point in the scene. If a performer
delays her stage entrance by even a second, it may be too late: Another
actor may have already jumped out on stage during the wait.

   The second problem with reductionism is a more fundamental
theoretical one: With some emergent phenomena, the pattern that
emerges takes on its own independent existence, and begins to influence
the lower level from which it emerged—a phenomenon called *downward
causation*.[2] Unlike the emergent bird flock—where no single bird knows
anything about the overall shape of the flock—every improvising actor
knows the emergent dramatic frame; thus, the performers' mental states
are changing constantly throughout the performance, as they listen
closely to the ongoing flow of the improvisation, remember certain bits
of dialogue, and make connections with prior plot events. In Chapter 6,
we saw that conversations have both emergence and downward causation at the same time. Speakers create their conversational settings
through collaborative emergent processes; then the conversation "takes
on a life of its own," as Goffman wrote, and it begins to constrain the
future improvisations of the speakers.[3]

   When there is both emergence and downward causation
between levels of analysis, reductionist analysis is incredibly difficult,

and may be for all practical purposes impossible. Even after some hypo-thetical point in the future at which computer technology is capable of modeling every neuron and every thought process of each actor, a pure-ly reductionist model will still fail to represent the emergent, higher-level entity—the collaboratively created conversational frame.

Whenever we're trying to understand human behavior, we tend to have a preference for reductionist explanation; if there are competing explanations, we prefer lower levels of analysis. This accounts for our current fascination with genetic explanations for behavior—because genetic explanations are at a fairly low level of analysis. If we can explain a type of behavior—for example, violence in adolescents—in terms of a certain gene, we think that's a more valuable explanation than if a sociologist identifies a strong relationship between that behavior and neighborhood, income level, or family structure.

When it comes to the study of social phenomena, this lower-level bias combines with a distinctly American cultural assumption: that the individual is primary. This individualistic bias—known as *method-ological individualism*—leads us to assume that we can explain everything about society in terms of individual personalities and decisions.[4] Although we assume that explanations at lower levels of analysis are more scientific—and in particular, that psychological explanations for social phenomena are more scientific than higher-level ones—there's no rational basis for this belief. Explanations at any level of analysis can be scientific; there are thousands of sociologists, anthropologists, and econ-omists who are actively engaged in scientific research.

This cultural bias towards reductionist, individualist explana-tions translates into research dollars and media exposure; you'll see examples of this bias every day on the evening news and in the newspa-pers. For example, there's a large body of psychological research that studies individual personality and the child's development in social groups; almost none of this research is reported in the media. But in 1998, when researchers identified genetic differences between "extro-verted" and "introverted" worms, the *New York Times* covered the story, with several hypotheses about how such research could help us under-stand human social behavior.[5]

And of course, this bias affects research funding, with the social sciences getting a small percentage of total government science dollars. If I could identify the gene that makes people good improvisers, I would get a heck of a lot more grant money than I do by going to theaters and inter-viewing actors. But using biology to study social life is like the nearsighted man who searches for his lost glasses under the streetlight, even though he lost them in the dark shadows by the bushes. When asked why he's look-ing in the wrong location, he answers, "Because the light is brighter here."

The lower-level phenomena of biology or physics, compared to higher-level social phenomena, are easier to control, easier to reproduce, and tend not to vary with context. And our popular definition of science is closely associated with reproducible, context-independent phenomena; this kind of science leads to general predictions that will hold true in the future. When you repeat a physics experiment, you can expect your instruments and your materials to respond the same way every time; physical sciences depend on the reproducibility of experiments. But when the object of study is conversation, every situation is a little different. And creativity, by definition, is rare, unique, and unrepeatable. That's why creating conversations are not easy to control in an experiment, and our research findings are often difficult to generalize. But that's a fact of life that social scientists have to live with, because this variability is exactly what we want to explain: How do people behave differently in different situations? If we remove the context, so that we can reproduce our results in Tokyo or Timbuktu, it's no longer "social" science.

The science journalist John Horgan started a debate about the state of science with the 1996 publication of his book, *The End of Science: Facing the Limits of Knowledge in the Twilight of the Scientific Age*.[6] Horgan argued that pure science has entered its twilight. No more will there be a Darwin or an Einstein; there is less left to discover today. Many scientists perceived this as an attack on science itself, and most of the published responses to Horgan's book were highly critical. One of these critical responses appeared in *MIT's Technology Review*, an article by Robert M. Hazen in July of 1997.[7] Hazen countered Horgan's claim by listing 14 important, unanswered questions. How many of Hazen's unanswered questions addressed the social sciences? Less than one; Hazen's list included only one about human behavior: "Is behavior dictated by genes?" In 1997, James Trefil responded to Horgan's book with a book of his own, *The Edge of the Unknown: 101 Things You Don't Know About Science and No One Else Does Either*.[8] As with Hazen's article, all 101 items were details in the grand architecture of the physical sciences— medicine, astronomy, and technology. Horgan, Hazen, and Trefil— despite their disagreements—all overlooked the area of our greatest ignorance, the social sciences, where there is still no grand architecture, and where we still have more questions than answers. For every chapter in *Creating Conversations*, I could list 10 or more questions begging to be studied, including:

- Chapter 1: How do people decide to use a catchphrase? Why are some situations more scripted than others? What does scriptedness communicate to the participants?

- Chapter 2: Can we measure the creativity of a conversation? Will some metatalk techniques result in greater creativity? How can collaboration result in increased creativity?
- Chapter 3: How do people creatively select an audience? How do they manage to speak to multiple audiences simultaneously? Why do different cultures have different concepts of the fourth wall in performance?
- Chapter 4: What is the role of oral culture in children's development? Do children's improvisations vary in cultures with different conversational rules, and what can this tell us about child development? What bits of oral culture propagate successfully, and why?
- Chapter 5: What is the relationship between the characters provided by a culture and the individual personalities that form? Why do some situations require more "stock" characters, whereas other situations allow more flexibility? Are personalities different in different cultures, and is there any pattern to these differences?
- Chapter 6: How can people from different backgrounds communicate effectively? What are the exact processes and mechanisms that people use to collaboratively create the setting? In what contexts are participants less able to influence the setting, and why? Can we describe the dialectic of bi-directional influence between speakers and settings?
- Chapter 7: How can we make a business organization more creative—what's the relationship between individual creative insight and organizational creativity? How can we characterize good, creative teaching, and how can we teach this skill? How does conversation contribute to friendship, and to a fulfilling, meaningful life?

I'm not sure why so many science writers ignore the issues that I've discussed in this book, when they'll jump on a story about introverted worms. Why don't we see more about social science in the newspapers or on TV? Trefil's list of 101 unknown items displays one of the hidden assumptions of science: If we don't know how to answer a question, then the question must be unimportant. Scientists who are working down in the trenches don't spend much time wondering about where their questions come from—"theirs is not to reason why." But sociologists and philosophers—who study the big picture of science—have examined why some questions tend to be studied to death, whereas other equally important questions remain neglected for decades. As government has picked up more and more of the funding of scientific research, the general public is asking the same questions: Are scientists using our tax dollars to explore the questions that we want them to?

Perhaps the most famous theory about why scientists focus on some questions to the exclusion of others is the "paradigm" theory of the late Thomas Kuhn.[9] A paradigm is a scientific worldview that defines certain kinds of questions as "interesting." Young scientists internalize their discipline's paradigm in graduate school and may never think to ask any other types of questions; any other questions are usually considered to be unscientific, simply because they are not "officially approved" questions. There are a few exceptions; some scientists occasionally pause from their work to examine the history of question-asking in their own disciplines. When they do, they find that the questions aren't necessarily studied because they're the most important questions; rather, they're the questions that can be answered with the methodology available at the time. For example, the psychologist Gerd Gigerenzer has analyzed the history of psychological research and discovered that psychologists always focus on questions that can be answered by the statistical tools that they have available.[10] As new statistical tools were developed by mathematicians, psychologists predictably started to ask new sets of questions.

Despite our increasing awareness of how science works to exclude certain important, valid questions, many practicing scientists continue to think that questions that can't be answered with existing methods are simply not "good" questions. Most of the questions I've raised in this book—about conversation, creativity, and social context—are difficult questions, and no one is really sure how to go about answering them. In Kuhn's terminology, these sciences are *pre-paradigmatic.*

In the history of science, it's typical that during a pre-paradigmatic period, there are theorists—usually non-scientists—who argue that the phenomena cannot be studied scientifically. In the 1920s—before the grand synthesis of evolutionary biology and genetics—there were spirited debates about the evolutionary emergence of life: How could life emerge from non-living matter? Many philosophers of the time argued that biological science was incapable of answering this question.[11] But by 1930, once the grand synthesis was firmly established, these debates fizzled out. Following this pre-paradigmatic pattern, some contemporary scholars—post-modernists in literary theory, philosophy, and cultural studies—argue that "discourse" can never be scientifically understood—because conversation is socially constructed, or because the researcher participates in its construction, or because of its fundamentally subjective quality.[12] There is much that is insightful and helpful in this recent body of work, and in many cases, these theories do a better job of explaining conversation than the reductionist attempts of psychologists and linguists. Nonetheless in this book I have very consciously used the language of "science," to emphasize my belief that conversation can be studied scientifically. Although I believe that conversation can be studied scientifically, I don't think its study can follow a reductionist methodology—because conversation displays emergent processes. Echoing Durkheim's emergence argument of over 100 years ago, I believe that the social sciences cannot be reduced to the natural sciences.[13]

One scientific way to study conversation, even in the current pre-paradigmatic state of the field, is to conduct *qualitative* research, and this has been the usual approach in conversation research—to conduct a close analysis of one or two interesting examples of conversation. Most of the research I've reported in this book has been of this type. Many scientists are biased against qualitative methods, because they lack many of the advantages of experimental methods—generalizability and reproducibility. Descriptive and qualitative methods are quite appropriate in the early, pre-paradigmatic stages of a scientific discipline. But as the field develops a more elaborated scientific paradigm, I believe that conversational emergence will eventually be studied using quantitative, statistical methods, and using computational models.

Scientific ignorance is greatest when scientists don't know what questions to ask. As E. O. Wilson has written, we usually think of the social sciences as the "soft" sciences, but in reality, social science questions are the "hard" questions.[14] Creativity and conversation are two of the most difficult human phenomena that science has tried to explain; for example, even after decades of research, computers are still miserable conversationalists, and computers still aren't very creative. Before we can look for answers, we have to ask the right questions; one goal of this book has been to ask good questions about creating conversations. When I think about the creativity of everyday conversation, as a scientist I am humbled; there is much that we don't know.

What's the best way to get answers to the mysteries of creativity and conversation? We haven't dedicated many resources to these questions. It makes sense for our brightest minds and our tax dollars to focus on saving lives and improving technology. But Horgan may be partly right about "the end of science": As the physical sciences mature, they will eventually reach a point of diminishing returns. In the 20th century we may find that we can no longer neglect the social sciences. In fact, several of our leading scientists are beginning to realize the untapped potential of the social sciences. Psychologists and medical researchers referred to the 1990s as the "decade of the brain"; a committee of leading social scientists has proposed that the first decade of the 21st century be referred to as the "decade of behavior."[15] These scientists argue that *peo-*

ple should be the scientific focus of the 21st century—that human psychology, society, and culture are, after all, as important as particle physics or the genome of weird insects.

If we respond to these calls, we may finally dedicate more resources to the sciences of everyday life—to small talk, to daily creativity, to the ways that we change to match our situation. To how people work together in groups, and how we find fulfillment in our relationships and our daily encounters. To how cultural differences are reflected in different ways of talking, so that we can take advantage of this diversity and benefit from these encounters. To creating conversations, and the performances of everyday life; after all, these are what make us human.

Notes

PROLOGUE

1. Jaques, in *As You Like It*, Act ii, scene 7, line 139. "All the world's a stage, and all the men and women merely players: They have their exits and their entrances." Probably written in 1599, the play was first registered in August 1600, but not published until the First Folio (1623). The "life as theater" metaphor was widespread in England at that time. Biking through Forest Park in St. Louis, I was surprised to find a plaque with a similar quotation, by the English playwright Thomas Heywood (1574?-1641), a contemporary of Shakespeare. The plaque was mounted on the wall of the outdoor public theater, the MUNI: "The world's a theatre the earth a stage/Which God and nature do with actors fill."
2. In referring to Goffman's theory as a game metaphor, I am following Geertz's (1980) interpretation of Goffman as a form of game theory. For an example of Goffman's repeated claim that we are less spontaneous than we think we are, see Goffman (1959, pp. 73-74).

CHAPTER 1: SCRIPTS AND IMPROVISATIONS

1. Goffman (1959, p. 72).
2. Kahn (1995) outlines several methods of collaboration for directors and playwrights.

3. Schank and Abelson (1977b). An extended treatment can be found in their book from the same year (Schank & Abelson, 1977a). Abelson published an important elaboration in 1981, which discussed script variations (pp. 723-724) and a more generalized version of scripts called *metascripts* (pp. 724-727).

4. For a discussion of "event schemata" and related terms, see Mandler (1984). A nice integrative summary of all of these approaches—script, frame, event schemata—is found in Tannen (1979).

5. Langer (1989, 1997). However, in his 1981 article, Abelson pointed out a difference between script theory and Langer's focus (in the 1970s) on the automaticity of mindless behavior; for Abelson, scripts are cognitive structures available to consciousness, and thus scripts can be applied mindfully (1981, p. 723).

6. The Champs-Elysees advertisement appeared in Fall 1996, perfume by Guerlain Paris.

7. The Improv Institute and ImprovOlympic examples are from my own collection. There are several good books that document the Chicago improv scene, and the history of the first group, Second City. These include Coleman (1990), Halpern, Close, and Johnson (1994), and Sweet (1978). The original sourcebook is Spolin (1963).

8. Canby (1998b).

9. Halpern, Close, and Johnson (1994, p. 9).

10. Calvin (1996).

11. American Psychiatric Association (1994, pp. 66-71).

12. Brody (1997).

13. The ImprovOlympic example is from Halpern, Close, and Johnson (1994).

14. The ImprovOlympic example is from Halpern, Close, and Johnson (1994).

15. Csikszentmihalyi (1990).

16. See Bakhtin (1981), especially pages 279-281 on the *internal dialogism of the word*. Bakhtin identified several different forms of dialogism: in analyzing novels, he also used the terms *hybrid constructions* (pp. 304-318), and *double-voiced discourse* (p. 324).

17. Sahlins interview in Sweet (1978).

18. Speech styles are a major theme of Chapters 5 and 6. For an early review of sociological research into *styles of talking*, see Hymes (1974).

19. The term "indexicality," derived from Peirce's semiotic concept of the "index," was coined by the linguist Bar-Hillel in a classic 1954 paper; this is where the 90% estimate appears (Bar-Hillel, 1954). An important contemporary treatment is found in Silverstein (1995). "Indexicality" is used primarily by language philosophers; linguists tend to use the term "deixis," which refers to the same phenomenon but is derived from the Greek word for "pointing" rather than the Latin. See Chapter 2 of Levinson (1983).

20. Kuiper (1996).
21. Philips (1992).
22. Goffman (1959, p. 49).
23. Schegloff (1986, p. 125).
24. Levi-Strauss (1962/1966, pp. 16-36).
25. Many of the routines documented by the sociologist William Corsaro have strong emotional content, including the danger-rescue routine; see Corsaro (1985, pp. 192-208).
26. The Santa-Claus-Easter-Bunny example is from my own data. The psychologist Greta Fein (1985, 1987) proposed that the basic structure of children's group play is often centered on emotional themes. Even though each performance is different, the children are riffing on the same *affective template*.
27. On the commedia as oral tradition, see Fitzpatrick (1995). A paper by Kathleen McGill (1990) compares *commedia* to jazz and to folkloric performances and has additional references. Also see the essays in George and Gossip (1993). There is still some debate among scholars about the extent to which the *commedia* represents an oral tradition versus a literate one. In fact, until fairly recently, *commedia* was analyzed using the tools of literary scholarship and, at least implicitly, assumed to be no different from other types of written theater. There is also some debate about exactly how literate the early commedia actors were, and exactly how much improvisation occurred on stage. For example, directors rehearsed the most popular scenarios; it's possible that even in the absence of a script, the performances did not vary a whole lot. These debates reinforce this chapter's theme, that we need a more complex view of "improvisation": We don't have to decide whether the commedia was completely scripted or completely improvised, once we realize that improvisation can occur even within the structure of the scenario.
28. For more information on how the scene play was used in the early Compass theater, see Coleman (1990).
29. Goldstein quotations are taken both from personal communication and from Rigby (1994). Goldstein also drew on the work of linguists who have attempted to map out the possible ways that a story can be told by developing complicated flow charts that are called *story grammars*. For a review, see Mandler (1984).
30. For a discussion of *scenes à faire* and Hollywood legend, see Friend (1998a).
31. Friend (1998b).
32. *New York Times*, October 20, 1996, Section 4, p. 1.
33. Olson (1994). Also see Goody (1987) and Ong (1982).
34. For example, G. H. Mead commented on how often we erroneously think the present is predictable from what came before, in Mead (1932).
35. Structuralism is primarily associated with French theorists— including de Saussure, Levi-Strauss, and Barthes—who study stat-

ic and synchronic systems of signs, in language, myth, advertise-ments, clothing, and so on. French structuralism is based on the foundational ideas of the Swiss linguist, Ferdinand de Saussure (1915/1959). Some scholars use de Saussure's term "semiology" in a way that is synonymous with "structuralism."

36. Anthropologists and scripts: For an example, see Wierzbicka (1996).
37. Bourdieu (1977).
38. de Certeau (1984).
39. Resnick (1996). Several researchers have written computer pro-grams that simulate bird flocks using emergence principles—where each bird's local actions are programmed, but no bird is the leader (Heppner & Grenander, 1990; Reynolds, 1987). From these local rules, the recognizable shape of a flock emerges.
40. Meyer and Brown (1998).
41. For a discussion of emergence in social groups, see Sawyer (1999b).

CHAPTER 2: DIALOGUES

1. *Six Characters in Search of an Author,* written in 1921, opened at the New Oxford Theater on June 15, 1925. See the English translation in Pirandello (1991). Also helpful is the analysis in Sogliuzzo (1982, pp. 127-155).
2. For examples of avant-garde performance in New York, see Canby (1998a); Marks (1997).
3. Goffman (1974).
4. Schiffrin (1980). In this paper, Schiffrin analyzed two types of metatalk. In the first type, "informational," a speaker uses metatalk to introduce or conclude a story, an explanation, or an entire con-versation. The second type, "evaluative," is typically used during arguments. Evaluative metatalk is found in "evaluative brackets," such as "I don't agree with that" or "That's not the point." But note that both of Schiffrin's examples of metatalk are relatively explicit; they're easy to identify because the speakers stop what they're doing to metatalk.
5. Bateson (1955/1972); Silverstein (1976, 1993).
6. The preference for explicit metatalk is not inherent in the English language; Gumperz, Aulakh, and Kaltman (1982) compared the use of metatalk in British English and Indian English and found that Indian English speakers use much less explicit metatalk (pp. 54-56).
7. An excellent summary of Grice's theory can be found in Chapter 3 of Levinson (1983).
8. For a more elaborate analysis of children's metatalk, see Sawyer (1997).

9. Bakhtin (1981, p. 324).

10. Korolija (1998).

11. For a discussion of teacher revoicing, see O'Connor and Michaels (1996).

12. For a good overview of research on reported speech, see the collection of articles in Lucy (1993).

13. There hasn't been much research on retellings of events in everyday conversation—perhaps because the researcher has to gather a lot of naturally occurring conversation to find one example of filling in, and because a full understanding of the event requires an analysis of both the retelling and of the entire prior conversation. The most relevant recent study is Norrick (1998).

14. Goncu (1993).

15. Bruner (1996).

16. The example is taken from Sawyer (1997, p. 98). The 50% rejection rate is also reported in this book. Chapter 5 of this book contains an introduction to recent psychological research on play entry.

17. Paley (1992).

18. For a study of the entrance strategies of everyday adult conversation, see Schegloff (1968). For a corresponding study of the exit strategies of everyday adult conversation, see Schegloff and Sacks (1973).

19. The classic discussion of turn-taking is a famous article by Sacks, Schegloff, and Jefferson (1974). This article defines "conversation" by referring to the improvised, collaborative nature of turn-taking. For a discussion of turn-taking as an emergent phenomena, see Clark (1996, Chapter 11).

20. A good review of interruption research is in Aries (1996, Chapter 4).

21. Yamada (1989).

22. The data on Finland are from Lehtonen and Sajavaara (1985). The information on Denmark and Northern Sweden is on page 112 of Reisman (1974).

23. Burke (1993, p. 94).

24. Tannen (1989). For New York Jewish style, also see Tannen (1981).

25. Reisman (1974).

26. This example is from Sawyer (1997, p. 156).

27. The Prague School of linguists worked in Prague between the two world wars. The most famous of these was Roman Jakobson, who migrated to the United States and taught at the New School, Harvard, and MIT for the rest of his career, introducing generations of American linguists to Prague school concepts and theories. The best-known exposition of his "poetic function" is Jakobson (1960). However, Jakobson had published these ideas in Czech as early as 1921, and this theme runs through many of the Prague school theorists; see Shapiro and Shapiro (1988, Chapter 4).

28. For a broad review of creoles and pidgins, see Reinecke (1964). For a review of research on *creolization*—when pidgins develop into a language, especially through first-language acquisition—see Bickerton (1981), Sankoff (1980). For an interesting study of the emergence of a pidgin sign language among deaf adults and children who were brought together in a single community in Nicaragua, less than 12 years ago, see Kegl, Senghas, and Coppola (1999).
29. Burke (1993). Also see the collected papers in Cope (1992).
30. King (1994). Gabor (1983) is another example of the how-to genre.
31. The creativity research project is described in Csikszentmihalyi (1996). The quotations that I use here are from Csikszentmihalyi and Sawyer (1995).

CHAPTER 3: AUDIENCES

1. Although its importance is widely recognized, body language is studied by only a small number of researchers. Most of the research on *kinesics*, or *body language*, was done between the 1950s and the 1970s; the topic seems to have become less popular among researchers after 1980. However, very little of this research focused on the relation of body language to conversational interaction; most of it focused on how individuals communicate specific messages—for example, emotions—nonverbally. In Michael Argyle's (1988) overview of the field, only Chapter 7 is devoted to conversation.
2. The term "back channel" was coined in Yngve (1970).
3. Goodwin (1981). The first example is from page 57; the second, from page 67.
4. Hickey (1991). Also described in Kuiper (1996, pp. 90-91).
5. Goodwin (1986).
6. Most linguists use the term *conduit metaphor*, a term coined in an influential article by Reddy (1979). The *football metaphor* is a term I borrowed from Michael Silverstein (personal communication). The football theory was first presented in formal terms by Shannon and Weaver (1949; see particularly the figure on page 98). This model influenced the next decade of research in cybernetics and communication theory. Because it was so successful as a framework for computer and network communication, it was perhaps too readily applied to human linguistic communication. Most scientists of human conversation do not accept the football theory. Perhaps the first critic was Birdwhistell, a kinesics researcher, who noted that the football theory could not account for the parallelism of back channel nonverbal messages (1970, pp. 65-79). Like my argument in this chapter, Irvine's (1996) critique is based on its simplistic

notion of speaker and hearer. David Olson (1994, pp. 270-271) has argued that the football metaphor only becomes widespread after the onset of literacy.

7. Goffman's famous essay "Footing" (1981) identified several types of audiences. Also see the elaboration in Levinson (1988).
8. Bakhtin (1981, pp. 280-282; 1986, p. 99).
9. Levinson (1983, pp. 17-18).
10. For speech act theory, the classic reference is Austin (1962).
11. Morgan (1996).
12. Fisher (1976); first quotation on page 231, second on page 234.
13. Dixon (1972). Dixon discussed the mother-in-law language on pages 32-34, and the group's history on pages 34-37.
14. The conversational dynamics of talk show discourse is surprisingly neglected as a research topic. Doug Glick's (1996) research is one exception, an analysis of a talk-show interview on Israeli television.
15. Austin (1962).
16. The two most widely accepted industry standards as of 2000— KQML and FIPA—are both based on a speech act model (Sawyer, 2000b).
17. An excellent discussion of the problem posed by indirect speech acts is in Levinson (1983, pp. 263-283). Also of interest is the brief summary of recent critiques of speech act theory in Bauman and Briggs (1990, pp. 62-66). For critiques of speech act theory as applied to children's language socialization, see Cook-Gumperz (1986, pp. 44-48).
18. The only study of these writings that I know of is a study of how their style reflects the closeness of the relationship (Giordano, 1995).
19. This example is taken from Heath (1984).
20. There's a long-standing belief among psychoanalysts that all conversations involve transference (e.g., Meerloo, 1952, pp. 210-212; Willoughby, 1932), although Freud himself only used the term "transference" to refer to the analyst-patient relationship. For a brief introduction to Freud's concept of transference, see the two lectures (Freud, 1958, 1966).
21. Psychologists have not paid much attention to this phenomenon; I am only aware of one study of gravesite "conversation" with the deceased (Josephs, 1998), an interview study with German Christians, which found that such conversations were common.
22. Kristof (1996).
23. Philips (1974).
24. Several examples of this pattern, in both verbal and musical performance, are described in Sawyer (1996b). Bauman (1977, p. 28) also observed that, across cultures, ritual performances have the most bounded "fourth wall."
25. The classroom discussion of Plutarch's Lives is from Wortham (1994, pp. 83-102).

26. Several researchers have discussed the formalization of ritual over time, including Bloch (1975), DuBois (1992), and McDowell (1983). Tambiah used the term *ossification* (1985, Chapter 4).
27. Olson (1994) explored the psychological effects of living in a literate culture.
28. Mulkay (1986).
29. For a theoretically informed study of electronic discourse, see Davis and Brewer (1997). However, their study analyzed interactions between 1989 and 1993, and etiquette has evolved rapidly since then; see Hafner (1998).
30. For some examples of new proposals for electronic communication, circa 1999, see Caruso (1999). This article described many projects, including one called Web Lab: www.weblab.org.
31. Foucault (1972). For a recent clarification of Foucault's concept of "discourse," see Sawyer (1999a).
32. Iser (1978). Iser argued that the literary text provided something like a script to the reader; the reader's job is to create an aesthetic experience by performing—or reading—the text. Reader-response theorists also include even more radical literary theorists; most famously, Stanley Fish has argued that there is nothing in the text that is not put there by the reader. Note that Iser's German word, *wirkung*, doesn't translate as "response," but means something more like a mechanical effect or result—clearly emphasizing the causal role of the original text. The term also doesn't carry the same psychological connotations as the American term "response," which I think subtly reinforce American perspectives such as Fish's, which emphasize the subjectivity of the reader's experience. The differences between "response" and "working" are subtle but substantial. For an example of how reader response theory might look if the word had been directly translated from German, see John Dewey's (1934) discussions of "art working." Dewey used the noun "working" in the German sense in 1934: "There is a difference between the art product and the work of art. The first is physical and potential; the latter is active and experienced. It is what the product does, its working" (Dewey, 1934, p. 162).
33. Anderson and Meyer (1988).
34. See the references on pages 21-22, and Chapters 28 through 32, of Cobley (1996).
35. For an overview of approaches comparing painting and performance, see Sawyer (1995). Three classic treatments are Collingwood (1938), Wollheim (1980), and Dewey (1934). For a comparison of Collingwood and Dewey on the topic of improvisation, see Sawyer (2000a).
36. Picasso (1982).
37. Collingwood (1938).
38. Csikszentmihalyi (1988).
39. Gardner (1993).

CHAPTER 4: REHEARSALS

1. Piaget (1945/1962).
2. See Sawyer (1997) for a more detailed discussion of how the improvisations of play contribute to social and conversational development. The first transcript is taken from page 54, and the second from pages 63-64.
3. Role play has been a topic of developmental research since the 1970s. Overviews can be found in Corsaro (1993); Miller and Garvey (1984); and Sawyer (1997).
4. In applying the script metaphor to children's pretend play, developmental psychologists borrowed Schank and Abelson's first usage of the metaphor (see pp. 9-11). The first developmental application of this metaphor was Nelson and Gruendel (1979).
5. Berliner (1994).
6. Stanislavsky wrote several books describing his technique, and many of them have been translated into English. These include Stanislavsky (1936, 1962).
7. Traditionally, the flux and contingency of rehearsal has been opposed to the fixity of the performance itself. But—just as modern theater is breaking down the fourth wall—modern theater is also breaking down the barrier between rehearsal and live performance, with a nod of the head to Pirandello (pp. 44-45). For an overview of these issues, see Baker-White (1999).
8. Keith Jarrett quotation from Solomon (1997, p. 35).
9. This section on Mike Leigh draws from Ansen (1996) and Frost and Yarrow (1990, pp. 37-45).
10. For a detailed history of the early days of The Compass, see Coleman (1990).
11. Interview with Sahlins, in Sweet (1978, p. 188).
12. On jazz personnel receiving credit, see Ratliffe (1998).
13. This description of the Orpheus Chamber Orchestra draws on Traub (1996). Apart from a few ethnomusicologists, there has been almost no empirical study of interaction in musical ensembles. For an exception—a study of the collaborative negotiation of tempo in orchestra rehearsals—see Weeks (1990).
14. Baker-Sennett, Matusov, and Rogoff (1992).
15. Levi-Strauss (1964/1969, pp. 17-18).
16. I took this version of the history of the Neiman-Marcus cookie recipe from an urban legend web site created by Barbara and David P. Mikkelson, at http://snopes.simplenet.com/. Many urban legends have been collected and published by folklorist Jan Harold Brunvand (e.g., 1999, 2000).
17. In anthropology, these issues emerged in Chicago in the mid-1980s, at the privately funded Center for Psychosocial Studies. This group coined the terms *decentering, recentering, decontextualization,* and *entextualization*. There are two references to this work. The first

is the influential review article by Bauman and Briggs (1990). More recently, an edited volume has brought together many of the theorists working in this area; see Silverstein and Urban, 1996. In the 1950s and 1960s, rumor dissemination and transmission was a major concern of sociologists who studied *collective behavior*. Two representative texts are Shibutani (1966) and Buckner (1969). Unlike the linguistic anthropologists, those researchers did not emphasize linguistic and textual methodology and analysis, but instead focused on social networks and communication among individuals.

18. On memetics, see Dennett (1995). Several evolutionary biologists are quite critical of memetics, and its use of evolutionary metaphors for cultural products; see, for example, Gould (1997).

19. Iwamura (1980).

20. Opie & Opie (1959). Figure 4.1 is adapted from pages 10-11.

21. The classic references on the Serbo-Croatian epics are Lord (1960/1965) and Parry (1971). For the hypothesis that there was no composer of these epic poems, but that they emerged from an oral performance tradition, see Nagy (1996), and a subsequent review by Pelliccia (1997). For an analysis of how psychological constraints influence the structures of both counting-out rhymes and of epic poetry, see Rubin (1995).

22. Drewal (1992).

23. Fox (1974). On page 79, Fox estimated that a performer must know between 1,000 and 1,500 dyads to be minimally fluent as a chanter.

24. A good discussion of how literacy changes a culture's concepts of what performances are "the same" is found in Olson (1994).

25. The idea that conversation is partly new and partly historical is associated with Bakhtin's notion of *dialogism* (see p. 25).

26. *Groundhog Day*, directed by Harold Ramis, 1993. In 1996, when the *New York Times Magazine* asked "What works created in the late 20th century will still be discussed, viewed, read and cherished 100 years from now?", the Harvard professor of philosophy and movie critic, Stanley Cavell, chose this movie. September 29, 1996, p. 177.

CHAPTER 5: CHARACTERS

1. "Social constructionism" is a broad and amorphous theoretical position. The strong version holds that all knowledge about reality is socially constructed, and therefore that there is no objective, scientific, or rational knowledge. For a critical discussion of the strong version, see Hacking (1999). For a less critical statement of the strong version, see Burr (1995). Burr's view of the person as an "occupier of subject positions within discourses" is consistent with role theory (discussed later in this Chapter), because the term "dis-

courses" is used to refer to macro-structural relations (see Sawyer, 1999a). My approach is in this book is a weaker version of social constructionism. Like the strong version, I argue that conversation and language mediates all perceptions of the world, and I argue that researchers must focus on improvisational processes rather than static structures (as I emphasized at the end of Chapter 1). However, I believe that these mediational processes can be studied through the methods of objective science; thus, my approach is not postmodern, as is most social constructionism. An example of the sort of empirical, objective social constructionism that I advocate is found in my first book (Sawyer, 1997), and in (Nelson, 1996), which explores how a child's development is socially constructed through language. It is striking that so few strong social constructionists refer to empirical work on conversation.

2. Gabler (1998, p. 58). As we saw in Chapter 1, the idea that life is performative is not new; Gabler explores how new media, and the integration of media with life, can change the nature of this everyday performance. Other scholars have also explored the role of new media; for example, Abercrombie and Longhurst (1998) refer to modern society as a *diffused audience*, because people are both members of the audience, and simultaneously are performers themselves. They write: "The media are constitutive of everyday life . . . we live in a performative society" (p. 175).

3. Hornbrook (1998, p. 115).

4. Role play is one of the most common types of pretend play. See Note 3 of Chapter 4 (p. 229).

5. Hornbrook (1998, pp. 118-119).

6. More detail on the *commedia dell'arte* can be found in Chapter 1, pages 32-33.

7. Goffman (1967, p. 47).

8. "When an individual projects a definition of the situation and thereby makes an implicit or explicit claim to be a person of a particular kind, he automatically exerts a moral demand upon the others, obliging them to value and treat him in the manner that persons of his kind have a right to expect" (Goffman, 1959, p. 13).

9. The on-line Model UN is described in Wagner et al. (1996). For another educational example of performing a role, see the description of the Paideia classroom in Chapter 3, pages 94-96.

10. Some of these ideas are taken from a 1996 interview with Wayne Fields, a political scientist who studies the rhetoric of American politics (St. Louis *Riverfront Times*, October 11, 1996, p. 23). Also see Fields (1996).

11. James (1890, Chapter 10).

12. For a summary of the history of role theory, see Stryker and Statham (1985, pp. 330-341).

13. Specifics are taken from Brooks and Marsh (1995, p. 457).

14. Minsky (1985).

15. Ewing (1990).
16. Gergen (1967).
17. Bourdieu (1987).
18. Resnick (1996). Also see Chapter 1, pages 39-41.
19. Internal family systems therapy (Schwartz, 1995). Cast of characters work (Watanabe-Hammond, 1986).
20. The quotations are taken from an unpublished article by Jennifer Harris, Chicago, 1992. Also see Fine's (1983) sociological study of role-playing games.
21. Turkle (1995). New technologies are emerging rapidly, and any such references are bound to go out of date. Two other recent ethnographies of Internet communities are Cherny (1999) and Surratt (1998).
22. Goffman's exploration of the concept of "face" is found in "On face-work," the first chapter of Goffman (1967).
23. Barry (1999).
24. Carbaugh (1996, Chapter 2).
25. My study of children's group voice is described in Sawyer, (1996a).
26. Goffman first explored these ideas in 1974, pages 517-523. On pages 522-523, Goffman noted that the stage actor is analytically similar to the ventriloquist's puppet; the only difference is that the animation is done from different distances: after all, the stage performer "manipulates his own limbs and his own lips." A more extended and canonical treatment is found in Goffman (1981). The "primitive notions" quotation is on page 128; the discussion of speaker roles is on pages 144-152. Levinson (1988) further elaborated these subcategories into 10 "producer roles."
27. For many examples of indirect performance style play, see Sawyer (1997).
28. *Double voicing* is a concept associated with Bakhtin (1986). The term "ventriloquism" is often attributed to Bakhtin, but as best as I've been able to determine it was never used by him. Two prominent Bakhtin scholars, Jim Wertsch and Michael Holquist, have both told me that they've never seen it in Bakhtin's writings. In connection with Bakhtin, the earliest use of the term that I can find is in Holquist (1981, p. 181).
29. Schieffelin (1990).
30. Goffman (1959, pp. 252-253).
31. Geertz (1980, p. 170).
32. MacIntyre (1984, p. 32).
33. Typical books of the period include Clance (1985) and Harvey and Katz (1985).
34. James (1892, p. 216). This 1892 book was an abridged version of James's 1890, two-volume masterpiece, which contained the similar passage "that thought is itself the thinker" (1890, Vol. 1, p. 401). However, the 1892 version had some significant differences; in the 1890 work, James did not use the plural "mes," preferring instead

to write "selves"; and his discussion of the "I" was not as explicit. The I-me distinction is sometimes erroneously attributed to G. H. Mead (1934), who elaborated James's concepts within his discussion of the social foundations of the self (p. 173 passim).

35. Koven (1998).

CHAPTER 6: SETTINGS

1. See Chapter 2, note 7, page 224.
2. Bauman and Briggs (1990).
3. Pogo cartoon originally appeared on May 29, 1950; can be found in Kelly (1959, p. 27).
4. See Chapter 2, pages 62-65.
5. See Chapter 1, page 26.
6. Gumperz (1982); Spanish-English bilinguals, page 66 and Chapter 4 in general; the graduate student example and discussion are on pages 30-34.
7. Inoue (1979, pp. 285-296); Martin (1964).
8. In fact, there was a verb form of "thou" in the English of Shakespeare's era, when "thou" was used in English as an informal pronoun. The verb "thou" was used to express contempt: "I thou thee" meant something like "I spit on you" (Brown & Gilman, 1960, pp. 274-275).
9. Gumperz (1982, p. 133).
10. Friedrich (1971). *The Village of Stepanchikovo* example is analyzed on pages 244-245.
11. A seminal article by Brown and Gilman (1960) documented the connections between cultural ideology and language use.
12. In a survey of employees at Toronto companies, sociologist Bonnie Erickson (1996) found that the predominant cross-class topic, after work itself, was sports. Class was measured by job status— employee, supervisor, owner. She also found that knowledge about sports did not vary with social class. Because the companies included in the survey employed security guards and licensed investigators, 80% of her respondents were men.
13. Hijirada and Sohn (1986).
14. Poussaint (1967). For a general discussion of *terms of address,* and an interesting analysis of this interaction (on page 223), see Ervin-Tripp (1972). Also see the discussion of Ervin-Tripp's theory of address in Braun (1988).
15. Brown and Gilman (1960, p. 261).
16. Brown and Gilman (1960, pp. 265-266); Knowles (1997, pp. 105-106).
17. Goffman (1967, p. 95).

18. A more extended treatment of this theme—that more valued set-
     tings are more formalized—can be found in Sawyer (1996b). The
     discussion of *formalization* began with Bloch (1975). A quick sum-
     mary of the resulting controversy can be found in Bauman and
     Briggs (1990, pp. 62-63).
19. Caton (1990).
20. For Grice, see Chapter 2, pp. 48-49; for Austin, see Chapter 3, pp.
     86-87.
21. Bateson (1990).
22. Monson (1996).
23. Todorov (1984, p. 87).
24. Goodwin and Goodwin (1992).
25. Goffman (1974). Goffman's usage of "frame" has some interesting
     similarities to how the term was later used by artificial intelligence
     researchers, beginning with Minsky (1975).
26. Goffman (1974, Chapter 3). Goffman used the term "keying" to
     refer to an action that shifts the current interaction into a different
     frame; for example, when children who are play fighting suddenly
     get really angry and start genuinely fighting ("downkeying").
27. Goffman (1967, p. 113).

CHAPTER 7: PERFORMANCES

1. Guare (1990).
2. The phrase "conversational duet" was coined by Falk (1980). When
    good friends are engaged in a conversational duet, they often inter-
    rupt each other, but this type of interruption isn't perceived as
    rude (Coates, 1997; Tannen, 1989; see also Chapter 2, pp. 58-62).
    This collaborative speech style is also common among native
    Hawaiian speakers, and is called *talk story* (Watson, 1975).
3. See Chapter 3, back channelling, pages 74-75.
4. Dunbar (1996). An interdisciplinary overview of research on gossip
    for the general reader is found in Levin and Arluke (1987). This
    book focuses on gossip about famous public figures—politicians
    and movie stars—and many of their examples come from newspa-
    pers; for example, one chapter is a study of gossip columns.
5. Brenneis (1984). Many cultures allow for collaborative, joint story-
    telling and gossip. Watson's (1975) study of Polynesian talk story
    documented a similar sort of rhythmic, poetic structure to these
    collaborative tellings. Another interesting research report is Burns
    (1980).
6. Several researchers have observed that American women engage
    in the "conversational duet" style of conversation much more than
    American men (Coates, 1997; Tannen, 1989). Coates (1997) docu-
    mented the improvisational nature of these conversations, refer-

ring to them as verbal jam sessions.
7. Csikszentmihalyi (1990).
8. Sawyer (1997).
9. Cohen et al. (1997).
10. Schiffrin (1984). Also of interest is a critique of Schiffrin's article by Lee and Peck (1995). In pages 36-40 of this critique, Lee and Peck documented several cooperative features being used even in the midst of a heated disagreement. They concluded that all argument involves collaboration, not only the forms of Jewish argument studied by Schiffrin.
11. For an interesting theoretical discussion of how disagreements still require collaboration, see Matusov (1996). Many conversation researchers have studied the special type of conversation that occurs during disagreements. See the collection of research reports in Grimshaw (1990).
12. Tannen (1998).
13. Pine and Gilmore (1999, p. x).
14. *San Jose Mercury News*, 1996.
15. For a discussion of how the legal notion of "copyright" influences our assumptions about creativity, see Wertsch (1995).
16. Eisenberg (1990) seems to have first applied the jazz term "jamming" to organizational contexts, although this usage has been widely popularized by the Harvard Business School professor John Kao (1996), who has a Web site (http://www.jamming.com/) and a consulting business based on jamming.
17. The study is described in Csikszentmihalyi (1996). Also see Chapter 2, pages 69-71.
18. Eisenberg (1990, p. 159).
19. Goodwin (1995).
20. Bearison et al. (1999).
21. Ghoshal and Bartlett (1995).
22. Drucker (1988).
23. Gardner (1995); Simonton (1994).
24. Vygotsky (1978, pp. 84-91).
25. Rogoff (1990); Rogoff et al. (1993).
26. Singer & Singer (1990, Chapter 5); Taylor (1999).
27. There are many studies on the developmental effects of the amount of pretend play, and children's preferences for peers over parents, including Dunn (1986) and Haight and Miller (1993).
28. For a discussion of cross-cultural studies of children's play, see Sawyer (1997, p. 6).
29. O'Barr (1981).
30. Elizabeth Mertz has done studies of first-year law school classroom discourse, analyzing how the unwritten patterns of dialogue communicate implicit messages about "how to think like a lawyer." See, for example, Mertz (1996).

31.   Borko and Livingston (1989). Also see Janine Remillard's (1997) study of improvisation in mathematics teaching. Pineau (1994) argued that the metaphor of *improvisational* performance avoids the individualistic bias associated with some versions of the "teaching is performance" metaphor, because that metaphor often implies that teaching is a *solo* performance.

32.   Sawyer (1999c).

EPILOGUE

1.   Reynolds (1987).
2.   Sawyer (1999b).
3.   Goffman (1967, p. 113).
4.   For a collection of essays on the topic of methodological individualism, see the reader edited by O'Neill (1973).
5.   Wade (1998).
6.   Horgan (1996).
7.   Hazen (1997).
8.   Trefil (1997).
9.   Kuhn (1960).
10.   Gigerenzer (1994).
11.   Blitz (1992).
12.   Many theorists, including social constructionists and postmodernists, use the term "discourse" in a way that has very little to do with conversation per se. In this usage, "discourse" is often treated as a count noun: "a discourse," "many discourses," "discourses of power." What is typically meant by this usage is *not* a "conversation," but something more like a conceptual scheme, or what Goffman calls a *primary framework* (1974, p. 21). Although this usage is often attributed to Foucault, he never used the term this way; rather, he was always quite careful to restrict his notion of discourse to uses of language (Sawyer, 1999a).
13.   Durkheim (1895/1964).
14.   "The social sciences are hypercomplex. They are inherently far more difficult than physics and chemistry, and as a result they, not physics and chemistry, should be called the hard sciences" (Wilson, 1998, p. 183).
15.   The Decade of Behavior was originally proposed by the American Psychological Association. The committee later included sociologists, anthropologists, political scientists, and economists. See the web site: http://www.decadeofbehavior.org/

References

Abelson, R. P. (1981). Psychological status of the script concept. *American Psychologist, 36*(7), 715-729.

Abercrombie, N., & Longhurst, B. (1998). *Audiences: A sociological theory of performance and imagination.* Thousand Oaks, CA: Sage.

American Psychiatric Association. (1994). *Diagnostic and statistical manual of mental disorders, 4th edition.* Washington, DC: Author.

Anderson, J. A., & Meyer, T. P. (1988). *Mediated communication: A social action perspective.* Newbury Park, CA: Sage.

Ansen, D. (1996, September 30). A long day's journey into light. *Newsweek,* 74-75.

Argyle, M. (1988). *Bodily communication* (2nd ed.). New York: Methuen & Co. (Original work published 1975)

Aries, E. (1996). *Men and women in interaction: Reconsidering the differences.* New York: Oxford University Press.

Austin, J. L. (1962). *How to do things with words.* Oxford: Clarendon Press.

Baker-Sennett, J., Matusov, E., & Rogoff, B. (1992). Sociocultural processes of creative planning in children's playcrafting. In P. Light & G. Butterworth (Eds.), *Context and cognition: Ways of learning and knowing* (pp. 93-114). Hillsdale, NJ: Lawrence Erlbaum Associates.

Baker-White, R. (1999). *The text in play: Representations of rehearsal in modern drama.* Lewisburg, PA: Bucknell University Press.

Bakhtin, M. M. (1981). Discourse in the novel. In *The Dialogic Imagination* (pp. 259-422). Austin: University of Texas Press.

Bakhtin, M. M. (1986). The problem of speech genres. In *Speech genres and other late essays* (pp. 60-102). Austin: University of Texas Press.

Bar-Hillel, Y. (1954). Indexical expressions. *Mind, 63*(251), 359-379.

Barry, D. (1999, June 6). Dog never drops his guard—except during dessert. *St. Louis Post-Dispatch*, pp. EV2.

Bateson, G. (1955/1972). A theory of play and fantasy. In G. Bateson (Ed.), *Steps to an ecology of mind* (pp. 177-193.). New York: Chandler. (Reprinted from *American Psychiatric Association Research Reports*, 1955, *II*, 39-51).

Bateson, M. C. (1990). *Composing a life.* New York: Penguin Books.

Bauman, R. (1977). *Verbal art as performance.* Prospect Heights, IL: Waveland Press.

Bauman, R., & Briggs, C. L. (1990). Poetics and performance as critical perspectives on language and social life. *Annual Review of Anthropology, 19,* 59-88.

Bearison, D. J., Dorval, B., LeBlanc, G., Sadow, A., & Plesa, D. (1999). *Collaborative cognition: Children negotiating their ways of knowing.* Unpublished research report. New York: CUNY Graduate Center.

Berliner, P. (1994). *Thinking in jazz: The infinite art of improvisation.* Chicago: University of Chicago Press.

Bickerton, D. (1981). *The roots of language.* Ann Arbor, MI: Karoma.

Birdwhistell, R. L. (1970). *Kinesics and context: Essays on body motion communication.* Philadelphia: University of Pennsylvania Press.

Blitz, D. (1992). *Emergent evolution: Qualitative novelty and the levels of reality.* Dordrecht: Kluwer Academic.

Bloch, M. (1975). Introduction. In M. Bloch (Ed.), *Political language and oratory in traditional society* (pp. 1-28). New York: Academic Press.

Borko, H., & Livingston, C. (1989). Cognition and improvisation: Differences in mathematics instruction by expert and novice teachers. *American Educational Research Journal, 26*(4), 473-498.

Bourdieu, P. (1977). *Outline of a theory of practice.* New York: Press Syndicate of the University of Cambridge.

Bourdieu, P. (1987). The biographical illusion. In R. J. Parmentier & G. Urban (Eds.), *Working papers and proceedings of the Center for Psychosocial Studies, No. 14* (pp. 1-7). Chicago: Center for Psychosocial Studies.

Braun, F. (1988). *Terms of address: Problems of patterns and usage in various languages and cultures.* New York: Mouton de Gruyter.

Brenneis, D. (1984). Grog and gossip in Bhatgaon: Style and substance in Fiji Indian conversation. *American Ethnologist, 11,* 487-506.

Brody, J. E. (1997, February 4). Quirks, oddities, may be illnesses. *New York Times,* pp. B9, B11.

Brooks, T., & Marsh, E. (1995). *The complete directory to prime time network and cable TV shows, 1946-present.* New York: Ballantine Books.

Brown, R., & Gilman, A. (1960). The pronouns of power and solidarity. In T. A. Sebeok (Ed.), *Style in language* (pp. 253-276). Cambridge, MA: MIT Press.

Bruner, J. (1996). *The culture of education.* Cambridge, MA: Harvard University Press.

Brunvand, J. H. (1999). *Too good to be true: The colossal book of urban legends.* New York: Norton.

Brunvand, J. H. (2000). *The truth never stands in the way of a good story.* Urbana: University of Illinois Press.

Buckner, H. T. (1969). A theory of rumor transmission. In R. R. Evans (Ed.), *Readings in collective behavior* (pp. 120-136). Chicago: Rand McNally.

Burke, P. (1993). *The art of conversation* (1st ed.). Ithaca, NY: Cornell University Press.

Burns, A. F. (1980). Interactive features in Yucatec Mayan narratives. *Language in Society, 9,* 307-319.

Burr, V. (1995). *An introduction to social constructionism.* New York: Routledge.

Calvin, W. H. (1996). *How brains think: Evolving intelligence, then and now.* New York: Basic Books.

Canby, V. (1998a, Sunday, April 19). Bursting through that fourth wall. *New York Times,* pp. AR3, AR24.

Canby, V. (1998b, May 31). "Power Plays," something more than a family affair. *New York Times,* pp. 6, 18.

Carbaugh, D. (1996). *Situating selves: The communication of social identities in American scenes.* Albany: State University of New York Press.

Caruso, D. (1999, Monday, July 5). Digital commerce. *New York Times,* p. C3.

Caton, S. C. (1990). *Peaks of Yemen I summon: Poetry as cultural practice in a North Yemeni tribe.* Berkeley: University of California Press.

Cherny, L. (1999). *Conversation and community: Chat in a virtual world.* Stanford, CA: CSLI Publications.

Clance, P. R. (1985). *The impostor phenomenon: Overcoming the fear that haunts your success.* Atlanta, GA: Peachtree Publishers.

Clark, H. H. (1996). *Using language.* New York: Cambridge University Press.

Coates, J. (1997). The construction of a collaborative floor in women's friendly talk. In T. Givon (Ed.), *Conversation: Cognitive, communicative and social perspectives* (pp. 55-89). Amsterdam: John Benjamins.

Cobley, P. (1996). Introduction. In P. Cobley (Ed.), *The communication theory reader* (pp. 1-32). New York: Routledge.

Cohen, S., Doyle, W. J., Skoner, D. P., Rabin, B. S., & Gwaltney, J. M. (1997). Social ties and susceptibility to the common cold. *Journal of the American Medical Association, 277*(24), 1940-1944.

Coleman, J. (1990). *The Compass: The improvisational theatre that revolutionized American comedy.* Chicago: University of Chicago Press.

Collingwood, R. G. (1938). *The principles of art.* New York: Oxford University Press.

Cook-Gumperz, J. (1986). Caught in a web of words: Some considerations on language socialization and language acquisition. In J. Cook-Gumperz, W. A. Corsaro, & J. Streeck (Eds.), *Children's worlds and children's language* (pp. 37-64). New York: Mouton de Gruyter.

Cope, K. L. (Ed.). (1992). *Compendious conversations: The method of dialogue in the early enlightenment.* New York: Peter Lang.

Corsaro, W. A. (1985). *Friendship and peer culture in the early years.* Norwood, NJ: Ablex.

Corsaro, W. A. (1993). Interpretive reproduction in children's role play. *Childhood, 1,* 64-74.

Csikszentmihalyi, M. (1988). Society, culture, and person: A systems view of creativity. In R. J. Sternberg (Ed.), *The nature of creativity* (pp. 325-339). New York: Cambridge University Press.

Csikszentmihalyi, M. (1990). *Flow: The psychology of optimal experience.* New York: Harper and Collins.

Csikszentmihalyi, M., & Sawyer, R. K. (1995). Creative insight: The social dimension of a solitary moment. In R. J. Sternberg & J. E. Davidson (Eds.), *The nature of insight* (pp. 329-363). Cambridge, MA: MIT Press.

Csikszentmihalyi, M. (1996). *Creativity: Flow and the psychology of discovery and invention.* New York: HarperCollins.

Davis, B. H., & Brewer, J. P. (1997). *Electronic discourse: Linguistic individuals in virtual space.* Albany: SUNY Press.

de Certeau, M. (1984). *The practice of everyday life.* Berkeley: University of California Press.

de Saussure, F. (1915/1959). *Course in general linguistics* (W. Baskin, Trans.). New York: McGraw-Hill. (Original work published 1915)

Dennett, D. (1995). *Darwin's dangerous idea: Evolution and the meanings of life.* New York: Simon & Schuster.

Dewey, J. (1934). *Art as experience.* New York: Perigree Books.

Dixon, R. M. W. (1972). *The Dyirbal language of North Queensland.* New York: Cambridge University Press.

Drewal, M. T. (1992). *Yoruba ritual: Performers, play, agency.* Bloomington: Indiana University Press.

Drucker, P. F. (1988). The coming of the new organization. *Harvard Business Review, 66*(1), 45-53.

DuBois, J. W. (1992). Meaning without intention: Lessons from divination. In J. T. Hill & J. T. Irvine (Eds.), *Responsibility and evidence in oral discourse* (pp. 48-71). New York: Cambridge University Press.

Dunbar, R. (1996). *Grooming, gossip, and the evolution of language.* Cambridge, MA: Harvard University Press.

Dunn, J. (1986). Pretend play in the family. In A. W. Gottfried & C. C. Brown (Eds.), *Play interactions: The contribution of play materials and parental involvement to children's development* (pp. 149-162). Lexington, MA: Lexington Books.

Durkheim, E. (1895/1964). *The rules of sociological method.* New York: The Free Press. (Originally published as *Les règles de la méthode sociologique.* Paris: Alcan, 1895).

Eisenberg, E. M. (1990). Jamming: Transcendence through organizing. *Communication Research, 17*(2), 139-164.

Erickson, B. H. (1996). Culture, class, and connections. *American Journal of Sociology, 102*(1), 217-251.

Ervin-Tripp, S. (1972). On sociolinguistic rules: Alternation and co-occurrence. In J. J. Gumperz & D. Hymes (Eds.), *Directions in sociolinguistics: The ethnography of communication* (pp. 213-250). New York: Basil Blackwell.

Ewing, K. P. (1990). The illusion of wholeness: Culture, self, and the experience of inconsistency. *Ethos, 18*(3), 251-278.

Falk, J. (1980). The conversational duet. *Proceedings of the Sixth Annual Meeting of the Berkeley Linguistics Society,* 507-514.

Fein, G. G. (1985). The affective psychology of play. In C. C. Brown & A. W. Gottfried (Eds.), *Play interactions: The role of toys and parental involvement in children's development* (pp. 19-28). Johnson & Johnson Baby Products Company.

Fein, G. G. (1987). Pretend play: Creativity and consciousness. In D. Gorlitz & J. F. Wohlwill (Eds.), *Curiosity, imagination, and play: On the development of spontaneous cognitive and motivational processes* (pp. 281-304). Hillsdale, NJ: Lawrence Erlbaum Associates.

Fields, W. (1996). *Union of words: A history of presidential eloquence.* New York: Free Press.

Fine, G. A. (1983). *Shared fantasy: Role-playing games as social worlds.* Chicago: University of Chicago Press.

Fisher, L. (1976). Dropping remarks and the Barbadian audience. *American Ethnologist, 3*(2), 227-242.

Fitzpatrick, T. (1995). *The relationship of oral and literate performance processes in the commedia dell'arte: Beyond the improvisation/memorisation divide.* New York: Lewiston.

Foucault, M. (1972). *The archeology of knowledge and the discourse on language.* New York: Pantheon Books.

Fox, J. J. (1974). "Our ancestors spoke in pairs": Rotinese views of language, dialect, and code. In R. Bauman & J. Sherzer (Eds.), *Explorations in the ethnography of speaking* (pp. 65-85). New York: Cambridge University Press.

Freud, S. (1958). The dynamics of transference. In J. Strachey (Ed.), *The standard edition of the complete psychological works of Sigmund Freud, Volume 12* (pp. 97-108). London: Hogarth Press and the Institute of Psychoanalysis. (Original work appeared in 1912)

Freud, S. (1966). Transference. In J. Strachey (Ed.), *Introductory lectures on psycho-analysis* (pp. 536-556). New York: Norton. (First English translation published 1920; originally published in German in 1917).

Friedrich, P. (1971). Structural implications of Russian pronominal usage. In W. Bright (Ed.), *Proceedings of the UCLA sociolinguistics conference, 1964* (pp. 214-259). Los Angeles: Center for Research in Languages and Linguistics.

Friend, T. (1998a, September 14). Copy cats. *New Yorker*, pp. 51-57.

Friend, T. (1998b, September 28). Laugh riot. *New Yorker*, pp. 75-86.

Frost, A., & Yarrow, R. (1990). *Improvisation in drama.* London: The MacMillan Press.

Gabler, N. (1998). *Life the movie: How entertainment conquered reality.* New York: Alfred A. Knopf.

Gabor, D. (1983). *How to start a conversation and make friends.* New York: Simon & Schuster.

Gardner, H. (1993). *Creating minds.* New York: Basic Books.

Gardner, H. (1995). *Leading minds: An anatomy of leadership.* New York: Basic Books.

Geertz, C. (1980). Blurred genres: The refiguration of social thought. *American Scholar, 49,* 165-179.

George, D. J., & Gossip, C. J. (Eds.). (1993). *Studies in the commedia dell'arte.* Cardiff, Wales: University of Wales Press.

Gergen, K. J. (1967). To be or not to be . . . a single self. In S. M. Jourard (Ed.), *To be or not to be: Existential-psychological perspectives on the self.* Gainesville: University of Florida Press.

Ghoshal, S., & Bartlett, C. A. (1995). Changing the role of top management: Beyond structure to process. *Harvard Business Review, 73*(1), 86-96.

Gigerenzer, G. (1994). Where do new ideas come from? In M. A. Boden (Ed.), *Dimensions of creativity* (pp. 53-74). Cambridge, MA: MIT Press.

Giordano, P. C. (1995). The wider circle of friends in adolescence. *American Journal of Sociology, 101*(3), 661-697.

Glick, D. (1996, October). *At the intersection of language, ethnicity, and interpretation: Lessons from a Hebrew-language television interview.*

Paper presented at the Georgetown Linguistic Society conference, Washington, DC.

Goffman, E. (1959). *The presentation of self in everyday life.* New York: Anchor Books.

Goffman, E. (1967). *Interaction ritual: Essays on face-to-face behavior.* New York: Pantheon Books.

Goffman, E. (1974). *Frame analysis: An essay on the organization of experience.* New York: Harper & Row.

Goffman, E. (Ed.). (1981). Footing. In *Forms of talk* (pp. 124-159). Philadelphia: University of Pennsylvania Press.

Goncu, A. (1993). Development of intersubjectivity in social pretend play. *Human Development, 36,* 185-198.

Goodwin, C. (1981). *Conversational organization: Interaction between speakers and hearers.* New York: Academic Press.

Goodwin, C. (1986). Between and within: Alternative sequential treatments of continuers and assessments. *Human Studies, 9,* 205-217.

Goodwin, C., & Goodwin, M. H. (1992). Context, activity, and participation. In P. Auer & A. d. Luzo (Eds.), *The contextualization of language* (pp. 77-99). Amsterdam: Benjamins.

Goodwin, M. H. (1995). Co-construction in girls' hopscotch. *Research on Language and Social Interaction, 28*(3), 261-281.

Goody, J. (1987). *The interface between the written and the oral.* New York: Cambridge University Press.

Gould, S. J. (1997, June 26). Evolution: The pleasures of pluralism. *The New York Review of Books.*

Grimshaw, A. D. (Ed.). (1990). *Conflict talk: Sociolinguistic investigations of arguments in conversations.* New York: Cambridge University Press.

Guare, J. (1990). *Six degrees of separation.* New York: Random House.

Gumperz, J. J. (1982). *Discourse strategies.* New York: Cambridge University Press.

Gumperz, J. J., Aulakh, G., & Kaltman, H. (1982). Thematic structure and progression in discourse. In J. J. Gumperz (Ed.), *Language and social identity* (pp. 22-56). New York: Cambridge University Press.

Hacking, I. (1999). *The social construction of what?* Cambridge, MA: Harvard University Press.

Hafner, K. (1998, December 10). Tracking the evolution of e-mail etiquette. *New York Times,* pp. D1, D9.

Haight, W. L., & Miller, P. J. (1993). *Pretending at home: Early development in a sociocultural context.* Albany: SUNY Press.

Halpern, C., Close, D., & Johnson, K. (1994). *Truth in comedy: The manual of improvisation.* Colorado Springs, CO: Meriwether Publishing.

Harvey, J. C., & Katz, C. (1985). *If I'm so successful, why do I feel like a fake?: The impostor phenomenon.* New York: St. Martin's Press.

Hazen, R. M. (1997, July). What we don't know. *Technology Review*, 23-30.

Heath, C. (1984). Talk and recipiency: Sequential organization in speech and body movement. In J. M. Atkinson & J. Heritage (Eds.), *Structures of social action: Studies in conversation analysis* (pp. 247-265). New York: Cambridge University Press.

Heppner, F., & Grenander, U. (1990). A stochastic nonlinear model for coordinated bird flocks. In S. Krasner (Ed.), *The ubiquity of chaos* (pp. 233-238). Washington, DC: AAAS Publications.

Hickey, F. (1991). *What Penelope said: Styling the weather forecast.* Unpublished Master's thesis, University of Canterbury, Canterbury, NZ.

Hijirada, K., & Sohn, H. (1986). Cross-cultural patterns of honorifics and sociolinguistic sensitivity to honorific variables: Evidence from English, Japanese, and Korean. *Papers in Linguistics, 19*(3), 365-401.

Holquist, M. (1981). The politics of representation. In S. J. Greenblatt (Ed.), *Allegory and representation* (pp. 163-183). Baltimore: Johns Hopkins University Press.

Horgan, J. (1996). *The end of science: Facing the limits of knowledge in the twilight of the scientific age.* Reading, MA: Addison-Wesley.

Hornbrook, D. (1998). *Education and dramatic art* (2nd ed.). New York: Routledge.

Hymes, D. (1974). Ways of speaking. In R. Bauman & J. Sherzer (Eds.), *Explorations in the ethnography of speaking* (pp. 433-451). New York: Cambridge University Press.

Inoue, K. (1979). Japanese: A story of language and people. In T. Shopen (Ed.), *Languages and their speakers* (pp. 241-300). Cambridge: Winthrop Publishers.

Irvine, J. T. (1996). Shadow conversations: The indeterminacy of participant roles. In M. Silverstein & G. Urban (Eds.), *Natural histories of discourse* (pp. 131-159). Chicago: University of Chicago Press.

Iser, W. (1978). *The act of reading: A theory of aesthetic response.* Baltimore: Johns Hopkins University Press.

Iwamura, S. G. (1980). *The verbal games of preschool children.* New York: St. Martin's Press.

Jakobson, R. (1960). Closing statement: Linguistics and poetics. In T. A. Sebeok (Ed.), *Style in language* (pp. 350-377). Cambridge, MA: MIT Press.

James, W. (1890). *The principles of psychology.* New York: Henry Holt.

James, W. (1892). *Psychology.* New York: Henry Holt.

Josephs, I. E. (1998). Constructing one's self in the city of the silent: Dialogue, symbols, and the role of "as-if" in self-development. *Human Development, 41*, 180-195.

Kahn, D. (1995). *Scriptwork: A director's approach to new play development.* Carbondale: Southern Illinois University Press.

Kao, J. (1996). *Jamming: The art and discipline of business creativity.* New York: HarperCollins.

Kegl, J., Senghas, A., & Coppola, M. (1999). Creation through contact: Sign language emergence and sign language change in Nicaragua. In M. DeGraff (Ed.), *Language creation and language change: Creolization, diachrony, and development* (pp. 179-237). Cambridge, MA: MIT Press.

Kelly, W. (1959). *Ten ever-lovin' blue-eyed years with Pogo.* New York: Simon & Schuster.

King, L. (1994). *How to talk to anyone, anytime, anywhere: The secrets of good communication.* New York: Crown.

Knowles, G. (1997). *A cultural history of the English language.* New York: St. Martin's Press.

Korolija, N. (1998). Recycling cotext: The impact of prior conversation on the emergence of episodes in a multiparty radio talk show. *Discourse Processes, 25*(1), 99-125.

Koven, M. E. J. (1998). Two languages in the self/the self in two languages: French-Portuguese bilinguals' verbal enactments and experiences of self in narrative discourse. *Ethos, 26*(4), 410-455.

Kristof, N. D. (1996, September 29). For rural Japanese, death doesn't break family ties. *New York Times,* pp. 1, 8.

Kuhn, T. S. (1960). *The structure of scientific revolutions.* Cambridge, MA: MIT Press.

Kuiper, K. (1996). *Smooth talkers: The linguistic performance of auctioneers and sportscasters.* Mahwah, NJ: Lawrence Erlbaum Assocates.

Langer, E. J. (1989). *Mindfulness.* Reading, MA: Addison-Wesley.

Langer, E. J. (1997). *The power of mindful learning.* Reading, MA: Addison-Wesley.

Lee, D. A., & Peck, J. J. (1995). Troubled waters: Argument as sociability revisited. *Language in Society, 24,* 29-52.

Lehtonen, J., & Sajavaara, K. (1985). The silent Finn. In D. Tannen & M. Saville-Troike (Eds.), *Perspectives on silence* (pp. 193-201). Norwood, NJ: Ablex.

Levi-Strauss, C. (1962/1966). *The savage mind.* Chicago: University of Chicago Press. (Originally published as *La Pensée Sauvage.* Paris: Librairie Plon, 1962).

Levi-Strauss, C. (1964/1969). *The raw and the cooked: Introduction to a science of mythology: 1* (J. Weightman & D. Weightman, Trans.). New York: Harper and Row. (Originally published as *Le Cru et le Cuit,* Paris: Librairie Plon, 1964).

Levin, J., & Arluke, A. (1987). *Gossip: The inside scoop.* New York: Plenum Press.

Levinson, S. C. (1983). *Pragmatics.* New York: Cambridge University Press.

Levinson, S. C. (1988). Putting linguistics on a proper footing: Explorations in Goffman's concepts of participation. In P. Drew & A. Wootton (Eds.), *Erving Goffman: Exploring the interaction order* (pp. 161-227). Camridge, UK: Polity Press.

Lord, A. B. (1960/1965). *The singer of tales.* New York: Atheneum. (Harvard Studies in Comparative Literature, No. 24. Originally published by Cambridge University Press, 1960).

Lucy, J. A. (Ed.). (1993). *Reflexive language: Reported speech and metapragmatics.* New York: Cambridge University Press.

MacIntyre, A. (1984). *After virtue: A study in moral theory.* Notre Dame, IN: University of Notre Dame Press.

Mandler, J. M. (1984). *Stories, scripts, and scenes: Aspects of schema theory.* Hillsdale, NJ: Lawrence Erlbaum Associates.

Marks, P. (1997, April 22). When the audience joins the cast. *New York Times,* pp. B1, B7.

Martin, S. (1964). Speech levels in Japan and Korea. In D. Hymes (Ed.), *Language in culture and society* (pp. 407-415). New York: Harper & Row.

Matusov, E. (1996). Intersubjectivity without agreement. *Mind, Culture, and Activity, 3*(1), 25-45.

McDowell, J. H. (1983). The semiotic constitution of Kamsa ritual language. *Language in Society, 12,* 23-46.

McGill, K. (1990). Improvisatory competence and the cueing of performance: The case of the commedia dell'Arte. *Text and Performance Quarterly, 10,* 111-122.

Mead, G. H. (1932). *The philosophy of the present.* Chicago: University of Chicago Press.

Mead, G. H. (1934). *Mind, self, and society.* Chicago: University of Chicago Press.

Meerloo, J. A. M. (1952). *Conversation and communication: A psychological inquiry into language and human relations.* New York: International Universities Press.

Mertz, E. (1996). Recontextualization as socialization: Text and pragmatics in the law school classroom. In M. Silverstein & G. Urban (Eds.), *Natural histories of discourse* (pp. 229-249). Chicago: University of Chicago Press.

Meyer, D. A., & Brown, T. A. (1998). Statistical mechanics of voting. *Physical Review Letters, 81*(8), 1718-1721.

Miller, P., & Garvey, C. (1984). Mother-baby role play: Its origin in social support. In I. Bretherton (Ed.), *Symbolic play: The development of social understanding* (pp. 101-130). New York: Academic Press.

Minsky, M. (1975). A framework for representing knowledge. In P. H. Winston (Ed.), *The psychology of computer vision* (pp. 211-277). New York: McGraw-Hill.

Minsky, M. (1985). *The society of mind.* New York: Simon & Schuster.

Monson, I. (1996). *Saying something: Jazz improvisation and interaction.* Chicago: University of Chicago Press.

Morgan, M. (1996). Conversational signifying: Grammar and indirectness among African American women. In E. Ochs, E. A. Schegloff, & S. A. Thompson (Eds.), *Interaction and grammar* (pp. 405-434). New York: Cambridge University Press.

Mulkay, M. (1986). Conversations and texts. *Human Studies, 9,* 303-321.

Nagy, G. (1996). *Poetry as performance: Homer and beyond.* New York: Cambridge University Press.

Nelson, K., & Gruendel, J. M. (1979). At morning it's lunchtime: A scriptal view of children's dialogues. *Discourse Processes, 2,* 73-94.

Nelson, K. (1996). *Language in cognitive development: Emergence of the mediated mind.* New York: Cambridge University Press.

Norrick, N. R. (1998). Retelling stories in spontaneous conversation. *Discourse Processes, 25*(1), 75-97.

O'Barr, W. M. (1981). The language of the law. In C. A. Ferguson & S. B. Heath (Eds.), *Language in the USA* (pp. 386-406). New York: Cambridge University Press.

O'Connor, M. C., & Michaels, S. (1996). Shifting participant frameworks: Orchestrating thinking practices in group discussion. In D. Hicks (Ed.), *Discourse, learning, and schooling* (pp. 63-103). New York: Cambridge University Press.

O'Neill, J. (Ed.). (1973). *Modes of individualism and collectivism.* New York: St. Martin's Press.

Olson, D. R. (1994). *The world on paper: The conceptual and cognitive implications of writing and reading.* New York: Cambridge University Press.

Ong, W. J. (1982). *Orality and literacy: The technologizing of the word.* New York: Methuen.

Opie, P., & Opie, I. (1959). *The lore and language of schoolchildren.* New York: Oxford University Press.

Paley, V. (1992). *You can't say you can't play.* Cambridge, MA: Harvard University Press.

Parry, M. (1971). *The making of Homeric verse: The collected papers of Milman Parry.* Oxford: The Clarendon Press.

Pelliccia, H. (1997, November 20). As many Homers as you please. *The New York Review of Books,* pp. 44-48.

Philips, S. U. (1974). Warm Springs "Indian time": How the regulation of participation affects the progression of events. In R. Bauman & J. Sherzer (Eds.), *Explorations in the ethnography of speaking* (pp. 92-109). New York: Cambridge University Press.

Philips, S. U. (1992). The routinization of repair in courtroom discourse. In A. Duranti & C. Goodwin (Eds.), *Rethinking context: Language as an interactive phenomenon* (pp. 311-334). New York: Cambridge University Press.

Piaget, J. (1945/1962). *Play, dreams, and imitation in childhood* (C. Gattegno & F. M. Hodgson, Trans.). New York: Norton and Company. (Originally published as *La formation du symbole chez l'enfant: imitation, jeu et rêve, image et représentation*, Neuchâtel: Delachaux & Niestlé, 1945).

Picasso, P. (1982). *The mystery of Picasso* [Film]: MK2 Diffusion and Ines Clouzot.

Pine, B. J., & Gilmore, J. H. (1999). *The experience economy: Work is theatre and every business a stage.* Boston: Harvard Business School Press.

Pineau, E. L. (1994). Teaching is performance: Reconceptualizing a problematic metaphor. *American Educational Research Journal, 31*(1), 3-25.

Pirandello, L. (1991). Six characters in search of an author. In *Pirandello's major plays* (pp. 65-120). Evanston, IL: Northwestern University Press.

Poussaint, A. F. (1967, August 20). A Negro psychiatrist explains the Negro psyche. *New York Times Magazine*, p. 52.

Ratliffe, B. (1998, April 5). The sideman moves out of history's shadows. *New York Times*, Sec. 2, p. 38.

Reddy, M. J. (1979). The conduit metaphor: A case of frame conflict in our language about language. In A. Ortony (Ed.), *Metaphor and thought* (pp. 284-324). New York: Cambridge University Press.

Reinecke, J. E. (1964). Trade jargons and creole dialects as marginal languages. In D. Hymes (Ed.), *Language in culture and society* (pp. 534-546). New York: Harper and Row.

Reisman, K. (1974). Contrapuntal conversations in an Antiguan village. In R. Bauman & J. Sherzer (Eds.), *Explorations in the ethnography of speaking* (pp. 110-124). New York: Cambridge University Press.

Remillard, J. T. (1997, March). *Mathematics teaching as improvisation: A problem for policy implementation.* Paper presented at the Annual Meeting of the American Educational Research Association, Chicago, IL.

Resnick, M. (1996). New paradigms for computing, new paradigms for thinking. In Y. Kafai & M. Resnick (Eds.), *Constructionism in practice: Designing, thinking, and learning in a digital world* (pp. 255-267). Mahwah, NJ: Lawrence Erlbaum Associates.

Reynolds, C. W. (1987). Flocks, herds, and schools: A distributed behavioral model. *Computer Graphics, 21*(4), 25-34.

Rigby, J. (1994, December). Virtual TV. *The University of Chicago Magazine, 87*, pp. 16-19.

Rogoff, B. (1990). *Apprenticeship in thinking: Cognitive development in social context*. New York: Oxford University Press.

Rogoff, B., Mistry, J., Goncu, A., & Mosier, C. (1993). Guided participation in cultural activity by toddlers and caregivers. *Monographs of the Society for Research in Child Development, 58*(8, Serial No. 236).

Rubin, D. C. (1995). *Memory in oral traditions: The cognitive psychology of epic, ballads, and counting-out rhymes*. New York: Oxford University Press.

Sacks, H., Schegloff, E., & Jefferson, G. (1974). A simplest systematics for the organization of turn-taking in conversation. *Language, 50*(4), 696-735.

San Jose Mercury News. (1996, May 30). At MBA schools, communication skills are no joke. *San Jose Mercury News*, pp. 1C, 2C.

Sankoff, G. (1980). *The social life of language*. Philadelphia: University of Pennsylvania Press.

Sawyer, R. K. (1995). Creativity as mediated action: A comparison of improvisational performance and product creativity. *Mind, Culture, and Activity, 2*, 172-191.

Sawyer, R. K. (1996a). Role voicing, gender, and age in preschool play discourse. *Discourse Processes, 22*(3), 289-307.

Sawyer, R. K. (1996b). The semiotics of improvisation: The pragmatics of musical and verbal performance. *Semiotica, 108*(3/4), 269-306.

Sawyer, R. K. (1997). *Pretend play as improvisation: Conversation in the preschool classroom*. Hillsdale: NJ: Lawrence Erlbaum Associates.

Sawyer, R. K. (1999a). *A discourse on discourse: An archeological history of an intellectual concept*. Unpublished manuscript.

Sawyer, R. K. (1999b). The emergence of creativity. *Philosophical Psychology, 12*(4), 447-469.

Sawyer, R. K. (1999c, April). *Script-think, classroom discourse, and curriculum design*. Paper presented at the AERA, Montreal.

Sawyer, R. K. (2000a). Improvisation and the creative process: Dewey, Collingwood, and the aesthetics of spontaneity. *Journal of Aesthetics and Art Criticism, 58*(2), 149-161.

Sawyer, R. K. (2000b, July 9). *Simulating emergence and downward causation in small groups*. Paper presented at the The Second Workshop on Multi Agent Based Simulation, Boston, MA.

Schank, R. C., & Abelson, R. P. (1977a). *Scripts, plans, goals, and understanding: An inquiry into human knowledge structures*. Hillsdale, NJ: Lawrence Erlbaum Associates.

Schank, R. C., & Abelson, R. P. (1977b). Scripts, plans, and knowledge. In P. N. Johnson-Laird & P. C. Wason (Eds.), *Thinking: Readings in cognitive science* (pp. 421-432). New York: Cambridge University Press.

Schegloff, E. A. (1968). Sequencing in conversational openings. *American Anthropologist, 70,* 1075-1095.

Schegloff, E. A. (1986). The routine as achievement. *Human Studies, 9,* 111-151.

Schegloff, E. A., & Sacks, H. (1973). Opening up closings. *Semiotica, 8,* 289-327.

Schieffelin, B. B. (1990). *The give and take of everyday life: Language socialization of Kaluli children.* New York: Cambridge University Press.

Schiffrin, D. (1980). Meta-talk: Organizational and evaluative brackets in discourse. *Sociological Inquiry, 50*(3-4), 199-236.

Schiffrin, D. (1984). Jewish argument as sociability. *Language in Society, 13,* 311-335.

Schwartz, R. (1995). *Internal family systems therapy.* New York: Guilford.

Shannon, C. E., & Weaver, W. (1949). *The mathematical theory of communication.* Urbana: The University of Illinois Press.

Shapiro, M., & Shapiro, M. (1988). *Figuration in verbal art.* Princeton, NJ: Princeton University Press.

Shibutani, T. (1966). *Improvised news: A sociological study of rumor.* New York: Bobbs-Merrill.

Silverstein, M. (1976). Shifters, linguistic categories, and cultural description. In K. Basso & H. Selby (Eds.), *Meaning in anthropology* (pp. 11-55). Albuquerque: University of New Mexico Press.

Silverstein, M. (1993). Metapragmatic discourse and metapragmatic function. In J. A. Lucy (Ed.), *Reflexive language* (pp. 33-58). New York: Cambridge University Press.

Silverstein, M. (1995, April). *Indexical order and the dialectics of sociolinguistic life.* Paper presented at the SALSA III, Austin, TX.

Silverstein, M., & Urban, G. (1996). *Natural histories of discourse.* Chicago: University of Chicago Press.

Simonton, D. K. (1994). *Greatness: Who makes history and why.* New York: Guilford.

Singer, D. G., & Singer, J. L. (1990). *The house of make-believe: Play and the developing imagination.* Cambridge, MA: HarvardUniversity Press.

Sogliuzzo, A. R. (1982). *Luigi Pirandello, director: The playwright in the theatre.* Metuchen, NJ: The Scarecrow Press.

Solomon, A. (1997, February 9). The jazz martyr. *New York Times Magazine,* pp. 32-35.

Spolin, V. (1963). *Improvisation for the theater.* Evanston: Northwestern University Press.

Stanislavsky, K. (1936). *An actor prepares.* New York: Theatre Arts.

Stanislavsky, K. (1962). *Building a character.* New York: Theatre Arts Books.

Stryker, S., & Statham, A. (1985). Symbolic interaction and role theory. In G. Lindzey & E. Aronson (Eds.), *The handbook of social psychology* (3rd ed., pp. 311-378). New York: Random House.

Surratt, C. G. (1998). *Netlife: Internet citizens and their communities.* Commack, NJ: Nova Science Publishers.

Sweet, J. (1978). *Something wonderful right away: An oral history of the Second City & the Compass Players.* New York: Avon Books.

Tambiah, S. J. (1985). *Culture, thought, and social action: An anthropological perspective.* Cambridge, MA: Harvard University Press.

Tannen, D. (1979). What's in a frame? Surface evidence for underlying expectations. In R. O. Freedle (Ed.), *New directions in discourse processing* (pp. 137-181). Norwood, NJ: Ablex.

Tannen, D. (1981). New York Jewish conversational style. *International Journal of the Sociology of Language, 30,* 133-139.

Tannen, D. (1989). Interpreting interruption in conversation. In B. Music, R. Graczyk, & C. Wiltshire (Eds.), *Papers from the 25th annual regional meeting of the Chicago Linguistics Society.* Chicago: Chicago Linguistics Society.

Tannen, D. (1998). *The argument culture: Moving from debate to dialogue.* New York: Random House.

Taylor, M. (1999). *Imaginary companions and the children who create them.* New York: Oxford.

Todorov, T. (1984). *The conquest of America: The question of the other.* New York: HarperCollins.

Traub, J. (1996, August 26). Passing the baton: What CEOs could learn from the Orpheus Chamber Orchestra. *New Yorker, 72,* 100-105.

Trefil, J. (1996). *The edge of the unknown: 101 things you don't know about science and no one else does either.* New York: Houghton Mifflin.

Turkle, S. (1995). *Life on the screen: Identity in the age of the Internet.* New York: Simon & Schuster.

Vygotsky, L. S. (1978). *Mind in society* (A. Kozulin, Trans.). Cambridge, MA: Harvard University Press.

Wade, N. (1998, September 8). Can social behavior of man be glimpsed in a lowly worm? *New York Times,* pp. B9.

Wagner, B., Gregory, S., Bierck, R., Daniel, M., & Sapers, J. (1996, December 2). Where computers do work. *U.S. News & World Report,* pp. 83-93.

Watanabe-Hammond, S. (1986). Cast of characters work: Systematically exploring the naturally organized personality. *Contemporary Family Therapy, 8*(1), 75-83.

Watson, K. A. (1975). Transferable communicative routines: Strategies and group identity in two speech events. *Language in Society, 4,* 53-72.

Weeks, P. (1990). Musical time as a practical accomplishment: A change in tempo. *Human Studies, 13,* 323-359.

Wertsch, J. V. (1995). Sociocultural research in the copyright age. *Culture & Psychology, 1,* 81-102.

Wierzbicka, A. (1996). Japanese cultural scripts: Cultural psychology and "cultural grammar," *Ethos, 24*(3), 527-555.

Willoughby, R. R. (1932). The functions of conversation. *The Journal of Social Psychology, 3,* 146-160.

Wilson, E. O. (1998). *Consilience: The unity of knowledge.* New York: Alfred A. Knopf.

Wollheim, R. (1980). *Art and its objects.* New York: Cambridge University Press.

Wortham, S. (1994). *Acting out participant examples in the classroom.* Philadelphia, PA: John Benjamins.

Yamada, H. (1989). *American and Japanese topic management strategies in business conversations.* Unpublished PhD dissertation, Georgetown University, Washington, DC.

Yngve, V. H. (1970). On getting a word in edgewise. *Papers from the sixth regional meeting of the Chicago Linguistic Society, April 16-18, 1970* (pp. 567-578). Chicago: Chicago Linguistics Society.

Author Index

A

Abelson R. P., 9(n3), 11(n5), *249*
Abercrombie, N., 135(n2), *237*
American Psychiatric Association, 15(n11), *237*
Anderson, J. A., 100(n33), *237*
Ansen, D., 114(n9), *237*
Argyle, M., 74(n1), *237*
Aries, E., 58(n20), *237*
Arluke, A., 188(n4), *246*
Aulakh, G., 48(n6), *243*
Austin, J. L., 79(n10), 86(n15), *237*

B

Baker-Sennett, J., 119(n14), *237*
Baker-White, R., 112(n7), *237*
Bakhtin, M. M., 25(n16), 52(n9), 76(n8), 153(n28), *238*
Bar-Hillel, Y., 26(n19), *238*
Barry, D., 149(n23), *238*
Bartlett, C. A., 199(n21), *242*
Bateson, G., 48(n5), *238*

Bateson, M. C., 177(n21), *238*
Bauman, R., 87(n17), 93(n24), 121(n17), 162(n2), 174(n18), *238*
Bearison, D. J., 199(n20), *238*
Berliner, P., 110(n5), *238*
Bickerton, D., 66(n28), *238*
Bierck, R., 139(n9), *251*
Birdwhistell, R. L., 75(n6), *238*
Blitz, D., 217(n11), *238*
Bloch, M., 97(n26), 174(n18), *238*
Borko, H., 208(n31), *238*
Bourdieu, P., 39(n37), 143(n17), *238*
Braun, F., 171(n14), *238*
Brenneis, D., 189(n5), *238*
Brewer, J. P., 98(n29), *240*
Briggs, C. L., 87(n17, 121(n17), 162(n2), 174(n18), *238*
Brody, J. E., 15(n12), *239*
Brooks, T., 143(n13), *239*
Brown, R., 167(n8), 170(n11), 172(n15), 173(n16), *239*

253

Shapiro, M., 64(n27), *250*
Shibutani, T., 121(n17), *250*
Silverstein, M., 26(n19), 48(n5), 121(n17), *250*
Simonton, D. K., 200(n23), *250*
Singer, D. G., 205(n26), *250*
Singer, J. L., 205(n26), *250*
Skoner, D. P., 191(n9), *240*
Sogliuzzo, A. R., 44(n1), *250*
Sohn, H., 171(n13), *244*
Solomon, A., 113(n8), *250*
Spolin, V., 12(n7), *250*
Stanislavsky, K., 111(n6), *250*
Statham, A., 142(n12), *251*
Stryker, S., 142(n12), *251*
Surratt, C. G., 146(n21), *251*
Sweet, J., 12(n7), 25(n17), 116(n11), *251*

T

Tambiah, S. J., 97(n26), *251*
Tannen, D., 10(n4), 60(n24-n25), 187(n2), 189(n6), 193(n12), *251*
Taylor, M., 205(n26), *251*
Todorov, T., 177(n23), *251*
Traub, J., 119(n13), *251*
Trefil, J., 215(n8), *251*
Turkle, S., 146(n21), *251*

U

Urban, G., 121(n17), *250*

V

Vygotsky, L. S., 201(n24), *251*

W

Wade, N., 214(n5), *251*
Wagner, B., 139(n9), *251*
Watanabe-Hammond, S., 143(n19), *251*
Watson, K. A., 187(n2), 189(n5), *251*
Weaver, W., 75(n6), *250*
Weeks, P., 119(n13), *252*
Wertsch, J. V., 194(n15), *252*
Wierzbicka, A., 38(n36), *252*
Willoughby, R. R., 90(n20), *252*
Wilson, E. O., 218(n14), *252*
Wollheim, R., 101(n35), *252*
Wortham, S., 95(n25), *252*

Y

Yamada, H., 59(n21), *252*
Yarrow, R., 114(n9), *242*
Yngve, V. H., 74(n2), *252*

Subject Index